Daring All Things – as seen on the BBC's 'Antiques Roadshow' First World War Commemoration Special – is a unique and extraordinary autobiography, which is published for the first time 55 years after its completion (shortly before The Rev George Kendall died suddenly in 1961, aged 79). The book is the life story of a man born into a working-class rural Yorkshire childhood in the late Victorian era – who through self-education, piety, ambition and sheer hard graft, projected himself onto the then British Empire's biggest stages. Kendall chose the life of a Primitive Methodist minister and, initiated through First World War duty, also pursued a dual career as a military chaplain, which lasted 30 years in war and peace.

Using his Christian faith, humour and straight talking, Kendall became a confidante to British royalty, prime ministers and religious leaders throughout the first half of the 20th century. Using his initiative, bravery and patriotism, he became both participant and eyewitness at many of the epoch-making moments during the most intense period of the United Kingdom's and Ireland's histories: Two World Wars, the rise of women's rights, the rise of working people's rights, the rise of *Sinn Féin*, the creation of the NHS and the Welfare State, and the development of the modern police and prison systems were all within his compass.

The Rev Kendall always ensured that a keen sense of morality – both public and private – was always to the fore; however, he was no staid clergyman: he delighted in life and its colourful characters. As one of the last of the great polymaths, Kendall was able to advise and educate both in private and public arenas. Speakers' Corner, which he described as 'the greatest forum in the world', became his open-air pulpit – and he was its most well-loved speaker by the 1930s and through the Second World War, when he again served as a military chaplain in London.

By the final years of his life, Kendall was the country's most war-experienced chaplain – having spent eight years on the front lines in four different countries and serving a further three years post-First World War with the first British Army on the Rhine. In 1920, he was given the responsibility of being in charge of the exhumation of the battlefields of Belgium and France, and building the war cemeteries we know today. His work there culminated in the highly secretive process to select the body that became 'The Unknown Warrior' – and he ensured his safe passage to England, to be buried at Westminster Abbey.

George Kendall's life was shrouded in mystery – much of it unrecorded formally. *Daring All Things* finally reveals the enormity of his experience and provides new historical information that will lead to academic revision of many of the events he lived through. Ultimately, the purpose of the book is to explain in the clearest of terms The Rev Kendall's belief in divine providence in both his – and anyone's – life who believes in it; this has been understood as 'God's Hand' at work on Earth. If this most remarkable of accounts doesn't make you a believer, nothing will. In order to promote the primacy of Kendall's testimony, the modern-day equivalents of the individual national leaders he met and worked with provide forewords to selected chapters. Each reflect on the man they encounter – and the cumulative effect is both a memorial and reassurance that hats might change, climates change and priorities change, but the underlying nature of the British establishment remains (if a little frayed) in modern times. Hope is indeed alive.

George Kendall was a clergyman, historian, patriot and adviser, as well as a modern prison, health, and education service pioneer, lecturer, musician, impresario, orator, antiques expert, humourist and writer, who lived in Britain between 1881 and 1961. From a working-class background, his vocation led to him living and working throughout Britain and Ireland. Kendall also served for more than six years abroad for the British Army – becoming a senior chaplain and being honoured with one of the first Military OBEs awarded by King George V at the end of the First World War. Refusing further official honours, Kendall spent most of the last 35 years of his life living and working amongst the poor in the East End of London.

The book contains hundreds of names – famous, infamous and neither – that personally moulded, educated and informed George Kendall and his life mission. Their cumulative legacy was the country that, by the late 1950s, could rightfully claim to be the most advanced in the world.

Kendall was married twice – firstly to Emily, who died in 1933, and then Winifred, with whom he had four children. Son David and his only daughter, Rosemary, survive – living respectively in Poole, England and Vancouver, Canada.

Daring All Things

The Autobiography of George Kendall (1881-1961)

George Kendall

 Helion & Company Limited

Helion & Company Limited
26 Willow Road
Solihull
West Midlands
B91 1UE
England
Tel. 0121 705 3393
Fax 0121 711 4075
Email: info@helion.co.uk
Website: www.helion.co.uk
Twitter: @helionbooks
Visit our blog at http://blog.helion.co.uk/

Published by Helion & Company 2016
Designed and typeset by Farr out Publications, Wokingham, Berkshire
Cover designed by Paul Hewitt, Battlefield Design (www.battlefield-design.co.uk)
Printed by Short Run Press Limited, Exeter, Devon

ISBN 978-1-911096-62-7

British Library Cataloguing-in-Publication Data.
A catalogue record for this book is available from the British Library.

For details of other military history titles published by Helion & Company
Limited, contact the above address, or visit our website: http://www.helion.co.uk

We always welcome receiving book proposals from prospective authors.

This book is dedicated to my grandfather's children
and my own dearest, Jasmine Georgina.

'To live in hearts we leave behind is not to die' – Thomas Campbell

Tim Kendall, London 2016
Grandson of The Reverend George Kendall

Each contributor was provided with only the chapter they have written their forewords to. The rest of the book, except the scantest of detail, was a mystery to them – the conclusion being the sum of their parts.

Contents

Part 3 – Home Again: The Second Great War and the Battle of London

Foreword

My father lived in the present and not in the past – and in consequence, his story has been a voyage of discovery for me: a journey into the unknown, for he rarely spoke of his earlier years. In common with most who experienced the trauma of the First World War, my father never shared his wartime experiences with the family. The young Yorkshire boy born in the latter part of the last century would never, in his wildest dreams, have imagined the significance of the life which stretched before him. His entry into the Methodist ministry and the advent of the First World War opened the doors of a new life for him. As a minister, he had pastoral responsibility for churches in Scotland, Wales and many parts of England; as an army chaplain, he was present at many of the major battles of the Great War – serving in France, Belgium, the Dardanelles, Ireland and Germany. Twenty years later – and now an RAF chaplain – he again was on the front line, but this time it was right on our doorstep, in London.

My father was so vital, so enthusiastic, such an understanding and wonderful companion that the life of the family revolved around him. The love which radiated from him encompassed all his fellows, and such was the exuberance of his personality that almost all whom he met became his friends.

The Bible which my father carried with him throughout the First World War still survives, and it is marked to show a passage from the Psalms which he read to countless soldiers in the last days or hours of their lives, or at their graveside after death – a passage which can also stand as a testimony to the faith which he lived by:

> The Lord is my light and my salvation; whom shall I fear?
> The Lord is the strength of my life, of whom shall I be afraid?
> Though a host shall encamp against me, my heart shall not fear;
> Though war should rise against me, in this I will be confident'.[1]

David Kendall
Dorset, 2016

---

1   Psalm 27: 1-3.

Preface

I have often been asked to tell what has happened to me in the strange, winding road of the life I have travelled. I have always fought shy of the task and I have had such a busy life that it has been difficult to find the time. Now I am supposed to live in retirement (I say 'supposed' because I am as busy as ever), but at the insistent demands of my family and my many friends I have at last found the time to record the happenings of the way. There are some things in my story that are historical as well as personal. You will find humour as well as tragedy.

Some years ago a journalist whose name I never knew, and who just added the initials 'P.A.E.', wrote an article about me entitled 'The New Men of the Morning'. I liked the title for I love the morning and all that is implied by the word but his description of my birth was very far-fetched, even if it caused a great deal of amusement. 'The village of Hoyland', he wrote, 'did not know that a human dreadnaught had howled that day as gently as a sucking dove'. I know that 'howling' is a sign of life in the new born babe, but not in the afterlife. I have never looked upon myself as a 'dreadnought', although I have battled with many things, especially during the two Great Wars and my thirty years as a so-called 'Soap-Box Orator' in Hyde Park. There is the story, too, of how I battled with my horses in France and the sad one when I was knocked out in the boxing ring! I am not by any means the kind of man who fears nought. Any man who said he was never afraid, especially during the two Great Wars, is a liar.

Sometimes I rub my eyes with astonishment to think that a fatherless boy living in what was then an isolated Yorkshire village should have had so many strange things happen to him in this bewildering and interesting world. I had no material advantages and in the Victorian period of nearly eighty years ago there were no scholarships to aid a boy in his career. I am, however, profoundly thankful to those who helped and inspired me in the days of my youth. I had a rich heritage in a good home and my philosophy of life was 'What you think and plan day by day you will get. A thing dreamed of is already won. But ambition is not enough; there must be prolonged and intense work'. The final judgement is, in those well-known words, 'By their fruits ye shall know them'.

G.K.
London, February 1961

Acknowledgements

My deepest gratitude to all the contributors, both great and good. My thoughts also of the late Bishop of London William Wand and to the 'Secret Knight' Sydney Walton – my grandfather's great friends, who didn't have the opportunity to write their forewords.

My thanks to Duncan for stopping to listen and to Kathryn for typing up the original manuscript and for being a great support.

Tim Kendall, 2016

Part 1 – In the Days of My Youth

1

My Home 1881–6

We of this generation have lived through dramatic events perhaps unequalled in any other age. I have survived three wars – serving in two of them. I have seen the shaking of thrones and, in my Windsor days, saw some of the Kings who were cast forth from their countries. I have in my lifetime seen astounding revolutions of science and thought. Born in the Victorian era, I have seen in our own land two Queens and three Kings, one Coronation postponed, one abandoned and four others filled with joyous splendour. These upheavals, many sudden and violent and many which will pass in history as the greatest in mankind, have not dimmed the recollections of my boyhood or of the strange experiences I have had in the winding road of life.

My father

My father Charles Kendall died when I was two and a half years old. He was a policeman in Hoyland, a Yorkshire town, where I was born on 10th October 1881. He was well on the way to promotion when death claimed him at thirty-six. He had passed through strenuous times in connection with colliery strikes when rioting was the order of the day and had suffered a great blow when his superintendent, a great friend of ours, shot himself. It was a few days after this sad event when, largely as a result of shock, my father died. When off duty, he used to attend the Methodist Chapel and everybody loved him. He had a policeman's funeral and, in spite of the fact that I was only a baby, I can remember the long column of the men in blue who followed him to his grave. For his sake, and because I love the men who protect our homes and take care of the little children crossing our dangerous streets, I have always taken a great interest in policemen. I talk to them at the corners of the street, sometimes I was with them and for many years, at Caledonian Road, Islington, I had a wonderful policeman's church parade, accompanied by their band – all so moving for me, and, I am sure, for them also.

My mother was a farmer's daughter and the man in blue fell in love with her, and at the same time with the old farm kitchen. In the fragrance of a July morning in the year 1877, when my mother was only eighteen, they were married in the lovely old Saxon church of Tankersley, Yorkshire. The result was eight years of happily married life and three children, two daughters and me, the youngest.

My maternal grandfather

After my father's death we went back to the farm and how I loved it! The charm of a well-kept country farm is indescribable, especially when that farm is in Yorkshire – Yorkshire of broad acres, stalwart men, pleasant and attractive women and Yorkshire pudding. Cattle and horses, rabbits and pigeons, meadows and woodland all make up the picture, but the central figure was my grandfather – the typical Yorkshire farmer of the bygone generation. He always wore a silk hat and frock coat and was well groomed, especially on Sunday mornings, by my grandmother. He had a handsome ruddy face which used to beam with the joy of religion. He used to say: "I went out at five o'clock this morning and the birds were singing so sweetly, and yet not one of them knew where its breakfast was coming from. How ungrateful I should have felt if I had not praised the Lord, for I know that mine was frizzling in the oven and would be ready when I got back." And I knew that too for I was generally to be found waiting by his side at table for a tit-bit of bread dipped in the bacon fat. My grandfather realised the blessedness of praise and I often went with him into the woods and fields. I had a passionate love for the birds and flowers, to me 'all things were bright and beautiful, all creatures great and small'. I could look through nature to nature's God. I went out with my grandfather on his last walk on earth – 'and he was not, for God took him', took him to that land where 'everlasting spring abides and never-withering flowers'. This is one of life's precious memories and it has followed me all the days of my ministry.

My maternal grandmother

We left the old farm to live in a house on the top of a hill which was near a beautiful wood. It was my grandmother's home. She was born there and died there at the age of eighty-seven. She was given to hospitality – tramps and gipsies and the hurdy-gurdy grinder, with his pet monkey balanced precariously on his shoulder, were always welcomed. We often had many strange visitors in those days and this taught me to love all peoples, especially the poor and homeless – a priceless inheritance for a minister of the gospel.

There is an old song: 'In the days we went a gipsying a long time ago'. This song brings back many memories, for my grandmother used to take me to visit a large gipsy encampment. It was a relic of old England. How full of fascination! There were all kinds of caravans and many dogs and horses. The gipsies all knew her and it was a great experience for me. This has brought fruits in my ministry for in one country circuit, where the gipsies used to camp, I paid them regular visits. Somehow or other there was a band of union – did it come from the past? Yes! Anyhow those gipsies used to come to my village church – strange worshippers; they looked ill at ease but were soon made at home by the welcome which they received. You could not patronise them for they were very proud but you could win their affection by kindness.

My grandmother was a very strong and yet a charming woman of great intellect. She had a visual memory and could learn a recitation by reciting it through once and then she would be word perfect. How well I remember her reciting such old poems as 'Mary, the Maid of the Inn'. I have a very vivid picture of her sitting in an old armchair in a corner by a table and, with the aid of an oil lamp, reading the Bible to me.

Often as she did so, she would quote Charles Wesley's great hymn:

> When quiet in my house I sit
> Thy Book be my companion still,
> My joy Thy sayings to repeat,
> Talk o'er the records of Thy will
> And search the oracles divine,
> Till every heartfelt word be mine.

Her reading to me covered many biographies of good and famous men, also the books that children love – 'Robinson Crusoe', 'Uncle Tom's Cabin', 'The Red Indian Yarns of Fennimore Cooper', Bunyan's 'Pilgrim's Progress' and books of travel covering all parts of the world. Is there any wonder that I have collected a fairly varied library of books and have been an omnivorous reader? This was the reason that, whilst I was a senior chaplain of exhumation work in France and Belgium, I collected a library of 4,000 volumes for the men engaged in that gruesome and yet sacred task. I revelled in those books which I obtained from all kinds of places, some from ruined huts and houses previously occupied by the troops in the war and many sent from home. All this thirst for literatures is a direct legacy from my grandmother. Some evenings we would linger over the experiences of the past. The past was always present with us. Her father, John Peaker, was born in 1796, and died the year that I was born. Her grandfather Hobson was born in the middle of the eighteenth century. Her husband's father, John Moulson, was born in 1763, and she would tell me stories dating back to the reign of Queen Anne – all handed down from generation to generation. I gaze sometimes at a Queen Anne table and mirror I possess and recall the vivid picture she painted me of the morning her mother was bride, how she went into the garden and plucked a red rose and placed it in the bosom of her crinoline dress, gazed in the mirror and then dropped the rose into an old bowl – which I also possess – all so moving to recall those days so long ago. She would talk to me of an uncle who came to visit her from South Africa; he was one of the pioneer gold-miners and he brought home a bag of gold which he poured onto the table.

Again there were stories of men who had been at the Battles of Trafalgar and Waterloo – these men, some with wooden legs, came to her home when she was a girl. There were stories too of the Indian Mutiny, of the Crimean War and others. I was often thrilled by her description of the Great Eastern ship which she visited, of her first ride in a railway train with its quaint carriages and wooden seats, of the abolition of the slave trade, of great Prime Ministers such as Sir Robert Peel, the Duke of Wellington, Disraeli and Gladstone. She also told me of the uncle who was coming on a visit but perished in the Tay Bridge Disaster and of many more events of the past, when life seemed to move more leisurely than today. All this thrilled my imagination and gave me a real love of history.

Another memory which I have is of her sweet voice; she was a good singer and often sang me to sleep in my childhood days. There are no songs like hers of years ago – I can hear her singing "Work for the night is coming." Its tune and words have always lingered in my mind. When very old, she sang in the minor key, often of rest for the weary. She feared nothing and, living in lonely places, she had many adventures. Once a man forced his way into the farm kitchen but he did not stay long for, seizing a broom she belaboured him to such an extent that he ran away and climbed the wall outside – but she followed him over the wall! Whoever he was, he avoided our abode afterwards. On another occasion, she was going with her sister to market – a long lonely road, when a man accosted them and tried to take her sister's basket. Without the slightest hesitation, she gave him a beautiful uppercut to his chin and sent him spinning – he too ran away. In those days, our women folk needed to be brave and fearless for they had many dangers to face which we, in these days, think nothing of.

Yet she was kind and gentle – "Kind, kind and gentle is she, kind is my Mary," so grandfather could sing, for Mary Moulson was known far and wide for her good works. She was clever in her medical knowledge and her simple remedies for all kinds of ills proved effective. I know this from experience for she dosed me with pills more than once! I hated the wretched things and often chewed them – which reminded me of the proverb: 'Never chew your pills or they will leave a bitter taste in your mouth'. Her turkey, rhubarb and magnesia were just as bad but were very effective and when I went to college, she took great care that a parcel of this was placed in my trunk. "It is the best medicine in the world," she would say, "share it with your fellow students when they are out of sorts." I did, and they walked the corridors throughout the night but were better the next morning. Once she was called at four o'clock on one dark winter's morning to visit a little child who was seriously ill. It meant a four-mile walk through woods and lanes but she went and she saved the child's life.

Yes! I certainly remember her pills and plasters, her embrocation and simple mixtures of herbs and ointments. So is there any wonder then, in my ministry, I always interested myself in people's ailments and have given many old-fashioned remedies which have removed the ills of the flesh. How many miners' wives in South Wales had cause to bless my healing ministry! And again I have frequently lectured on health in Hyde Park – at Marble Arch – and also in various churches. I emphasised also, as my old grandmother did, another good medicine which you can read of in the Bible – 'A merry heart doeth good like medicine', for she had the music of a merry heart. Is it not true that a good jaw-aching, side-splitting laugh is the best tonic in the world, whilst anger and resentment make the very pepsin of the stomach lose its power? Again I believe that a hearty laugh, open and free, will allow you to indulge in pickled lobster, ice cream and ginger beer without any ill effects!

My grandmother trained me in the way that I should go and she carefully guided my budding judgement with Heaven-given principles. To teach me to be kind and loving to old people, she would pack me up, each Sunday afternoon, a basket of comforts – oranges, cakes and sweets, and send me to visit the old ladies in the alms-houses at the other side of the wood. There I would read a chapter from the Bible and sing to them hymns, especially one favourite entitled 'The world is very beautiful'. The gifts were welcome but the visit of the cheery red-haired boy – a boy from the outside world to the lonely and the aged – was even more appreciated.

The Peaker family

My grandmother was proud of her family – a fine old Yorkshire family. She would take me to the churchyard surrounding the old Norman Church at Ecclesfield, a cathedral-like church known in history as 'The Minster of the Moors'. There she would point out to me the tombs of my ancestors – flat tombstones with many names, dating from the seventeenth and eighteenth centuries. There 'the rude forefathers of the hamlet slept'.

I pictured these ancestors of mine living through many periods of joyous and troublous history in our land. Perhaps they too answered the beacon fires from the many hills around and assembled with the clans at what was known as the 'stone of ages', a landmark of ancient Britain on the top of Jawbone Hill, one thousand feet up where the vista is too beautiful for words.

One great joy to me was the frequent visits of my great aunts, all sisters of my grandmother. They were tall, handsome women who had married well. I lost count of their number. There were Esther, Jane, Caroline, Fanny, Maria, Hannah, Polly and others. Gathered round the tea table they would talk of days gone by. Of their brothers, twins who died at the age of five, of their eldest brother who had spent a holiday in the Isle of Man – a great journey in those days – and who caught a serious cold through sleeping in a damp bed and died a short time after his return as a result. Oh, the stories they told, stories of ghosts, highwaymen, murders and disasters, stories too of the joyous side of life, love stories, marriage stories, stories of little children; sometimes they would laugh and sometimes they would cry. One thing, however, sticks in my memory, sometimes they gave me a penny and sometimes threepence and I was always wondering whether I should be lucky in receiving the threepence.

I am afraid that I was often a source of anxiety to both my mother and grandmother. Once I crushed my finger in the mangle, on another occasion I rolled down the stairs and on still another rolled into a pond. I seemed to have no fear and this was seen one day when I was found in a wall-in yard of the farm calmly trying to play with the bull – the bull was supposed to be very savage but I came to no harm. Always in mischief, I would be tied occasionally to the table leg in the kitchen and given enough rope to reach the door but the rope was not always effective.

My grandmother was devoted to the Mount Pleasant Wesleyan Methodist Church. I have a class ticket issued to her over one hundred years ago. She sat under the ministry of The Rev Morley Punshon and many other famous ministers of those days.

When I have gone to take services in this old church her memory has thrilled me. I am glad that I showed my love to her in all sorts of ways. On her birthday I used to buy her a cap with flowers on it – they were used by all ladies in those days – I generally tried one on in the shop before buying, saying to the astonished assistant "If it suits me, it will suit my grandmother!"

She died as she had lived – a very brave death. I was a minister in Scotland at the time and she sent for me. I travelled all night from near Glasgow and reached home in the early hours of the morning. She simply said to me, when I entered the room, "George, I am going to die. Your grandfather has been dead for ten years and I want to join him." I sent for the doctor and he told me that she had no disease of any kind but she had willed herself to die. I remember the nights I sat up with her and all that she said to me. The vicar of the parish came one afternoon to see her and we celebrated Holy Communion together and a day or two later she passed away 'and all the trumpets sounded for her on the other side'. A great number of relatives and friends came to her funeral, for she was well known and respected and we sang her favourite hymn – 'The strife is o'er, the battle done'. She, being dead still speaks to me in my old age and of her I can say, "Blessed are the dead who die in the Lord: Even so, saith the Spirit, for they rest from their labours; and their works do follow them."

The Duckett/Kendall family

I never knew my father's family. His mother Elizabeth was a member of the well-known family of Ducketts. She had ten brothers and sisters and was born in 1824, in Settle, near Skipton. She died at the early age of forty. Her brother Edward left for Australia in 1848 and founded a flourishing business in Melbourne. It is still one of the most important businesses in the city. Her brother Charles and sister Sarah also went to Australia two years after Edward.

His father's name was John Kendall. I have in my possession his indenture of apprenticeship as a shoemaker to George Redmayne of Settle for six years. His aunt, Mary Wilman, paid for this the sum of eighteen pounds and the date is 20th October 1830.

The indenture is quaintly worded:

> The apprentice must dwell, remain and serve, shall keep his master's secrets, shall not commit adultery or fornication or haunt taverns of ale-houses, shall not play at dice, cards, tables, bowls or any other unlawful games and all this for a boy to observe, signed, sealed and delivered under a government stamp of one pound in the reign of our Sovereign Lord King William.

I often wished that I could have lived in Settle and known my paternal grandparents and the other members of the family. It was a joy to me, however, to welcome some members of the Duckett family when they came on a visit from Australia in 1957, and by a singular coincidence I found, in talking to Dr Wand, who was then the Bishop of London, that he had stayed as the guest of my aunt when he was the Archbishop of Adelaide and he told me of her beautiful residence and of the important part the family played in the City of Melbourne.

My mother

I have written at length about my grandmother, Mary Moulson, because she took the place of my father and was the guiding influence of my life. It was a very big task for her to take into the old home my mother and her three children but she gladly undertook the task and never murmured. I want, however, to pay tribute to my mother. Her name was Ann. She was more like a playmate to me for she was hardly past her girlhood when I was born. Sorrow had come to her just as she had expected sunshine and song. But, alas, the music of her life had been broken in the sudden death of my father – eight years only of married life followed by a long widowhood. She was a handsome girl with a warm, all-embracing love for us all. My two older sisters, Mary and Annie, shared the home and that love.

I like to think of the bright Sunday afternoon my mother, along with my father, took me to the Tankersley Parish Church to be baptised. My mother's only brother John was the Sunday School superintendent and served in this office for forty years. I have a faint recollection of my mother nursing me in the old-fashioned rocking chair. She took me everywhere with her and carried me on her back when I was tired. I never remember hearing her complain, she quietly accepted her lot and my grandmother was glad to have her and her children in the home.

The first break I had with her was in 1904 when I went to college. I remember very vividly the morning that I left home. My mind was full of what I thought would be the glorious future in store for me with little thought of how she would feel without my companionship. I went downstairs for breakfast and found her waiting to join me. I noticed how quiet she was and then she began to cry and I cried with her. In that moment I realised what her sacrifice meant and that life, for her, would never be the same again. One of my greatest joys was to welcome her in my own home, after my marriage. She generally stayed two or three weeks. Once when she came to see me in London I went to St Pancras Station to meet her. She wrote and told me that she would be wearing a new brown costume. I saw a lady walking down the arrival platform wearing such a costume and she was the image of my mother. In my excitement I went up to her, seized her travelling case and kissed her, then to my horror, I saw my mistake for there was my mother smiling at the lady's back. Apologising, I said, "I do hope you will forgive me, I do not want you to think that it is the custom for parsons in London to meet ladies on the platform and kiss them." She replied, "Please do not apologise, I liked it!"

We lived in Kilburn when my mother paid her last visit in 1935. She came to see my little baby son David, just a week or two old. At the end of two weeks she said that she must return home. She said goodbye to my wife and kissed the baby and I left with her to take her to the station. We had got to the corner of Queen's Park, a few yards beyond our front door, when she began to cry. I said, "Don't cry, mother, come back with me." She dried her tears and came back and stayed another week and then she went home. Not long afterwards she passed away in the old home at the age of eighty and I laid her to rest in the village cemetery not far from the grave of my grandmother and grandfather. I am always glad that she returned with me for that extra week.

Sometimes, when silence seals the day and bears me on my homeward way I can see her smile and hear her voice. The long day closed for her and after life's fitful fever she sleeps well. A good mother is life's greatest blessing and her children arise up and call her blessed.

2

Childhood Days 1886–95

We never forget the scenes of our childhood and yet it is difficult to recapture its lost legend. Hazy shapes always seem to emerge from memory's sunset air. Faint sounds seem always to be re-echoing across the years. Do we ever lose the source of wonder and adventure? I have not found it so even though I am nearing the age of eighty. All the days of childhood and youth seem to colour age and recollections can bring joy and comfort. Well might Job cry, as he did when old, 'Oh that I were as in months past, as in the days when God preserved me; as I was in the days of my youth when the secret of God was upon my tabernacle'. Often have men made this cry as they have travelled earth's pilgrimage and so have I; but in spite of the changeful scenes of life, I have found that life is good and I know that 'all things work together for good to them that love God'.

My childhood, after the age of five, was spent in Burn Cross, a typical Yorkshire village. I have always thought that it was a pretty name, no doubt derived from the fact that whichever way you entered the village you had at some point to cross a burn. Tennyson would have delighted in these burns just as he did, and wrote about, the burns he knew near his Lincolnshire home at Somersby. 'Men may come and men may go, but I go on forever'. That is a parable of life with all its changing scenes of trouble and joy. The burns of my childhood thrilled me. How I loved sailing paper boats on them or paddling in the clear, sparkling water on a hot summer's afternoon.

Then there were glorious woods – Spring Wood, Greno Wood. I lived under the shadow of the former and it was always full of cuckoo flowers and bluebells in the spring. I once described this wood to a prisoner in Holloway Prison for Women who was awaiting trial for the murder of her child. I was doing locum duties for the chaplain at the time. This woman had remained silent since her arrest so I was asked to break that silence. It was a sunny afternoon and I sat by her side in the cell and talked of the woods of my childhood, of the flowers, trees, singing of the birds and the sighing of the wind through the trees. I saw that her interest was awakened and then she began to cry and told me of the tragedy of her life, too pitiful for words. I was thus able to help her and bring her to take some interest in life. She was not executed, the verdict being 'guilty but insane'. The same thing happened when I was the chaplain and education officer of the General Hospital near Cologne, during my service with the army of occupation after the First Great War. One bitter winter's night the officer commanding – a doctor – sent for me. He told me of a man in one of the huts who was dying. He said there was hope for him if his interest in life and a desire to recover could be aroused. "See what you can do Padre," he said. It was after midnight. Outside the snow was drifting and it was bitterly cold. I went in and sat beside the man and began to talk of the bluebells, cuckoo flowers, trees and hills, of the God of nature and of grace and I said, "It is winter now, the storm is raging outside. I want to live to go back to dear old Blighty again and see another spring." After a prayer, I left him. He had not spoken to me and I thought that my visit had been in vain until next morning, after breakfast in the mess, the colonel came and said, "You cured the man I sent you to see, Padre. This morning he is talking about bluebells and the springtime and says that he is going to live," and so he did.

The trees too! How I loved them. I could climb them like a monkey, swinging from branch to branch and this gave me breadth of shoulder and strong arms. Again this was to prove of great value to me in the Great War. I was never afraid of climbing to dizzy heights. Once I climbed to an observation post at the top of Arras Cathedral, during the Battle of Arras. It was a risky climb up a perpendicular ladder with shells screaming about. On another occasion I climbed to the top of the Cloth Hall at Ypres and walked along the crumbling masonry and a still more thrilling experience in the bay of Mudros, at the mouth of the Dardenelles. I put off in a rowing boat from another ship to board the Aquitania which was then a transport. When I arrived, a sailor shouted, "Shall we send down a sling to hoist you up, sir?" I replied "No" and so I climbed a rope ladder with the boat rocking below – a great height but my tree climbing as a lad came in good stead and the sailors on deck were astonished at my performance for I had my pack on my shoulders. For some reason or other there were no steps operating at the time and the ship was anchored out in the bay.

Greno Wood, the other wood that had an influence on me, was a romantic place. It was part of an extensive ancient forest. There were stone quarries and winding paths, thick undergrowth and dark avenues of trees, through this wonderland I climbed and met with many adventures. One emerged from the wood after an upward climb onto the old stage-coach road and here the view and the breezes repaid with interest the stiff climb. On one side, as far as the eye could see, there are hills and dales, farms and villages, and the smoke rising from the chimneys of distant coal mines. On the other side are the moors and the hills of the Pennine Range and in between Wharncliffe Crags – the home of the legendary Dragon of Wharncliffe. This is the scene of Sir Walter Scott's opening chapter of 'Ivanhoe' in which he speaks of pleasant districts of merry England watered by the River Don and running through the valley is this river which means so much to Sheffield and the surrounding countryside. Onward the river runs, fighting with stones, letting its life be dominated by the huge rocks that heap themselves on one another, that fall in showers down the hillside, forming a stony pathway leading at last to new shapes of grass and moss and fern.

It was impossible for me to live in this country without loving it deeply. Year in, year out I wandered amid these lovely scenes, often as early as five and six o'clock in the morning, shouting and singing and glad to be alive. I knew the patterns, forms and vagaries of the clouds. I saw the tender greys, the gorgeous blues and the flaming reds. I saw them in troops as they danced and quivered round the sun. I watched the deer wander at will, chased the rabbits and saw the buzzards soaring in the air. In winter I revelled in the sun-drenched snow. I filled my lungs with the pure air of those everlasting hills, so pure and health-giving that once when I had an attack of influenza I made the climb and the flu vanished as if by magic.

I once heard my old friend The Rev Edward McLellan give a lecture on 'The music of a merry heart'. I certainly had, through the influence of this lovely countryside, that music which he so vividly described.

In fact, my soul was full of music and like Thomas Moore I could sing with joy:

> Thou are, O God, the life and light
> Of all this wondrous world we see:
> Its glow by day, its smile by night,
> Are but reflections caught from Thee:
> Where're we turn, Thy glories shine,
> And all things fair and bright are thine!

This ministry of nature has been wonderful to me and has had a profound influence on my life. This influence too was experienced in another way. The romance of it all inspired my imagination. The result was that I wrote a serial for a West Riding weekly paper entitled 'The Mysterious Horseman'. The editor featured it but alas he only gave me seven shillings and sixpence for it. Still even that sum, in those days, was a lot for a village boy in his teens. Years afterwards I reached what some might call the dizzy heights of success, for on my return from the Middle East, during the Great War, the editor of the *Manchester Guardian* accepted and published my article on 'The long white road to Monastir', and whilst serving on the Rhine with the Sheffield and Bradford troops, I became the special correspondent of the *Sheffield Daily Telegraph*, describing each week the activities of the West Riding men. I also wrote many descriptive articles for our local army paper *The Cologne Post* and subscribed to many army publications. My stories too were welcomed by several magazines and periodicals at home and all this resulted from the seeds sown by the influence of the hills, woods and crags of my boyhood years.

In another direction, from the area I have just described, one could see the Thorncliffe Ironworks and Collieries. These were in a valley surrounded by woods and here men toiled for their bread. These works were founded in 1874 by good Methodists who gave their names to the firm – Newton-Chambers. My grandmother, who knew them well, often told me stories of George Newton and Thomas Chambers. They were greatly beloved and used to conduct classes at the old Mount Pleasant Methodist Church. They were God-fearing men. There was no snobbishness about them and they were greeted by their men by their Christian names 'George' and 'Tom'; in fact, the whole works had a family atmosphere. So greatly beloved and honoured were they that once, when times were bad and it looked as if the finances were on the rocks, the men worked a week for no wages in order to help to pull things round.

This sacrifice did pull things round, so it was not in vain. Later on it was returned to the men, pressed down and running over, when more prosperous times came. There were no trade unions in those days and, in fact, there was no need for them when such understanding and sympathy was manifested by masters and men. My grandfather Peaker built some of the warehouses and workshops for the firm and later on he carried out many improvements both here and throughout the districts.

Here and there dotted over the countryside were splendid mansions – Wharncliffe Hall, the seat of the Earl of Wharncliffe, at Wortley; Wentworth Woodhouse, the seat of the Earl Fitzwilliam, near Rotherham; Barnes Hall, where I spent much of my time; Whitley Hall, an Elizabethan mansion which my great-grandfather Peaker helped to restore. In those days these great houses were the centre of hospitality, all were welcome – rich and poor. They are now taken over by the nation and trade unions and we have lost a good deal, lost a vital part of old England, lost that which maintained the life of the villages around these estates and, was productive of so much good.

Burn Cross itself, was a long street of chiefly stone houses, with the common at one end and Bracken Hill at the other. There was one side road leading to the top of the hill and here I lived in the midst of a cluster of houses built by my great-grandfather Hobson; round the corner were some brick houses and opposite a farm. My great-grandfather built three houses in a row with gardens in the front and in them lived my grandmother, her deaf and dumb sister Hannah, cared for by my grandmother until she died, and her sister Caroline. There was only one public building in the village, the Methodist Chapel, erected in 1865, although for many years before that there had been the 'Little Chapel'. This chapel, which had been used at times as a day school, was to prove the greatest influence in my life and in the lives of many others.

The village had many quaint houses and two public houses and in my boyhood days strange things happened at times. At Christmas, pigs were slaughtered in the streets and the block would always be surrounded with children. I remember the squeals of the dying pigs as their throats were cut and the scraping of the body after it had been soaked with boiling water.

When a man was idle and neglected his work he would be tarred and feathered and pushed around the village in a wheelbarrow. At each public house great quantities of beer were poured down his throat and the throats of his tormentors. Whenever they came to a pond he was thrown in. This treatment generally proved effective but it was a sorry spectacle for any boy to see. He much preferred the German bands which came at times and the man with a dancing bear.

I saw, at times, fearful fights. Once I saw two navvies, stripped to the waist, fighting. One was knocked out and had his face beaten in by a woman whilst he was lying on the ground. The woman used a tin can for the purpose. I have seen the effigies of enemies burned in gardens and, in those days, it was hardly safe for girls and women to be out in the dark. I recall several criminal assaults. I remember one woman being knocked onto a heap of stones. It was a lonely road between two woods. She had an umbrella in her hand and whilst the tramp, who had assaulted her, was bending over her, she pushed the point of her umbrella stick into his eye. This brought about her escape and the tramp's arrest. I was knocked down on the road one day by a tramp and bore the marks of the blow for some years.

The most vivid experience of my five-year-old period was beginning school. The school – a board-school – was built the year I was born. It was a fine stone-built structure with a large playground. We paid one penny a week in those days. I suppose this was a token payment. Here, in the infant school, I had the first sorrow of my life. The headmistress, Miss Crossland, whom I still remember, was an ideal mistress, kind and gentle and passionately fond of little children. In my second year she died. I went, with the other infants, to her funeral in the adjoining cemetery and remember how we stood around her grave and sang that rather haunting hymn – 'Sleep on, beloved, sleep, and take thy rest' – with the refrain after each verse, 'Good night! Good night! Good night!'

Later on I graduated into the junior school, a school where in those days we completed our education by the age of fourteen. We had no opportunity of sitting for a scholarship but we did receive a very sound education, especially in the three 'Rs'. The headmaster, whose full name we always used, Francis Lucas Elliott, was a bachelor and very keen for the success of his school and proud of it too. He was passionately fond of horses and hired a stagecoach and four horses to take his teachers out from time to time. I kept in touch with him throughout the years until he died. He was coming home from his holiday, somewhere on the south coast, when he died suddenly in the train.

The assistants in the junior school were a mixed lot. One I had great respect for was Miss Redfern who died at the ripe old age of over ninety. She had lived in the village all her life and hundreds of boys and girls had passed through her hands. She was also a Sunday School teacher. Another, Harry Wilson, inspired me but later on he gave up teaching and became a very successful businessman. There were others who were tyrannical and the only impression they left on me was of their ignorance of the mind of a child or how to educate him. One, a Welshman, seemed to have a real delight in thrashing us and he always began by pulling down his bottom lip and saying, "I will give you five or six, you thick monkey." How well I remember that threat. Another was of the same kind – a hot-tempered Welshman. He thrashed me one afternoon. I was holding my pen and he caught his arm on the nib. His rage then knew no bounds and he continued his thrashing, from which I suffered for some time and which caused my grandmother to give him a solemn warning as to what she would do to him in the future if he tried to lift a finger against me. Anyhow, he met his doom when he tried to thrash a bigger boy – the butcher's son. The boy promptly knocked him down and the fight, long to be remembered, took place. In a subsequent argument with the headmaster about the incident, he again lost his temper and in a rage hit him and so, to our joy and relief, was instantly dismissed from the school. There was no sadness of farewell on this tyrant's departure. One form of punishment we all hated was the wearing of the dunce cap. I have a vivid recollection of this lunatic contrived creation. Great ingenuity must have been used in the making of these fantastic, horrible things. It was a real torture to stand in the corner wearing them and to be laughed at by the rest of the school. If this form of punishment was in use today the Royal Society for the Prevention of Cruelty to Children would surely step in.

A great joy came to me when the first school library was formed – an innovation in those days. The best boy in the class during the week was allowed to take home a book to read. I contrived to qualify for this real treat and many were the glorious hours I spent reading Dickens, Scott, Kingsley and other writers. The school concert was an event we always looked forward to, especially when we formed a troupe of which I was the centre boy. Before the happy day arrived I sent out letters to the big houses and halls stating that I proposed to bring my troupe at a certain time and we received no refusals. It was a novelty for the Christmas house parties at these mansions and much was the astonishment of the guests to see a troupe of small boys. I had prepared a fixed programme of songs and jokes and I accompanied the songs on my melodeon which I had won for reciting at a district competition. We were feasted at each place we visited, so much so, that before the day ended our stomachs rebelled. We also got so rich by the cash we received that I employed a boy, at the rate of threepence, to carry my overcoat.

I was six at the time of Queen Victoria's Jubilee and we celebrated it by attending a service in the Ecclesfield Parish Church and afterwards by a glorious tea and the present of a souvenir mug, long since lost. Ten years later I shared in the Queen's Diamond Jubilee celebrations and received a medal. I once walked several miles to Sheffield to see the Queen when she visited the city. The dear old lady, sitting in her state coach, seemed to me like any boy's grandmother. The pageantry of the procession naturally impressed and delighted me along with the thousands of others who lined the streets. I little thought in those days that I should visit Buckingham Palace and attend a King George V Levee at St James' Palace – but that is another story. We never know where the winding road of life will lead us. Strange coincidences happen to all of us. They have happened to me.

Memories of school days still crowd upon one. The chums and games that we had and the thrilling experiences viewed from the angle of childhood. We lived on the hill top and there were some nine other boys in the gang that we formed. In the summer we had our cricket pitch on the grass verge of the road. There was hardly any traffic, it was an ancient road leading to a couple of farms and onto the fields we loved so much. I remember one particular evening when we had a so-called cricket match. One of our team, and a member of our gang, known by the name of Jo Willie got very tired of bowling at me, so he smashed the stumps in his rage. In returned I smashed Joe Willie and then he smashed me by throwing a brick which cut my head very severely. I have the scar to this day. Another game we played on that road was Knur and Spell – a game played with a ball (knur), trap (spell) and trapstick. This game is played chiefly in the North of England. We also managed to raise a football team. As most of us had only one penny a week pocket money, we raised the necessary cash to buy a ball and some posts by going round with a collecting box. I wrote the appeal and did most of the begging. One of our farmer friends allowed us to use his field and what exciting matches we had! Disaster came one year. I had collected a good sum of money and handed the same to another boy who was our treasurer. Unfortunately, his mother was in need of money and so she used ours and could not repay it, so we had to make the most of a bad job by joining, that particular season, a more prosperous club.

I had a great desire to possess a bicycle. I used to see the penny farthing ridden by one man in our village. How I envied him! The next stage was the development of what is known as the 'bone-shaker'. I saw one of these which had been discarded by a man I knew. He had thrown it into the corner of a coal shed. I thought, "here is my chance," so I asked him to give it to me. This he generously did. It was very rusty, the brake and tyres were missing, but I got to work and first of all cleaned off the rust and then polished the rims with boot blacking – I could not afford paint. I got some rubber from a pram and tied it on the wheels with string and pieces of wire. There was my bone-shaker, and a shaker it was! I took it out proudly and began on the top of the hill. My first attempt landed me in a thorn hedge. I tried the other side of the hill and down I went – remember I had no brake on the machine – up the hill came a girl. She had been to the village shop to purchase a jar of jam. I met her on that hillside half-way down and we collided, falling down together in the dust. The jam jar was smashed but being anxious to help her and, as I thought, save her from a scolding at home, I helped her to scoop up the jam and place what we could of the mixture in the broken jar. Fortunately, neither of us was hurt. I persevered with that machine until I could ride it. There was a cycle club of the more fortunate young people, and some adults, in the village. I wanted to join the club but they would not have me – one look at my machine decided that and, of course, my penny a week was no good to any club. Still the roads are free and I thanked God for that. One Saturday afternoon the club went out for a run and much to the disgust of the members I followed at the back. Riding along what we called the top road, I felt some strong thumps in my back. I thought someone was throwing stones at me and I cried out "Stop throwing!" I then found some of the others laughing at me. What had happened was that the old pram tyres of the back wheel had come loose and with each revolution of the wheel the tyre was hitting me in the back. That was my last trip on the old bone-shaker. Later on, there was a jumble sale in our schoolroom and being a generous kind of boy, I gave my old cycle to the sale and it actually fetched ten shillings – a lot of money in those days – and wishfully I thought of all I could have done with it. I did not possess another bicycle until I began my ministry in Horncastle, Lincolnshire at the age of twenty-four. When I arrived there, a brand new 'Rudge Whitworth' machine was delivered to the door of my lodgings. I naturally took it in. Who gave it to me I have never found out but it was a God-send, as I had some twenty-one village churches to visit and my average of journeys in this visitation was one hundred miles a week. To return to my gift, I received it on the Saturday. On the Sunday I had to go over the Wolds to Donnington-on-Bain, a distance of some ten or so miles each way. I had not ridden a bicycle since the old bone-shaker days twelve years before but I got on that brand new machine and cycled off perfectly as if I had been riding each day. Hence, if you can ride the bone-shaker you can also ridge the new machine.

The farm opposite my home was always a joy to me. The very smell of it awakened memories of the old farm at Tankersley. It was owned by a man called Redfern who, I was told, had emigrated to Australia and returned home and, with the money he had earned, bought the farm. I often helped in all sorts of ways, cleaning out the stables, haymaking, harvesting and also the very back-tiring job of singling the turnip field, for this work the old farmer would give me an occasional threepence, and often I shared with him and his one labourer the bread and cheese and herb beer he served by way of lunch. How sweet that tasted to a hungry boy! His wife was one of the kindest women I have ever met. Her memory is fragrant.

Another thrill was when the woodmen came to fell the trees in the Spring Wood. Some of these trees I had climbed like a monkey and I always felt like saying:

> Woodman spare that tree,
> Touch not her gentle bough,
> In youth it sheltered me,
> And I'll not forget it now.

Yes, that was an old song I loved to sing, and when the trees fell by the woodmen's axe, my heart at times was sad. I was always on the spot at these times and gathered the chips and branches for firewood.

3

Early Influences

I have elsewhere mentioned the building of the chapel. It was always called the 'chapel' and not 'church'. Built of local stone, it was approached by some steps and was surrounded with high railings. Underneath was the schoolroom and there was a small yard at the back. There was no other place of worship in the village and it formed part of what was, then known, as the Sheffield Third Circuit of the Primitive Methodist Connexion. In those days one never anticipated that in 1932 all the various sections of the Methodist Church would be united to form one great church.

I began my spiritual pilgrimage in the Sunday School at the age of five. The school itself was very plain. In the centre were a large slow combustion stove and a boiler to heat the chapel above. The stools were without backs and there were no other rooms. The infant class was in one corner and as we progressed year by year, we just moved round the room with the stools placed in so many squares. At one end was the superintendent's desk and also steps up to a trap door which opened into the chapel, where the young men held a Bible class after they had attended the school opening. It was, I think, a sensible arrangement that the infants had A B C boards to learn the alphabet, for that helped them with their day school work.

The teachers were all from the village and we always called them by their Christian names. I recall those names now, Luther Winkley, also the school secretary, who had lost his leg and wore an iron rod – a strange device with which he could hop along and jump with anybody. John Steele, the superintendent, who worked as foreman of the fettling shop in the local steel works. He was a big man with a large head and twinkling eyes – a stalwart Yorkshireman who loved a joke and could laugh with us. He used to read stories to us at the close of the school. Then there was James Parkinson, who worked in the engineering part of the local works. He was one of the kindest men I have ever met and his family, too, radiated gladness. Charles Woodward, the blacksmith, a local preacher who became, for a time, a parish councillor. Agnes Redfern, also a day school teacher, who nursed me when I was unruly and gave me sweets. Lucilla Sausby, who married my old friend, another teacher, Harry Wilson.

So very many I could mention, they are to me:

Sweet dreamland faces passing to and fro
Telling of the memories of long years ago.

These were the men and women who helped to mould my character, who deeply influenced me for good, who made it possible for me to believe the highest ideals. They were not wealthy, and had to earn their daily bread but they held aloft the standard of principle and maintained the true dignity of human character. Much has been written about the influence of the village chapel in those days of seventy and eighty years ago but let it be said that at Burn Cross the leaders, both in the Sunday School and the church, made every effort to brighten the lives and to inspire the people of the village. The chapel was a living centre of beneficent activity.

Who can forget the thrill of the Magic Lantern, the concerts with local talent, talent that in some cases won fame in the great city; the excursions we had to seaside and country. To the seaside – Scarborough, Bridlington, Cleethorpes – we went in trains with hard, bare seats. At about five in the morning you would see the exodus of practically the whole of the village to the railway station with tin boxes full of food. The country excursions in the farm wagons, with the schoolroom seats placed in them, were even more thrilling. The plod, plod of the farm horses, the singing of the children, the rolling countryside – all brought infinite delight.

The Sunday School Anniversary was always a red letter day for all the village. The platform occupied the whole end of the chapel and nearly reached the ceiling. The orchestra was augmented from other villages, violins, cellos, flutes, with a local conductor. The anthems were generally from the Messiah and nothing can beat a Yorkshire Sunday School choir singing these and the hymns. Then on the week-night, there were the recitations. I said my first at the age of five and later on I recited at the competition organised for all the Sunday Schools and won the first prize on the two occasions that I took part. The prizes being a case of paradise birds and a melodeon. So much for my training as a reciter. The lanes and roads of these Yorkshire villages are full of children forming themselves into a long procession. There are some eight Sunday Schools and they march with banners flying, headed by the local band. It is the day of all days – Whit Monday, a day of singing and of rejoicing. Some of the banners are very beautiful, depicting Christ blessing little children – ours was rather a severe one showing a big eye which gazed upon us and a Bible. I have never seen a banner like this anywhere else and I and the other children would have preferred those showing the little children surrounding the Saviour. From early morning we had been awake putting on our new suits and anticipating the joy set before us. We had two well-known places where we sang our hymns, the Market Place at Chapeltown, a good walk away from our village, and the ten acre. Crowds would line the roads and gather in these places to hear us sing. Our school was the first to leave as, for many years, we had gone to sing in front of Barnes Hall just on the village outskirts. After singing the special hymns once again, we all marched under our flag to receive a large and very welcome bun. The rest of the day was spent in one of the Barnes Hall fields where we played games. The closing hours – and often as the sun was sinking – we revelled in the kiss-in-the-ring game, singing the ditties that had been sung for ages.

'King William was King David's son', 'Oats and beans and barley grow', 'When the trees were all covered', 'In and out the window'. What a thrill to be chosen by some girl playmate as we sang, "Open the ring and take one in."

I was always fond of one particular verse sung after the nuptial ceremony had been sealed with a kiss:

> Now you're married you must obey,
> You must be true to all you say,
> You must be kind, you must be good
> And help your wife to chop some wood.

Where is now the merry party of those days so long ago? Scattered and gone! The few that remain are old like I am. We used to sing a hymn in the school in those days telling us that

'Childhood days will soon be over' – with the haunting, yet true, thought:
> Soon we part it may be never
> Never more to meet again.

And that again is a picture of life.

Sometimes we had another experience connected with the chapel, ten or fourteen days' revival services. Generally some well-known revivalist preacher came along. Gipsy Tom was one I remember. I do not know if he was a real Romany but he excited us with his stories. Looking back I can see how crude his sermons were. He preached with vigour the burning, torturing flames of Hell, contrasted with the joys of Heaven where all good boys would wear crowns and play harps. After these sermons he would appeal for converts and generally the children would be the first to respond. I was always ready to go to the front for I did not want to burn in Hell and I certainly longed for a crown and a harp. Some of these evangelists were really excellent and we felt the impact of their services. I remember several genuine conversions and these always created a great stir in the life of the village. There is an intimate association in village life and a change of heart and life affecting one of the community affects many. There is a lighter side to one incident during the closing night of a revival service. This evangelist said that all he wanted for his services were his railway fare, hospitality and the collections on the last Sunday, and also his final service.

I remember the appeal he made for a good collection finishing by quoting the lines of a hymn:
> Whatever Lord, we lend to Thee,
> Repaid a thousand fold 'twill be.

I had one shilling and one halfpenny in my pocket. The shilling I had saved for our local feast – a wonderful collection of roundabouts and shows which I looked forward to – and the halfpenny I had brought for the collection. The collection box came round, "Shall I make the sacrifice?" I wondered, "If I do, will it be repaid a thousand-fold?" My decision was made, into that box went the whole of my earthly wealth – one shilling and one halfpenny. I am afraid I looked for a long time afterwards for the repayment promised – "Repaid a thousand-fold!" That was the way a Yorkshire boy looked at things. It is easy to laugh about it but anyone knowing the mind of a child will understand. I might say that gift has been repaid a thousand-fold, not perhaps in the literal way I expected – but in other ways far better. My spiritual awakening began in that chapel, not at any revival service but simply and unostentatiously. I was just an ordinary boy and lived like others. There was nothing exciting about it, no dreams, no spiritual struggles. I had read and heard of wicked men who became saints, I had read Bunyan's 'Pilgrim's Progress' and how Christian fled from the wrath to come. I suppose that some natures need something catastrophic to change them, but we should remember that Christ said that the Kingdom of God is like a harvest field – 'First the blade, then the ear, then the full corn in the ear' and you hardly notice it growing. That always appealed to me. Like others I could often say, "We are growing up for Jesus" and I, and so many others, have grown up loving Him. The seed had been well sown and fostered by the good men who dedicated their lives to the children of that Sunday School and so my soul was awakened and all things became new. I joined the Band of Hope and the Christian Endeavour – both great movements for building up life and character and I took part in the meetings held.

From my earliest days I felt called to become a minister and again I received every encouragement from the leaders of the chapel. I preached my first sermon in the schoolroom, I was just fifteen at the time. My text was 'Come unto Me, all ye that labour and are heavy laden'; I can see the manuscript now. It was written in large, boyish handwriting and I read it. My next attempt was a disaster. I wrote a sermon on a text which appealed to me: 'Remember now thy creator in the days of thy youth, while the evil days come not, nor the years draw nigh, when thou shalt say I have no pleasure in them'. I memorised what I had written and, probably with the feeling that I must make an impression on my congregation, I determined to preach without notes. This is where the disaster came and a well merited know-out to my vain desire. It was a hot summer's evening. Some thirty people were present in the schoolroom for the week evening service. I stood by a table near to the stove in the centre of the schoolroom. It had been well and truly black-leaded seeing that the summer had come. All went well until I came to give out my text. I began, "This is a warning to all young people which we must remember" – then my mind went blank, I could not remember anything. The perspiration poured from my forehead and I put my hand on the stove and drew it across my wet forehead, I suppose for inspiration – then the congregation laughed. I forgot my manners and said, "What are you laughing at?" They said, "Look at your face!" I left my place and looked into a little mirror which we had in the room and then I could see why they had laughed so much! I went away in confusion and someone closed the service. I did not give up but tried again and again. I am glad that I was taught one lesson, not to be vain and too self-confident. There were other lessons which I had the sense to profit by.

Not only did I preach but I also went around the village visiting the people and sometimes holding cottage prayer meetings. What a welcome I received. Even in those early days I stood by the bed of the dying and offered up my simple prayers – there are no prayers like the prayers of childhood and looking back, I know that this was my greatest preparation for my future ministry and in it I can see the Hand of God.

I was for many years one of the managers of a group of London County Council schools in North London. I was visiting one of the schools one day – a very large school, and I said to the headmistress, "Do you know the lines written by Isaac Watts: 'Happy the child whose tender years receive instruction well?'" She replied, "Yes," and there in that London schoolroom the whole of the past came back to me 'through memory's sunset air', and before us sat the children of the present generation. They looked so happy and I rejoiced that they were having far better opportunities than ever I had and yes, in the old village Sunday School, the foundations were well and truly laid for which I thank God.

Life is moulded by a thousand subtle influences; by example and precept; by love and literature; by friends and neighbours; by the world in which we live as well as the spirits of our forefathers, whose legacy of good deeds we inherit, and by ourselves and all this I have found abundantly true and especially in the days of my youth.

4

Working Days 1895–1903

I remember on one occasion, visiting a large grammar school and I was deeply moved by one sentence in a prayer that the five hundred scholars repeated in unison: "O Lord, help those who have gone out from this school into the world to fight the battle of life." I needed that prayer when I left school at the age of fourteen. I suppose that nearly all children look forward to the end of their school days. Is it not true that in childhood we are never satisfied? I know that I often stood by the window of my home and looked out and looking, felt that there was something in the world better than I had ever had. Where was it? My eyes and thoughts were always enquiring, searching for something I had not realised. I expect that childlike, I wanted to live faster than my time.

Later on I found out the truth and wonder of Browning's advice given in his poem 'Rabbi Ben Ezra':

> Grow old along with me!
> The best is yet to be,
> The last of life, for which the first was made;
> Our times are in His hands
> Who saith, "A whole I planned,
> Youth shows but half; trust God,
> See all, nor be afraid."

One Sunday afternoon, a few weeks after I had left school, George Harvey, my grandmother's nephew, paid us a visit. He was the manager of one of the departments of the iron and steel works section of Newton-Chambers Thorncliffe Ironworks and Collieries. My grandmother said to him, "Will you give George a job at the works?" "Yes," he replied, "but it will be no collar and cuff job. He will have to rough it like the rest." 'Rough it' I did! I had to rise at 5am and leave home half an hour later to walk across the fields to the works. In my hand I carried a can of tea and a basket with provisions to feed me during the long day. I was given a check with a number, it was of brass, the size of a penny, and this had to be deposited in the box before the bell finished at six o'clock and collected at five o'clock in the afternoon when the day's work was done.

At eight o'clock we had half an hour allowed for breakfast and one hour for dinner between twelve and one. In those days the boys were not allowed to stay in the shops for meals and not the slightest attempt was made by the management to provide any place where we could stay. So we wandered about, searching for some warm place in winter and in the summer sat in the fields around the works. All this meant eleven hours at the works, nine and a half of which we were supposed to be working, and as the journey took half an hour each way, we had twelve hours away from home. The working week, including seven hours on Saturdays, was fifty-four and a half hours. Compare those long hours with those of today!

My pay was five shillings a week and the firm kept one week in hand in case any left without notice. I am sure of this, that we did five shillings worth of damage each week! After the First Great War I returned to visit the works and to give a lecture on my experiences. The managing director took the chair at the lecture and by a coincidence he was an ex-major of the 12th Division in France at the time that I was a chaplain to the same division. Prior to this, I was entertained to lunch in the splendid canteen at the works and I told them how that, in the days of my boyhood, I had wandered around finding a place to eat and contrasted it with the splendid provision made in the present days. I also stated the cost of the lunch I was then enjoying was paid for by the interest owing on the five shillings kept back for damage I had done in the course of my work!

My usual task for the first year was sweeping out one shop and lighting two fires between six and eight, then the rest of the day was spent filling in orders. My office was a cubby hole, without windows, and lighted by one gas jet. In between office work, I wandered round the works getting myself very dirty by tinkering with various things in the blacksmith and moulding shops, the dirt being added to by men who threw various things at me because I happened to be the boss' relative. In those days, so long ago, boys were often degraded and demoralised by men from whom something very different ought to have been expected – demoralised sometimes in the foulest way. In these days this condition of things would not be tolerated. You will, however, find the sadistic type of man in any community. Many of the men who threw things at me were of this type. True, there were exceptions and these were men of strong religious views and they saved me from despair – their memory is fragrant.

After the first year, I began working in the shops. I suppose it was attended by the manager, my relative, that I should receive training in fitting stoves, gutters, spouts, stabling equipment and all kinds of castings. My favourite job was in the rainwater pipes, spouting, gutters and drainage pipe shops. The reason was that sometimes it gave me the chance of leaving the works and going with the men to erect these pipes and fix the spouts along the eaves of the rooves of various buildings, cottages, farms, workshops and colliery engine houses. This meant climbing ladders and I always felt that it was a real thrill and adventure to do this. I never thought of danger and yet I remember, on one occasion climbing a ladder with a spout across my two arms to a very high building. The building was on a slope and I had nearly reached the top when the ladder began to slip. A man, called Billy Seal, who was in charge of the works, saw my danger and at once threw himself on the side of the ladder and saved it from crashing down. Later on, I was given what was considered a very important task: to study the various plans for work to be carried out and to measure the various castings and mark them with the necessary figures for the positions they were to be built into. I was always fond of my white paint pot and brush. I also helped to make plaster casts for mouldings. This enabled me to experiment with plaster of Paris to my heart's content!

In the meantime, I attended evening classes in the old school, often wishing I could spend the whole day studying. There were two books which had been given to me and which inspired me to make the most and best of myself. One was Todd's 'Self Improvement' and the other Samuel Smile's 'Self-help'. The latter impressed me the most, with its biographies and autobiographies of how the lives of the successful are supposed to have been shaped. Although Smile's book was published in 1859, it has, in recent years, come back into favour with a new edition. I remember having a chat with Mr R.A. Butler, when he was Chancellor of the Exchequer, it was at the close of the Public Morality Council Annual Meeting at the Caxton Hall. I said, "Have you ever read Smile's 'Self-help?'" and he replied, "Yes! And I wish the youth of today would read it." I little thought in those days that I should ask any chancellor a question like that or that I should give addresses at Rotary luncheons and at youth gatherings on that book. It helped me and it will continue to help others for years to come. I knew this, and in my old age I know it still, that life and our so-called career is bound to be an uphill business, a matter of constant climbing.

I continued this climb in the iron and steel works for the next five years, receiving, as a so-called suitable reward for my long hours and for my efforts, the princely sum of an increase of one shilling a year – so that at the age of nineteen my pay was ten shillings a week. One day I decided to launch out and break with the past. It was a glorious spring day in March 1900. I left the works at dinner time and went home and changed into my best suit. "Where are you going?" asked my mother. "To Sheffield," I replied. "What are you going for?" she asked. "To get a new job," I said. She tried to dissuade me but to no avail. I arrived in Sheffield and looked round the centre of the city for the best and most imposing office. This I found in Division Street. It was the office of J.G. Graves, who, a few years before, had begun a mail order business for which the firm became known throughout the country. I went into the lobby and asked to see the manager. "Have you an appointment?" I was asked. "No," I replied and I was about to be refused admittance when I saw the open door of a room on my left and noticed a large desk with a man sitting behind it. Without more ado, I pushed past the commissionaire and entered the room. The man, who was wearing glasses, looked up and said, "Who are you?"

"George Kendall from Burn Cross near Chapeltown" I replied. I had it pat and the direct answer amused him, as I could see by the twinkle in his eye. He asked me what I wanted. "A post on your staff," I replied. "Why on our staff?" he asked. "Well," I replied, "this seems to be the best looking office I have seen and I thought I should like to work in it!"

"What can you do?" was his further question. "I can do anything you want me to do if you give me a week or two to learn."

"Right," he said, "I will give you a post."

"You will have to wait for me as I shall have to give a month's notice where I am now employed," I explained. "A month's notice!" he exclaimed, "Astonishing, but I will wait for you." And so he did. On the twenty-second day of March in the year nineteen hundred I received a letter from J.G. Graves accepting me but adding, "Your age and experience do not warrant my offering you more than fifteen shillings per week to start with. It will depend afterwards entirely on your own efforts and the amount of ability you display."

The next morning, I returned to Thorncliffe and I went into the office and gave my month's notice. "What is this young fool up to and why does he want to leave?" asked the manager of a friend. "To get a better and a more pleasant job to suit his case," was the reply. And a better job it proved to be with the five shillings a week more than I had been receiving.

I still had to rise early in the morning, for I had half an hour's walk to the railway station to catch a train which left Chapeltown at 7 o'clock. The office hours were eight o'clock in the morning to six in the evening with one and a half hours for dinner. One of the most sensible things I did was to join the thriving YMCA in its excellent premises in Fargate, the centre of the city. There I could spend my spare time studying in the dinner hour. I also had many of my meals there and attended elocution classes. I took advantage of the city's many splendid evening classes and seldom arrived home before ten or eleven in the evening.

My work was altogether new. I began on approval ledgers, then went on to commission ledgers and finally became a correspondent, both answering and signing letters. Sometimes we were privileged to have a typist but more often they were written. Another of my duties from time to time, was to total up the sales figures for the accountants. All this was of good service to me and I found it of great value in later life.

I had four very happy years with the firm, with suitable increase of salary each year. J.G. Graves was one of Sheffield's great benefactors. He gave a park and art gallery to the city and these bear his name. He was a member of the Methodist Church and an inspiration to all his staff. When I left to prepare for college, I was given a set of Dickens' books and told that if I did not like the ministry he would gladly have me back. I kept in touch with him until he passed away.

5

College Days 1903–06

Foreword

I am very pleased to write these lines – introducing this chapter in the remarkable life of The Rev George Kendall. Two lines in particular struck me: firstly, the opening words: 'I had always known what my destiny would be' – namely, in his case, years of faithful service as a Methodist minister. He firmly felt a sense of being called and persevered in following his vocation, despite the highs and lows of subsequent years. His formative period at Theological College was an important one, and equipped him with many of the skills he would later need. In reading this chapter, there is a sense of joyful expectancy as he commits himself to this path. The other line is: ' … you never know where the winding road of life will lead you …' Kendall is referring to his first visit to London, when he stayed in the Manse in Queen's Park, where he would one day live, 30 years later. Life is indeed full of twists and turns; of chance meetings and seeming coincidences, which the perspective of faith attributes to God's guiding hand.

It is astonishing how Kendall had a front-row seat at some of the most significant moments in modern British history – not only two World Wars and the burial of 'The Unknown Warrior', but, as we see in the following pages, a memorable rally on 13 October 1905: Winston Churchill was campaigning for a seat in the Manchester area as a Liberal candidate. Turning up without a ticket, Kendall managed to sit with the dignitaries on the podium and recalled how the speeches 'aroused the enthusiasm of the great audience'. What he does not mention is that there was a disturbance over the question of Women's Suffrage, which landed Christabel Pankhurst and Annie Kearney briefly in prison. This caused much media interest and raised the profile of their cause. Little did Kendall realise how quickly the world was changing before his very eyes!

May his recollections inspire us all to be faithful in our duties and to realise that we are all involved in a great drama that goes beyond our individual lives.

HE Cardinal Vincent Nichols
Archbishop of Westminster

I had always known what my destiny would be and that was to become a minister of the Methodist Church. I had sat at the feet of many men of ripe experience and listened to the advice given to me. I had been inspired by many men who had served the church as lay preachers, men like Major General Campbell and Superintendent Bielby of the West Riding Police Force. These men were a tower of strength to the Methodist churches in Sheffield and the area around the city. The one to whom I owed everything was our local minister The Rev John Holland, who spent long hours coaching me for my examinations. He was one of the most remarkable men I have ever met and possessed outstanding gifts. He was generous in his treatment of young men. He was also a very hard worker and expected me to copy his example.

I will pass over the details of the struggles which I had to equip myself for my life's work – my one outstanding desire and for which I was determined to live. I could not foresee the future but I could prepare for it by seizing all the opportunities that came along. On occasions I got up at four o'clock in the morning and generally not later than five, then going off to my daily work and on my return working often until midnight, burning the proverbial midnight oil. To keep my health, I took long walks through the glorious woods and hills around. This, generally, at weekends. On Sundays I walked many miles to my preaching appointments in Sheffield and the villages around. All this preparation culminated in my oral examination when I was twenty-two. The year was 1903, and the examination centre was London. I remember the morning that I left home, dressed as was the custom in those days, in frock coat and silk hat, feeling very proud of myself but at the same time a little fearful of what awaited me in London. I was thrilled at the prospect of visiting, for the first time, the London I had read and heard so much about. I duly arrived and fortified myself with a lunch of roast beef and Yorkshire pudding, the latter proving how little the London caterers knew of the art of making it – to me it was like a slab of indigestible paste. I passed first of all the medical examinations and took the rest of the test, which lasted two days, in my stride. Having, at that time a visual memory, I could give the answers on the books I had studied simply because I had memorised them. Book answers in those days brought full marks. Later on I found that memory work was not as important as analysing a book and giving my own views on the contents.

I was billeted at the Manse of The Rev George Shapcott in Kilburn and reached the Queen's Park Station at midnight and stood bewildered. Where was Milman Road? I was on the bridge and a young lady passed me. I raised my silk hat and began to say, "Excuse me, madam, but can you kindly direct me to Milman Road?" and – without a word – she ran away. I thought it very strange, for in my Yorkshire village if I asked anyone to direct me, they would have said, "Aye lad, I'll tak thee." Eventually I asked a policeman and he gave me the direction. When I arrived at my billet I told my host what had happened and he very wisely said, "Young man, you do not accost ladies on bridges in London at midnight."

The Rev George Shapcott was very kind to me during my visit and after the examination he took me to Westminster Abbey, the Mint, the zoo and many other places. All this thrilled me. By a strange coincidence, showing that you never know where the winding road of life will lead you, I lived in that Manse in Milman Road thirty years afterwards and I became the minister of the church served by The Rev Shapcott. I also laid both he and his wife to rest. He had burglars the night before I arrived and, to complete the coincidence, I too had burglars who robbed me of all the presents and little treasures I had received.

Shortly after my return home I received word that I had passed the oral examination and then I prepared for the final written one. In the spring of 1904 I passed and preached my trial sermon in Doncaster. That took place at seven o'clock in the morning before a large congregation and it completed my various ordeals. Later in the year, I was admitted as a student at the Hartley Victoria Theological College, Manchester. This is the largest in the country and owes much to the late Sir William P. Hartley, who gave most of the money for its erection. Each student had a study and a bedroom. In the centre is the clock tower, a landmark in the Alexandra Park area of the city and there is a lovely chapel, library and spacious lecture rooms. In my time the principal was The Rev W. Johnson and the tutors – Dr A.S. Peake MA, Professor of Biblical Exegesis and Dean of the Faculty of Theology in the University of Manchester; Professor A. Lew Humphries MA, who taught Greek; and Dr W.T. Wardle MA, who taught Hebrew. We were also taught apart from the Theology and Exegesis of the Old and New Testaments, Homilies, Logic, Psychology, English, Philosophy, Elocution and other subjects. One ordeal was to preach, from time to time, to one's fellow students, the sermon forming a basis for criticism and discussion. On Sundays we served the pulpits in Manchester and the towns of Lancashire, Cheshire and even further afield. We also assisted in university and other missions. All this proved a sound training for the ministry. One could write of many interesting and amusing incidents of the days spent in college, of fellow students, sport and the numerous friends one made and the hospitality received – but this would involve a good deal of repetition. The main thing was our studies and the attendance at lectures. Occasionally we were able to attend concerts and theatres in the city. I remember vividly the night I saw Barrie's play 'The Little Minister'. One, too, met many girlfriends. I suppose some are fascinated by students and in several cases this fascination did eventually end in marriage.

In 1905, Sir Winston Churchill was fighting for the Liberal Party in Manchester and Oldham. I attended a Free Trade meeting that he addressed in the Free Trade Hall at Manchester on 27th January of that year. The other speakers were Lord Frederick Stanley and Sir John Gorst and the hall was packed. On Friday 13th October, Sir Winston was again at the hall, along with Sir Edward Grey and the Earl of Durham. This meeting advertised as a great Liberal rally. Unfortunately, I had not been able to secure a ticket but I was determined to attend. I put on my frock coat and silk hat and presented myself at the main entrance. "Have you a ticket, sir?" asked the police inspector. I had to confess that I had not but I tried to persuade him to let me in but he persisted in his refusal. I suppose you call it cheek, or any other word you like, but I was not going to be put off by a police inspector. I knew that Winston Churchill had not arrived, so I waited until I saw him making for the speakers' entrance. I then walked over to him, shook him by the hand and told him that we were in for a great meeting. I continued talking to him and noticed that the police inspector had come from the main entrance to the speakers' entrance. I walked up with Mr Churchill, the police inspector did not now ask me for my card but saluted us – and so we went in. I chatted with Mr Churchill and Sir Edward Grey in the anteroom and walked onto the platform with the speakers, sitting next to Mr Churchill. I suppose that neither Winston Churchill nor Sir Edward Grey knew why I was there. I expect they thought I was a member of the Liberal Party Committee. I achieved my purpose and enjoyed the speeches, which aroused the enthusiasm of the great audience. Winston Churchill was then a young man and a rising politician.

The memory of that first meeting has lived with me these fifty-five years during which I have seen him rise to power and become, what I really believe, the saviour of his country – the Great Wartime Prime Minister. Now he has reached the eventide of life, beloved by all. No doubt he can say, as Ramsay McDonald said at the end of his tenure of office as Prime Minister, "I feel certain that when the end comes and the evening dews begin to fall, one will be able to look back and say it was good. The chance of the future must spring from the soul of the past. Only by combining reverence with idealism can we live the life we expect to live in the present."

The two years at college passed over all too quickly. I longed for an extension but that was impossible. I suppose, like many others. I had experienced a great mental shake-up. Many of the theological views I had held in my teens were completely changed. I had been brought up in what one might term 'the old-fashioned school of thought'. The first lecture I had listened to from Dr Peake brought me up with a shock. I remember so well the opening sentences in his introduction to Old Testament Exegesis – "The history of the religion of Israel began with Moses," he said, "but no religion can have an entirely new beginning. It must link itself onto the past, taking up into itself older customs and beliefs." I had not counted on these 'older customs and beliefs' so I began an intensive study of comparative religion and my eyes were opened to entirely new views of the Old Testament. Dr Peake was the teacher of what was known in those days as 'Higher Criticism'. He was a brilliant scholar and author of many books, including his popular work known as 'Peake's Commentary'. I suppose this will always be a standard work. At the time it was published it aroused a good deal of opposition from the fundamentalists. Times, however, have changed and his views are now widely held by all scholars and students of the Bible.

My devotional life was enriched during those two years and the foundations for my future ministry well and truly laid. Looking back, I am profoundly grateful to my tutors for all they taught me and for the fellowship of the men I lived with. Many I have never met since and many have passed away.

I left college at the end of the summer term in 1906 and went home for my vacation. I spent it rambling through the haunts of my childhood, the lovely hills and dales surrounding my home, and to use a well-known saying, I felt like 'a giant refreshed with new wine'. I officiated at the Sunday services in the various chapels in the Sheffield area and eagerly awaited the appointment which was always arranged by the Stationing Committee of the Methodist Conference, to my first circuit.

6

Lincolnshire Days 1906–08

Foreword

The life of a Methodist minister at the beginning of the 20th century was very different from that of today. As he takes up his first appointment, George Kendall is plunged into rural life – complete with stampeding bulls and a preponderance of rabbit pie! With no Manse provided for the young minister fresh from college, he has to find his own lodgings. Paid once a quarter, he shares the experience of other ministers, who were often unable to feed their families, when the circuit fails to pay his full stipend. George is fortunate in having a generous grandmother to come to his rescue.

I was amused to read of the 'slow-combustion stove' in the corner of the chapel. I have been told that a kettle would be put on the stove – timed to boil at the end of the service. If it was an unpopular preacher, the kettle would only be half full! George also tells an amusing story of playing matchmaker for a local farmer, and a local preacher who borrowed a sermon.

What is tantalising in this chapter is what he does not mention, such as meeting and falling in love with the remarkable woman who was to become 'a power of strength in all his work'. As a Sunday School teacher, Emily must have been one of the first people he met on his arrival in Horncastle, but he is strangely silent about her. A relationship may have been unthinkable, as George was not allowed to marry for four years, until he had completed his probation. Perhaps, as an older woman, she did not take the young man's feelings seriously? Was his emotional state the real reason for his decision to leave Horncastle after two years? It is surprising that he feels it necessary to give a reason at all, as it would have been usual for a probationer to stay for only one or two years in his first appointment. It is interesting to note that George's love for Emily indicates his support for women preachers, which was a strong characteristic of the early Primitive Methodists.

George was held in great esteem by the Primitive Methodist Church, as seen in the 'sketch' about him which appeared in the *Christian Messenger* in 1921, as he was about to take up his fifth appointment as superintendent of the South Wales Mission. The article also mentions how The Rev John Holland influenced his decision to enter the ministry, which was to shape his life.

In this chapter, however, George appears cocooned from the outside world in a rural idyll, where we see glimpses of a now vanished world. There is no mention of external events such as the great centenary of Primitive Methodism, when half the world flocked to Mow Cop for the celebrations in 1907.

Dr Jill Barber
Vice-President of the Methodist Conference (2015-2016)
Director of Englesea Brook Chapel and Museum of Primitive Methodism

My first ministerial appointment only appeared on the list of stations. I was to serve the Horncastle Circuit, Lincolnshire – a circuit of twenty village churches with the central church in the town. As Lincolnshire is the county of John and Charles Wesley there is no wonder that in every town, village and hamlet you will find a Methodist chapel. They are even more numerous than those of the Church of England.

Horncastle itself is a market town of ancient origin and the centre of a thriving community. It had four streets – North, South, East and West – all converging on the market place. With its cobbled streets and old inns, in my days it seemed untouched by time's rude hand. Through it ran the River Bain, spanned by several picturesque bridges and flanked by old corn warehouses. The sale of sheep cattle and pigs on market days was always a source of interest to me, for one met the farmers from the various villages. The high-water mark of the year was the October Horse Fair when hundreds of horses lined the streets and crowds of gipsies and dealers come from all parts of the country. The streets on these occasions were full of shouting men, running their horses for the inspection of the buyers. George Borrow, on his journeys through England in 1825, gave a colourful description of this fair and the old inns with their immense stabling for the horses.

I arrived in Horncastle on the Friday preceding the first Sunday in July 1906, for on that particular Sunday my ministry began. I had to arrange for lodgings and so I selected the home of a retired farm labourer in West Street. It was a very old house and also very primitive but it was spotlessly clean and my rooms were comfortable. "How much can you pay me?" asked my landlord. "Thirteen shillings a week," I replied and he was completely satisfied for the farm labourers only earned ten or eleven shillings a week – a week of many hours of gruelling work. My salary (or stipend as it was called) was one pound a week, paid quarterly, so after paying my board I had a balance of seven shillings but my generous grandmother subsidised me and I shall never forget how on the Friday morning I left home she gave me eight golden sovereigns to begin with. It was a good thing she did so for, at the first quarterly meeting when I should have received thirteen pounds, I only had seven pounds as the funds were so low and the people so very poor. I collected the balance of six pounds in donations from my friends and again from my grandmother. Our housekeeper was the deaf and dumb elderly stepdaughter of my landlord. She was a splendid cook and a wonderful worker. Alice, as she was called, has a treasured nook in my memory. We lived a good deal on rabbits because they cost nothing and one could always get them from the farmers around. As we always had rabbit pie at the Harvest Festival suppers held in our twenty chapels I was soon fed up with the things and I have seldom tasted rabbit since!

We had some four hundred and five active members in the various chapels with probably another four hundred adherents. Some of the villages had picturesque names, such as Hagworthingham, Ashby Puerorum, Scamblesby, Chapel Hill, Sandy Bank, Mareham-le-Fen, Donington-on-Bain and White Pit. They were widely scattered and I averaged one hundred miles a week in my visitations. I hadn't much time to study Theology but I certainly studied 'Legology'! I sometimes cycled, at other times hired a horse and trap and when the snow was deep on the ground, or bad storms came I walked. I often walked twenty miles on a Sunday and sometimes during the week. The little chapels were often by the wayside. They were plain, with matting or carpet down a central aisle, lighted with paraffin lamps and heated with a slow-combustion stove in the corner. They were well attended and the centre of village life. There were only two ministers, helped by a large staff of lay preachers and stewards, to serve those chapels. Some of the farmers and farm labourers were lay preachers, men of great pulpit power and originality. Many were very quaint in their utterances. I remember one who prayed, "I thank Thee Lord that Thou has not made every smell a stink." He was, of course, right to be so thankful for he knew all the 'smells' of the farmyard. One of the most striking and original sermons that I ever listened to was by a farm labourer on the text from Jeremiah: "Break up your fallow ground and sow not among thorns." He knew what he was talking about and he got his message well over to a congregation which filled the Horncastle Chapel. Another was of a different type. He was like the famous Dr Joseph Parker in appearance and had a deep, arresting voice but alas I found that he had only one sermon and that was borrowed! I listened, amazed, at one week-evening service as he began: "As I was walking down the streets of New York," – then followed a brilliant word picture of that city, with many interesting and graphic illustrations, a sermon full of flowery language finishing with a moving appeal to enter in at the strait gate. In thanking him afterwards I said, "I didn't know you had been to New York."

"No!" he replied, "but it's in the sermon." I found that he had memorised one of Dr De Witt Talmadge's sermons from *The Christian Herald*. I was afterwards told that he had preached that same sermon for forty years, no matter what text he took it was always the same sermon!

Sometimes, on a week evening, I would take the town band with me into the country. I arranged to have a half-hour service in some field, the band accompanying the hymns, and afterwards they would play all kinds of selections, including waltzes. On these occasions, people came from all parts to join in and these kinds of meetings were fruitful of much good.

Not only did I preach in these villages each week but I visited the isolated farms and cottages, caring for the sick and dying, baptising children and interesting myself in the problems of daily life. In one village I used to visit a farmer who had an excellent housekeeper. I am not, and never was, a matrimonial agent but one afternoon as we were having tea he told me of his loneliness. I said, "Why not get married?"

"Whom can I marry?" he replied. I suggested that the best woman in the world was his own housekeeper. He pondered for a few moments and then said that he was too shy to ask her. I told him I would do it for him, went into the kitchen and asked his housekeeper, "Would you like to be married?" She blushed and I hastily added, "I'm not asking for myself," – I was twenty-four and she forty-five – "I am asking for the master." I shall never forget the woman's astonishment as she said, "What! The master wants to marry me!" Of course she said "Yes" and I took her to join the master in the dining room. A short time after that they both drove over one morning in the farm trap to Horncastle, ten miles away, and I married them and provided the wedding breakfast for the happy pair in my rooms. Whenever I visited the farm afterwards I was greeted with real warmth and they both said it was the best day in their lives when I popped the question for them.

I had the joy, one Sunday evening, to welcome into my pulpit The Rev Thomas Lord who was one hundred that day. He preached a very moving sermon to a crowded congregation. This fine old preacher of the Congregational Church lived to nearly one hundred and one. His family were all devoted workers at the local church.

What adventures one had on those winding grass banked roads! I remember one evening as I was cycling to Bardney I met a herd of bullocks being driven to the Horncastle October Fair. The night was very dark and the beasts were round a corner so that I had no idea of their presence until I suddenly burst upon them. Dazed by the brilliant rays of my acetylene gas lamp, they plunged about in all directions, one huge beast attacking me with his horns and throwing me into the ditch by the roadside. Fortunately I had a thanksgiving fund collecting box in my overcoat pocket and this took the force of the blow. I escaped with a severe shaking. This story was retold in many papers and one made a joke of it, saying: 'The Rev George Kendall of Horncastle, Lincolnshire is no gambler but a bull would have gored him but for a thanksgiving fund box which the reverend gentleman was carrying. The bull badly wanted to toss him for the contents!'

It should be said that in the Methodist Church, ministers, on leaving college, serve four years on probation before being ordained and, in my time, before they were allowed to marry. A rather heavy list of books on Philosophy, Theology, Church Administration, Hebrew and Greek had to be studied and an examination had to be taken at the end of each year. This, along with the care of so many churches, decided me to break my probationary period, so I thought I had better leave Horncastle at the end of two years. A farewell meeting was held at the end of June 1908, attended by leading townspeople and all the ministers of the other churches, including the centenarian The Rev Thomas Lord. I had served during my two years as the secretary of the Free Church Council and this was greatly appreciated. I went for a short holiday to Hunstanton and then, after a week at home, took up my duties as minister for Shieldmuir and Wishaw in Scotland.

7

Scotland Days 1908–10

I began my ministry at Shieldmuir on the third Sunday in July 1908. I arrived in Glasgow at 4 o'clock in the morning after an all-night journey from home. It was the Saturday of the Glasgow July Fair and the first thing I was offered as I arrived at the station was a bottle of whisky by an intoxicated man. As I am a teetotaller, of course I refused. I had on another occasion a brush with the whisky-loving man. I was about to board the Southern Express from Edinburgh when a gentleman said, "Are you going South, Padre? If you are, will you travel with me?" I noticed that he was travelling first class whereas I was a third-class passenger, so I refused as courteously as I could. He then turned to his valet and said, "Get me a bottle of whisky, William, I must have some spiritual comfort on my journey." We then parted.

To return to my new sphere of duty. In the place of twenty village churches, I now had sole charge of one. It was a tremendous change but I welcomed it. It gave me an opportunity to concentrate on my sermons and studies and to get to know my people more intimately. The chapel at Shieldmuir was a compact and attractive little building with a very large hall and rooms at the rear – ideal for work amongst young people in Sunday School and clubs. It was on the main road to Motherwell and opposite Lord Belhaven's park gates. There was a cosmopolitan population of Scots, English and Poles living in the crowded streets around and there were swarms of children. One street was called 'English Street'. I was not very proud of it. My plan of campaign was to visit every house and keep as constantly on the knocker as the postman and the insurance agent. I wore, as was the custom with all ministers in Scotland in those days, a silk hat and frock coat and, contrary to the opinions of some critics, I found that the people welcomed my visits in this dress.

I had some curious experiences during these visits. I called one day to see an old excise officer. He was notorious for his bad language and received me with suspicion. Shall I ever forget that afternoon of its conversation? The old man growled and grumbled and rapped out occasional oaths, with a fierce stamping of his wooden leg. I found at last a point of interest. I asked him to tell me of his travels as a seaman and found that he had sailed with Joseph Conrad and that he had met Mark Twain in America and had suffered a shipwreck. His face lit up as he spoke of his adventures in all parts of the world. By a little tact, I had been able to soothe and interest him. He came with me to the door and I was about to give him half a crown – for he looked in need of help – when he said, "Look here, young man, you're the first parson to take notice of a lonely old sinner. You're a brick, here's five pounds as a thank offering to help you in your work." With that five pounds I bought a crate of crockery and had a sale, realising twelve pounds towards my debt reduction scheme on my little church.

One thing that surprised me was that the people preferred to be married in their own homes. They had, of course, to produce the necessary licence before the ceremony. I remember one couple calling on me one night as late as ten o'clock to be married. I conducted the ceremony in my study and the happy pair went off to begin their honeymoon in Glasgow. On another occasion I married a couple in the kitchen of a very poor home. At the conclusion of the ceremony the bridegroom asked me, "Will Your Reverence kindly lend me seven shillings and sixpence?" I obliged him with the loan, which was never repaid.

When anyone died I was generally asked to call and say a prayer as the body was lifted from the bed into the coffin. The service for the funeral, three days afterwards, was always held in the home. I generally accompanied the mourners to the cometary and had the usual interment service. This was not the custom in Scotland in my time, however. The undertaker did the committal and as far as the minister's service was concerned, that ended with the service in the home. I never liked this and so adopted the English method. I had one rather distressing funeral in a very wretched home. I had just taken the usual service when the group around the coffin, under the influence of a good deal of whisky, began to sing, "We won't go home 'till the morning!" With the help of the undertaker and his men, I cleared the room and we left the mourners behind, proceeding to the cemetery on our own for the Last Rites.

Baptisms were numerous and again I was surprised by the fact that many women, especially the Poles, would bring their babies three days after birth to be baptised. Some had very large families and how they managed to bring them up was always a mystery to me.

My chapel was well attended and we had a thriving Sunday School. I found the people very kind. I remember a homeless boy who was taken into the home of one of our members and made one of the family. Years afterwards he came to visit the old chapel. He had gone to London as a young man and had made good. His position was one of importance in the city. He came, a handsome man in a silk hat and frock coat, and visited the school and told the children of those early days: "I owe everything to this world," he said, "to the members of this church and the teachers of this Sunday School and especially to my foster-father and mother who took me in. I was simply a little street child but I was welcomed just the same." It was all so very moving and to show his gratitude he gave a handsome donation of several pounds to the funds of the church.

In addition to my ordinary work, I began open-air services in Shield's Glen, a little beauty spot a mile or so from the church. I also conducted all kinds of services in the other churches. I was honoured by being asked to preach the sermon at the Bonkle Presbyterian Church on the occasion of Dr James Henderson's Jubilee. The famous Scots divine Dr A. Smellie had been asked to do this but could not come, so I was selected to take his place. The celebrations were continued on the Saturday, beginning with a lunch provided by Colonel Stewart of Murdeston Castle and followed by a gathering of some five hundred people. Dr Scott had served the church for fifty years, having succeeded his father who also served the same church for a period of fifty years. I was also appointed one of the Religious Knowledge examiners for the Cambusnethan School Board. Lord Blythswood, who was a Church of England clergyman, invited me several times with other ministers to his lovely home, 'Blythswood' Renfrew. We met many distinguished preachers and laymen on these occasions.

Another highlight of this period was the two weeks' mission which I conducted in Edinburgh. This lovely city appealed very strongly to me. Next to the large church where I held the mission, was a fairground and on the first Monday evening the music of the merry-go-round filled the church. It was not an easy thing to preach to the accompaniment of songs like 'Goodbye Dolly I must leave you!' The following day I visited the caravans and met with a courteous reception. I suggested holding special services for the fraternity and this was taken up with enthusiasm. The proprietor found me a portable organ and the singing was an inspiration. A most unexpected and, I should think, unexampled sequel followed. For the rest of the mission, the music of the merry-go-rounds and the noise of the shooting galleries was stopped each evening for an hour whilst my service was in progress. In return I had services for the people in the fairground. My pulpit was the steps of the proprietor's caravan and he provided a portable organ.

Often I have had a rather sneering question asked me, especially during my addresses from my platform in Hyde Park: "Do you parsons ever do any good by your Bible-punching and sermons?" My answer is: "Yes; you can save a soul and a life." And so it was during the period of which I am speaking. I was walking past the window of a house on my way from my lodgings to the morning service.

Inside that house a man in abject despair was preparing to commit suicide. He was just raising a cup of deadly poison to his lips when he glanced through the window and saw me pass. Afterwards in the vestry of the church he told me this:

> I saw you pass my window, as you had done many times before and I said, 'I'll give myself a couple more hours to live, the poison can wait. I'll go and hear what that chap has to say.' I followed you and sat in the back pew. All the hymns seemed to have been chosen for me. Why, for example, did you sing – 'Courage, Brother! Do not stumble though the path be dark as night?' Why did you preach from the text: 'But he himself went a day's journey into the wilderness and came and sat under a juniper tree, and requested for himself that he might die and said 'It is enough now, Lord, take away my life. I can begin afresh."

And so he made his confession as the tears ran down his cheeks. In that vestry he began a new life and on going home, threw away the poison. Why? Is it not true that in some way unknown to us, God's providence is always at work and out of our very sins and follies it pleases Him to unfold the opportunities of grace. I think this story supplies the answer to the sneering cynic.

In the last year of my probation, I had to add Political Economy and Apologetics to the other subjects I had to study for my final examination and this meant a lot of extra work. I was helped by being the guest in the comfortable home of the Grainger family. The two daughters Lily and Flora were my best workers. Whilst my stipend had been increased by five shillings a week, bringing it up to one pound five shillings, I hadn't too much to cover my daily expenses but my generous friends saw that I did not suffer in this respect. Having satisfied my examiners, I was duly ordained at the Synod held in the Pollockshaw's Presbyterian Church, Glasgow, kindly loaned for the service, on Saturday 30th April 1910. I preached my farewell sermons in Wishaw and Shieldmuir on the Sunday of 26th June following. On the night previously, I had attended a farewell tea and social, attended by all the ministers of the area and by a crowded congregation.

8

Village Days 1910–13

Foreword

George Kendall continues to tell us his story with modesty and a flair for vivid narrative. His time at Colnbrook is recounted with delightful freshness, although the subjects range from the distasteful (an army of rats) to the macabre (the murderous innkeeper and his wife). Underlying the more dramatic elements of his life in Colnbrook is the steady, unglamorous, invaluable ministry of an ordained minister. We catch glimpses of the visiting, the flourishing Sunday School, the renovation of buildings, the preaching, and the care of souls, but George makes no fuss about what would have been a very demanding life of long hours on his feet, at his desk, and on his knees. This is the stuff of local church ministry in whatever century it occurs.

When I was Bishop of Oxford, both Colnbrook and Eton/Windsor (the next chapter) were in that diocese of 815 local churches. What impressed me more than anything was the knowledge that, day in day out, the people of God – lay and ordained – were living out their faith in a thousand acts of loving service.

Every community has within it a considerable number of those agents of God's mercy seeking to transform both individual lives and the flourishing of their communities, and they are supported by the George Kendalls of this land – tireless promoters of peace and well-being; but in this chapter and the next, we begin to encounter the royal contacts which were to 'spice up' the familiar disciplines of George's ministry. George Kendall was to experience an extraordinary breadth of human society in the course of his ministry and, in each place, to make his mark as a man of God.

The Rt Rev John Pritchard
Bishop of Oxford (2009-2014)

On 4th July 1910 I was married to Emily Mary Ellis in the Horncastle Congregational Church, a church of which she was one of the best supporters and where she was a teacher in the Sunday School. The church was full for the service and the wedding breakfast held in the Oddfellows Hall. Thus began a partnership which lasted twenty-four years until her death.

My wife became a lay preacher and had the unique distinction of becoming the first lady minister of the church since the early days. This occurred when I was appointed chaplain to His Majesty's Forces and she took charge of my work until the appointment of my successor. My wife was also an admirable writer of short stories which were published in various periodicals from time to time, one serial 'Mary Laird' was used by two magazines.

After my ordination in Scotland, I had another surprise – a surprise because it equalled my previous change from Lincolnshire to Scotland, now it was from Scotland to Buckinghamshire. I became superintendent of what was known in those days as the Colnbrook and Uxbridge Circuit – a circuit of four churches: Colnbrook, Uxbridge, Staines and Colham Green. I arrived with my wife in Colnbrook on 23rd July 1910. The change from Scotland to this old-fashioned village was a rather strange experience.

Colnbrook is partly in Middlesex and partly in Buckinghamshire. It is a village of one street. We lived on the other side of the little bridge which spanned the River Coln, in Middlesex. The Manse, at that time, was a very old house which I was told had been an inn in the time of Dick Turpin, the highwayman. This must have been so, for the kitchen was panelled with wood and between that and the dining room was a cellar-like place which must have been used for the storage of beer barrels. There were no modern conveniences. The toilet was a good distance down a narrow path in a garden through which ran a river. The garden was full of apple trees and a wilderness but the river was well stocked with fish and that was one compensation for I became an angler and caught roach and chub from time to time. Next door was another old-fashioned house with stabling and we could hear the noise of the horses clanging their chains through the night. The house was full of rats and I had three dogs to keep them under control. We knew that there was something mysterious in the house because after tea on our first afternoon we went for a walk, leaving the tea on the table. When we returned, the food had disappeared! I also put a sack of potatoes in the kitchen cupboard and left them for winter use. When I went to open the sack, the potatoes had vanished. In the winter the rats would burrow under the floor by the fireplace and I had on a number of occasions to have the hearth stone removed to clear out the remains of those who had died. Sometimes the rats swarmed in hordes, seeking new quarters. The village greengrocer used to tell me how he was out with his horse and cart one night when he met an army of rats. He said that they covered the road and he had great difficulty in driving through them – a terrifying experience. I suppose the floods had something to do with it for the whole area was covered at times and we had to walk on planks; boats were also used.

Nearly opposite to my house was a remarkable building known as King John's Palace, used as a hunting lodge when the area was a part of Windsor Great Forest. Colnbrook used to be famous for its many-roomed inns but is now only a relic of its former self, especially since the bypass road was made. It grew up with the pack horse and coaching traffic being on the Bath Road. For centuries it flourished. Now it has sunk peacefully to its present lethargic condition. It had a corporation, a fair, markets and courts of pie powder. The innkeeper of the George Inn, named Buckingham, made so much money that he got into Parliament and eventually into the golden pages of Debrett's and, we are told, died in the odour of sanctity, a pattern to all men.

Near to my chapel in the centre of the main street stood, and still stands the most remarkable feature of Colnbrook – the Ostrich Inn, erected in the year 1106 and originally a Pilgrim's Inn or Maison Dieu. Here the spirit of a long-dead age seems to linger. For some centuries the upper part of it has looked as if it meant to topple over into the street beneath. It is the oldest licensed inn in England and has the blackest history of any. It was the site of some of the most gruesome murders imaginable; upstairs is a bedroom which might be suitably called 'the chamber of horrors'. It was told me that in those far-off days the bedstead in this room was placed on a hinged trapdoor above the brewhouse's boiling vat. A window at the back of the cupboard enabled the innkeeper to see whether his victim slept. You may guess what happened next! Sixty murders were committed before the innkeeper and his wife were brought to book. This is how it happened.

Thomas Cole, a Reading clothier, used this inn freely and as he carried large sums of money with him, he was marked down for slaughter. For some time, he escaped the innkeeper and his wife's intentions. On one occasion he fell sick and luckily stayed elsewhere; another time London was in flames and he pressed on there. "The third time pays for all," said the innkeeper's wife, but a friend came and stayed with the traveller on his third visit and so, in spite of the landlady's proverb, his doom was postponed. The innkeeper was struck with these coincidences but his wife nagged and abused him, calling him a cowardly fool and as the traveller was due again the arguments as to whether he should sleep in the chamber of death grew very heated. You can picture them huddled over the brewhouse fire during this dispute, but the wife prevailed and sturdily stoked up the fire in readiness. The traveller arrived but before he retired he asked the landlord to sign a paper; it was his will. This dreadful premonition more than every troubled the innkeeper and even more so when Mr Cole added his own presentiment of coming evil. The wife was gravely troubled also at the time but thought of the clothier's gold and the money they had already spent to fuel the fire underneath the vat. They made, however, a solemn agreement that he should be the last victim. And so Mr Cole went to his doom. Somehow or other his horse broke loose from the stable and went home rider-less and this led to strict enquiries. The crime of the pair was found out and many mysteries were solved. The innkeeper and his wife met their doom for both were hanged on the gibbet. Those were supposed to be the good old days but every time I passed this old inn I was thankful that I lived in a more secure age.

The quaint little chapel in the centre of such surroundings was built by the Roberts family over one hundred years ago. The deeds of the land dated from the time of Queen Elizabeth I. I always had a good congregation and we had a thriving Sunday School for the village children. It was held in two cottages next door. These had been converted into suitable rooms for our work. The other three churches I visited once a week. The riverside at Staines was always a delightful change and I made many friends there, addressing meetings in not only my church, but the Quakers' and the Congregationalists'. The same was true of the little town of Uxbridge, where I eventually was elected as President of the Free Church Council. Colham Green was a small wayside chapel with an excellent Sunday School run by two earnest women.

I carried out the complete renovation of our Colnbrook Church and to raise the money for this I organised a bazaar under the distinguished patronage of HRH Princess Christian. This proved most successful. The question of the new Manse, which was such a pressing need, was solved in a remarkable way. One Monday morning Mr Samuel Roberts, the son of the founder of the church and a lay preacher, called to see me. He was getting old and in the course of our conversation began to weep. He said, "I was deeply moved by the service we had last evening and I do not like to see you living in this house under such bad conditions. I have a house on the Bath Road and I want you to have it. Here is a contribution towards the cost." He handed me an envelope as he left. I opened it after I had seen him to the door, thinking perhaps that there would be five pounds but, to my astonishment, there was a very large sum made out on the cheque. The house became ours and was made over to the church as a Manse and our generous friend had every room decorated at his expense in addition to his other financial help. Although I lived in it for six months only I was very grateful for the kindly thought and others who followed blessed his name.

There were two royal occasions at this time that I witnessed, both at St George's Chapel, Windsor. The first was the sad occasion of the funeral of Prince Francis of Teck on 26th October 1910. The second was the Investiture of the Prince of Wales as Knight of the Garter on 10th June 1911. King George V and Queen Mary, together with other members of the Royal Family, attended on both occasions. I was very grateful to have a card of invitation to see these events, especially the historic procession at the Investiture. The last King of Portugal and King Alfonso of Spain were both present and all the knights of that period marched in their gorgeous robes and insignia, the pomp and splendour of this ancient rite was deeply moving to me. I also had another interesting experience when I attended the Great Review of the Troops of King George V in Windsor Great Park.

After three years' service at Colnbrook, I accepted an invitation to Windsor. At a crowded farewell meeting held the first Monday in July 1913 I received as a present a handsome inlaid mahogany bureau. I then left for a short holiday before commencing my new duties.

9

The Royal Borough of Windsor 1913–15

I moved to my new home by road. The village greengrocer packed my personal belongings, including my desk and boxes of books, onto his cart and I went with him. Ministers, in my church, have a furnished house with all rates and taxes paid and so it is easy to move. My stipend, at this time, was two pounds a week, paid quarterly but today a minister in the position I then held would receive at least six hundred pounds a year.

The new Manse, named 'Kingsmead', was a lovely little house on the borders of Slough and Eton College. I had a full-front view of the college and of Windsor Castle from my front windows. I was to superintend two churches in Slough, one in Windsor, Sunningdale, Winkfield Row and Bracknell. I was disappointed with the size of my congregation in Windsor so I visited each house in Denmark Street and the area around and began a series of open-air services. At the conclusion of my services in the streets, I decided on the second Sunday to go to the castle and took my stand on the plinth of Queen Victoria's monument at the entrance to the main gates. I had no idea of the far-reaching effect of this, my one object was to awaken the interest of the people of the Royal Borough. Two days after this I had a letter from Queen Mary's Lady-in-Waiting asking me to call. I was rather afraid that perhaps I was going to be censured for using the monument as my pulpit. Instead I had awakened the interest of Her Majesty who was always keenly interested in all the work carried on in Windsor and anxious to further this work and give her support. In passing, I wish to record that Queen Mary helped me until she passed away. The result of this invitation and my response to it was the great help I received from the ladies of the Royal Circle in my work in the poorer part of Windsor. I was able to completely renovate the church and I had many garments given to me for the poorer children of the Sunday School.

Altogether, apart from my usual service on a Sunday and the week nights in the various churches I had to superintend, I was keenly interested in the welfare of the Guards stationed in the garrison. I had two splendid men who were serving in the Coldstream Guards as members of my church, one was T.W. Briggs from Barnsley and the other W.S. Scruby, the latter, the son of a ministerial friend of mine and who later became an officer in the 12th Middlesex. I met both in France and both were killed in action. I invited these men and others to spend their Sundays with me and I asked our generous people to invite as many as they could because I knew how lonely they felt at times and how much they missed home life. My request was met with a great response. I then opened my schoolroom and other rooms as a club, providing papers, games, tobacco and other comforts. One day I went to see the commanding officer. He received me graciously and said, "Padre, I wanted to meet you to thank you for all you are doing for my men." Smiling, he added, "I have had a good many requests from them to change their denomination to yours." I had not expected this, my object being not to 'sheep steal' but simply to make their lives happier and give them a bit of home life. On the commanding officer's recommendation, I was appointed an officiating chaplain to the garrison. Thus began a happy period of service with the troops which culminated in my commission as a chaplain to His Majesty's Forces, a period which lasted in war and peace until I reached the retiring age of sixty.

I was thrilled one day to be asked by Bishop Gore of Oxford to attend the annual service held in St George's Chapel on St George's Day. This service, attended by the Military Knights of Windsor, is very moving. I walked in procession with the Bishop down the aisle of the crowded chapel. I had previously had a kind invitation from the Countess of Arran whose husband the Earl was a cousin of the Bishop, to visit her and have tea along with her and the Lady Winifred Gore. The Countess showed a great interest in the work I was doing and Lady Winifred was delighted with my Irish stories and a book I had read, which I loaned to her, on ghosts. This was by an Irish author Elliott O'Donnell.

In the midst of all my somewhat bewildering activities, I continued visiting the people of my churches and preached each Sunday and each night apart from Fridays. One interesting visit had rather a strange sequel. I went to preach in my church at Sunningdale one Thursday evening. Before the service I visited one of my members who was a fishmonger. He was a familiar figure in the village with his cry "Fish alive-o!" When I arrived I found him weeping. I said, "What is the trouble, my friend?" He replied, "My horse fell down dead this afternoon and I do not know what I shall do now." Rather impulsively I said, "Cheer up! I'll try and buy you another." He took my promise for granted and I went home pondering how I could, with my two pounds a week, manage to find the money for a horse. When I arrived home I told my astonished wife of my promise and she naturally asked how I was going to manage it. That night when I retired, I suddenly had a brain wave, "I'll go and tell Mrs Joicey about it!" Mrs Joicey lived in Sunningdale Park and some of her maids attended my church and this was my point of contact. The next day I put on my frock coat and silk hat and cycled up the Long Walk to the Great Park, passed the Ascot Racecourse, to the mansion. I suppose I am the only man who has cycled in such a rig-out through such aristocratic surroundings but I did not mind as I wanted to look impressive. Arriving, I cycled up the long carriage drive, put my bicycle by a rhododendron bush, took off my cycle clips, brushed my trousers and rang the doorbell. After a while a maid appeared and asked if I had an appointment. "No!" I replied, "but I think Mrs Joicey will see me," and so she did. I told her my story of the weeping man and the dead horse, saying, "No longer will the village hear his melodious voice unless a new horse can be bought for him." I told her how I had promised him a new one but alas I could not afford it on my stipend of two pounds a week. I then added, "I was thinking of you when I went to bed last night."

"Thinking of me!" she exclaimed and well she might for I had never met her before! "Yes," I said, "something told me to come and tell you as I was sure you would solve the problem for me by buying the horse required." This she promised to do and then asked me to stay for tea. During tea she asked me about my little church and was pleased to hear that her maids attended. She asked if I had any other problems and I told her of the debt on the building. "I will help you to clear it off," she said. The result was that the debt was cleared and she laughed as I added, "I wish some more horses would die!" The strange sequel is that when I joined the 5th Northumbrian Fusiliers on the Somme, the first man to greet me on my arrival was Lord Joicey who was an officer in another battalion I served – the 7th. I was able, in the midst of battle, to tell him of my visit to his relative and this was a real bond of interest between us.

I was in Windsor the day that the Austrian Archduke Franz Ferdinand and the Duchess arrived on their visit to King George and Queen Mary at the castle. I was struck by the Archduke's appearance and his smile at the reception he was given at the station. By a coincidence I saw them leave Windsor at the conclusion of their visit, en route for Sarajevo, Serbia. A few hours before they had listened to a concert given by a Yorkshire choir in the castle. They drove to the station and entered the brilliantly lit Royal Train which rushed off into the night – on into the strange unknown, on, on to their last journey on earth. Whether I am psychic or not is a matter I have often wondered about but I had a strange premonition that night – an uncanny feeling that some tremendous upheaval was shortly to take place. I can still see it all so vividly. A short time afterwards the world was shocked by the news of their assassination. I remember reading how the Archduke called to his wife, little thinking that she too was dying, "Sophie, Sophie! Don't die! Live for the children." So the upheaval came – it was an earthquake costing millions of lives and sending me and countless others when war was declared, on the long, long trail with all its horrors of mud, blood, poisonous gas, liquid fire, screaming shells and sniper's bullets. War more terrible than anything else in the history of the world.

The first thing that happened on the fatal morning after war was declared was the departure of the Guards to fight at Mons. I saw them leave and in the April following I received my commission as a chaplain to the HM Forces. My commission was signed by the King who stated that I was his 'trusty and well beloved' and that he reposed 'especial trust and confidence in my loyalty and piety and good conduct'. To receive this was a great experience for me and I fervently prayed that I might merit such confidence.

After this, life was never the same again. The change was indescribable; a new life with many dangers to face and at times incredible hardships. One had to be tough to endure it at all.

Part 2 – The First Great War: The Long, Long Trail

10

The Base (Le Havre) 1915

Foreword

On 14 May 1915, the *London Gazette* published the name of 30 men who had been appointed to be temporary chaplains to the Forces, 4th Class. The list included the name of The Rev George Kendall, who was commissioned into the Army Chaplains Department on 3 May 1915; he was 34 years old. Having previously worked in a Sheffield steel factory and as a clerk for one of the first mail order companies, before being accepted for training as a primitive Methodist minister, it is likely that Padre Kendall had both empathy and understanding of the working men who now filled the ranks of the armed forces in the First World War. Indeed, such was his love of soldiers and his sense of calling and vocation as an army chaplain that George Kendall extended his service – and on 27 April 1922, the *London Gazette* confirmed The Rev George Kendall OBE Honorary Chaplain to the Forces, 4th Class to be Chaplain, 4th Class in the newly-formed Royal Army Chaplains Department.

During the First World War, Padre Kendall served alongside the troops in France, Flanders, Salonica and in Germany – and in 1920, he was to return to France and Belgium to oversee the exhumations of the war dead and the provision of war cemeteries. It was in this capacity that he was involved in the selection of 'The Unknown Warrior' for reinternment in Westminster Abbey.

As the present Chaplain General to Her Majesty's Land Forces, it gives me great pleasure to commend the life and work of The Rev George Kendall OBE for his unfaltering and devoted service to soldiers during the Great War.

The Rev Dr David Coulter QHC CF
Chaplain General, British Army

The long, long trail which I have travelled has been unique and I doubt if there is anyone still living who had had the same experiences. Much of it covered the First Great War, culminating in the embarkation of The Unknown Warrior in which I took part in my capacity as senior chaplain of an area which covered the whole of Belgium to the German Frontier. Then there is the story of the many divisions with which I served, of my journey to the Balkans and, after the lapse of twenty-one anxious years in our history, of my service in the Second World War as officiating chaplain to the RAF London Balloon Command in the Docklands.

Following the receipt of the telegram announcing my commission, I visited the War Office. For several days I had been preparing for service overseas. Here was the painful process of inoculations, followed by thirty-two hours in bed with all kinds of sensations and finally, the winding up of my affairs at home. The morning of departure dawned. Every moment was precious. A lump rose in my throat as I looked round my old home and gazed out of the window to see the view I had always loved, that of Windsor Castle. It was hard to say goodbye; the future was mercifully hidden. I tore myself away and drove to the station. The train was due and my wife and friends gathered on the platform. The train began its journey and there came that inevitable feeling of loneliness – I have always found in life that there are some thoughts too deep for tears. I reached Southampton after dinner and reported to the embarkation officer. At 10pm we gathered at the wharf, a crowd of officers and men of all ranks including four other chaplains beside myself. It was a weird experience, the sea looked dark and the cold wind chilled. I wondered whether any German submarines would be lying in wait for us. I had a first-class bunk with a good bed for which I was thankful. For a couple of hours I talked to my fellow chaplains and several young officers before retiring at midnight.

At 4am I was awakened by the throb of the engines. The boat had started but I was tired and 'rocked in the cradle of the deep' I fell asleep again. I was not much inclined towards breakfast and so I went on deck and watched the escorting destroyers. At 10am the shores of France were in sight. In the distance I could see a huge hospital ship full of wounded soldiers returning home. There was a lot of excitement as we entered the harbour. On the wharf I noticed a motley crowd of Frenchmen and several staff officers. We disembarked and were soon in the car taking us to report to the base commandant, there to await instructions as to our posting. What scene this French seaport of Le Havre presented! British soldiers and officers by the thousand, Canadians, Australians, Indians, crowds of French soldiers in their baggy red trousers and blue overcoats. Scores of widows wearing long veils whose husbands had fallen for France. Along the street moved a funeral procession headed by priests with a coffin covered with a Tricolor and a company of soldiers in the rear. The crowds bared their heads and we stood to attention. We were permitted to use the Officers' Club and we had our first French lunch. Later in the day I, and the other four chaplains, received our instructions to report to the principal chaplain at Rouen. A first-class travelling warrant was given to us and we had a cosy compartment along with an Irish officer. The journey occupied three hours and we passed through well-wooded country with verdant fields and arable land, all in a high state of cultivation. I noticed that the cows were not allowed to wander but were chained to a post. At 10.30pm we arrived at our destination and proceeded to the Grand Hotel d'Angleterre.

After a night's sleep I awoke refreshed and reported to headquarters. I soon found myself in the presence of The Rev J.M. Simms DD KHC CB CMG who ranked as a major general and was the principal chaplain to the British Army in the field. Dr Simms was loved and admired by all the 2,000 chaplains who eventually served under his command. I was thrilled to meet him and was received with a smile and with words of advice and encouragement. It was my privilege at the end of the war to write a biographical sketch of his career and to attend the farewell dinner which we gave to him at Cologne. I little thought, as he interviewed me that morning, that all this would happen. The interview over, I was told to await orders so went back for a further day and night in Rouen. The hotel was very expensive and was overcrowded, so much so that I had to sleep with another officer. The charge was one pound a day and my pay ten shillings and sixpence a day with the usual allowances. I was, therefore, glad that my stay was limited. An amusing incident occurred as I left the hotel. All the waiters and sundry hangers-on lined up, as was their custom, for a tip. The staircase and vestibule was lined with them. I reluctantly gave them each one franc which I could ill afford. Another chaplain solved the problem in a better way. He shook each outstretched hand and murmured "God bless you" – they certainly did not appreciate this! I laughed at the look on their faces.

The order for my posting came. I was to return to our principal base Le Havre and, for a time, do duty there. I duly arrived at Le Havre and had to find my own billet. I was very fortunate in finding out another chaplain I had previously met in London – Padre E.L. Watson. He, at once, suggested that I should stay in his billet in a boarding house near the Grand Promenade. Madame, the proprietress, was glad to have me and gave me an excellent room with electric light, attendance and food for the modest sum of five and a half francs a day – equivalent to about four shillings a day at the rate of exchange fixed by the Army Pay Department at that period. My fellow boarders were three British officers, six Belgians and, occasionally, a few French civilians. Madame was born in Algiers, her mother being an Algerian and her father a French officer. She was married to a French officer who was at the Front. She was about forty and had no children. One thing I remember about her was her quick temper and her scolding of the servants. She presided in state each day at lunch and dinner. Her household staff consisted of a cook, kitchen maid and Eugenie who waited at table and attended to the bedrooms. Eugenie was a most remarkable girl, small and extremely plain. Madame was very, very wise in the selection of her principal maid. She was a treasure of a maid, the hardest working girl I have ever met; reliable, clean and honest and yet she was only paid one franc a day and was profuse in her thanks for the one franc a week the officers gave her for a tip.

One curious and rather mysterious thing occurred. I noticed one day a dark girl passing the house repeatedly. The next day she did the same thing but this time she rang the bell and asked to see Madame. She asked if she might come to lunch and dinner each day and Madame consented. I was most suspicious of her as soon as I saw her. She could speak perfect English and said she had travelled all over the world. The first day she talked a lot about herself, the second and third she began to ask a few questions about Le Havre and was particularly anxious to talk to the officers. Madame then did a very wise thing. She gave information to the authorities about the girl and one day she suddenly disappeared from our midst. Madame said in reply to our enquiries, "That girl! She is a spy."

My duties were many and varied. There were many camps and hospitals throughout the base where I arranged concerts and religious services. There were no compulsory church parades but I found, at all times, crowds of men who gladly attended and who loved to sing the old hymns. There was, for example, the Convalescent Camp. It was reached by a kind of mountain railway. The view from this camp was one never to be forgotten. Hundreds of feet below you could see the town, the huge docks and harbour. In the centre of the camp was a large and well equipped YMCA which was the centre of all our activities. It was always crowded with men who were being nursed back to health and were resting for a week or two before once more returning to the Front.

One huge hospital that I had charge of was right on the sea front. It was a lovely building with spacious halls used as wards. The men lying in bed could see the cruisers, transports and all kind of shipping in the bay. I remember arranging a concert in the main hall on the Whit Monday afternoon of 1915. In the front row was Sir Francis Villiers, the British ambassador to Belgium, with Lady Villiers and the consul general. The ambassador and party joined in the various songs and afterwards the ambassador entertained us all to tea.

I had to lay to rest one great fellow, Sergeant Major Moore. He was a great force in the 5th Division. The manner of his death was typical of his splendid life. He was instructing a squad of men in the use of hand grenades when something went wrong with the fuse of one. Even then Moore might have saved himself by throwing it away but he told me as he lay in bed that he held it and shielded his men with his own body. I shall never forget the majesty of his burial – the grave surrounded by officers and men.

One great problem which confronted us was the large numbers of men who had contracted venereal disease. The effect upon manpower was becoming serious. There were many prostitutes in all the base towns and in the villages. Officers and men were subjected to all kinds of temptations. Wherever one walked one was accosted by the street walkers and there were even small boys inviting men into their homes to meet their sisters. We had therefore one hospital for the treatment of men suffering from this malady. It was not my duty to condemn but to try to win them back to self-respect, self-reverence and self-control. I remember presiding over a meeting at this hospital. Dr R.J. Campbell, then the minister of the City Temple, had come to visit the troops in Le Havre and was asked to talk to the men. He began by saying, "You have that power within you which can either lift you up to Heaven or drag you down to Hell." It was a powerful address and fruitful of much good.

It was a real joy to me to welcome one day The Rev George Standing who had arrived from home for duty in France. I entertained him in my billet until he received his orders. Padre Standing, who was afterwards awarded the CBE, DSO and MC, became an assistant principal chaplain and later the deputy chaplain general at the War Office. He little knew then that all those honours would come to him. He was a kind and friendly man and throughout my army career proved of the utmost help and inspiration to me.

On another day Dr Edwin Smith came to take up duty and I also entertained him. His army career as a chaplain was short as he was called home to join the staff of the British and Foreign Bible Society. He was a brilliant writer and an expert of Africa. He eventually became the editorial superintendent of the society. This society made great gifts of Bibles and New Testaments to the troops throughout the war and all this proved of inestimable value to the men and to the chaplains.

There was one scene which will never fade from my mind. It was a parade of all the soldiers and officers of the French garrison on the Boulevard FranVois. Admiral Governor Biard was there to present decorations for bravery in the field. There was a Guard of Honour and the band played 'The Marseillaise'. The officers and men to be decorated stood under the Tricolor. Some had their arms missing, others their legs. The admiral pinned the decorations on their breasts and, as is the custom in France, kissed them on the cheek. Then an officer called out "Madame Haas!" and a tall, stately lady dressed in deep mourning, stepped forward. She was the widow of Captain Haas of the 129th Infantry Regiment. Then another called "Madame Ballus!" and forward stepped a young lady with a babe in her arms; she was the widow of Brigadier Ballus of the Dragoons. "Monsieur Sautreuil!" was called and a white-haired father in frock coat and silk hat stepped forward. There they stood, underneath the Tricolor with the sun shining on their tear-stained faces, two widows, one with a babe, mothers of France and the old white-haired father, to receive the decorations of their loved ones killed in battle. Afterwards Admiral Biard shook me by the hand and told me of his pride in investing the men and the mourners and I was proud to shake hands with each one.

11

Into Battle (The 12th Division)

Foreword

It is significant that The Rev George Kendall loaned my distant relation, Lady Winifred – then aged 13 – a book about ghosts. Chapter 9 reveals our family's distant connection – not just to my great-great grandfather the 5th Earl's second wife and their young daughter, but to my great-great uncle The Rt Rev Dr Charles Gore (then Bishop of Oxford), and it feels a bit like being haunted, in a nice way.

We naturally tend to know less about our relatives as each generation turns. These snapshots – a tea in pre-war Windsor; a bishop's guiding hand behind a young upstart minister – coming from more than a hundred years ago turn my thoughts to my forefathers and mothers, and in them is warmth and reassurance. If The Rev Kendall was big on anything, it was the importance of remembrance.

In this chapter, we are plunges into battle – 'a journey into the unknown', Loos and, as usual, The Rev Kendall, was with General Wing – one of three divisional commanders killed in the space of one week in October 1915 in the aftermath of the battle. He was knocked over by the same deadly blast, but lived to tell this tale and bury the general.

We also get another unique snapshot of the Duke of Windsor – Her Majesty The Queen's uncle. Again, The Rev Kendall is witness and confessor.

Despite its grim subject, the chapter is not without humour. Kendall recounts how he 'battled with my horses', as he, by necessity, learnt to ride.

As thoughts of my ghostly relatives – with the many 'greats' before them – flood my mind, it strikes me that this story is of Tim Kendall's grandfather, not a distant relative. The 5th Earl's second wife, also Lady Winifred, was a Lady-in-Waiting to Princess Helena – Queen Victoria's daughter – whom The Rev Kendall also knew in her later years. I was a grown man whilst he was still alive. Grandfather? Time traveller more like!

Arthur Gore
The 9th Earl of Arran

One day I received orders to leave Le Havre and join the 12th Division in the line. I was sorry to leave the many friends I had made and worked with. Madame and Eugenie wept as I said goodbye, I was sorry to leave my billet there. Soon I began my journey into the unknown. I proceeded to the railway station, armed with my warrant. I then went to the stores near at hand and drew my rations for the two nights' journey. They consisted of one big tin of small biscuits, tea and sugar, two tins of bully beef and one pound of cheese. All these rations were placed in a sandbag. Three other officers travelled in our first-class carriage and so we each had a comfortable corner seat. The carriage was lit by the feeble light of an oil lamp which, I remember, smoked so much that we put it out. The train was of great length and was full of officers and men representing many regiments, also a company of Indian soldiers. We had several vans full of horses. The grooms were with them all the time and slept on the hay between the stalls. For two days and nights we sped on. Whenever the train stopped, the men would jump out and rush to the engine to get hot water for tea. We broke our journey at one military centre and spent a few hours looking round the old world city. Here a titled lady had erected a hut and with some voluntary helpers from many a stately home, dispensed comforts to us and cheered us on our way.

It was a great relief to reach the railhead at last and depart to our various units on the Front. I found a car waiting for me to take me to a village on the outskirts of Armentieres to join the 39th Field Ambulance of the 12th Division. In those days our trenches were in the front of the town and the Germans shelled them continuously, yet the civilians remained in their homes. I was taken to my billet which had been a butcher's shop. We used the shop as the officers' mess. My bedroom was over the shop. Madame, who was a sweet old lady of seventy, still lived with her daughter and daughter-in-law and they were very good to me. The house had been hit by a shell but had escaped serious damage. They had two fierce black mastiffs and these dogs were their guardians. I remember one day they seized a cat and pulled it in two before anyone could interfere. Although the house was in danger of being demolished any minute by a shell, these women kept it spotlessly clean and calmly proceeded with their household duties each day. At the close of the war, I passed through the village and found that the house and church nearby had been completely destroyed. I have often wondered if those splendid women escaped.

The evening of my arrival gave me my first experience of the firing line. I had to bury a soldier killed that afternoon. We covered the body with the Union Jack and as I laid him to rest I repeated the old and dear words, "Yea though I walk through the valley of the shadow of death, I will fear no evil." The darkness was illuminated by star shells, there was the booming of the guns and a stable of straw was burning furiously a few yards away. We reverently saluted the grave of our comrade and returned to our quarters. I was out again at midnight. I had heard that a Yorkshire battalion was in the trenches and, being myself a Yorkshireman, was anxious to pay them a visit. A sentry challenged me. I saw that he was suspicious and was soon arrested but strange to say, the sergeant who came along lived in a Yorkshire village that I knew very well and doubts were soon removed. I found afterwards that a German spy had been masquerading as a chaplain and all units had been warned to keep a strict lookout for him. I happened to go along at an unfortunate time but the sergeant and my Yorkshire brogue saved me from any further trouble. I was well repaid for the risk I had taken and in the hours that followed I think I managed to cheer up those men.

The next morning, I held two informal services for the men who were going into the trenches that evening. One was in the corner of a field. The men sat round in a ring on the grass and we sang, "The King of Love my Shepherd is," with the appropriate lines – "Through death's dark vale I fear no ill with Thee, dear Lord, beside me." No sooner had we departed than the Germans shelled the very field in which we had worshipped. The next service was on the banks of a canal near a bridge which had been blown to atoms. All through these services the guns were booming.

On the Sunday morning I had once again three services in a field and in the afternoon I went into Ploeg Street Wood to visit the boys in the trenches. A line of trees a few hundred yards ahead claimed my attention for it was a favourite hiding place for German snipers. I ran across to the shelter of the wood which had been the scene of terrific fighting and had only been cleared at the point of a bayonet a short time before. I pressed on through the wood on roads laid out by our men and was reminded by the various boards nailed to the trees that I was in 'Piccadilly Circus', 'The Strand' and 'Ludgate Hill' and noticed that various dugouts were called 'Selfridges', 'Harrods' and 'The Corner House'. A shell came whistling over followed by others, cutting down the trees as if by one sharp cut of a woodman's axe. At last I reached the front line and, looking through the periscope, had my first view of the German trenches. I then visited the dugouts. They were not very deep ones in those days. The rain came in and there was mud everywhere. I talked to the men of home and loved ones and gave them cigarettes and sweets, soap and other useful presents. Darkness descended and I made my dangerous return back to my billet.

Oh, the ruined churches! There were no less than four blown to pieces in the district I travelled. More shells, roofs gone, altars broken down – though in one church the cross still stood. I dashed into one, one evening, when the shells were falling in the vicinity. I felt like a rat in a trap and found shelter in a confessional box which still remained. It was not very good protection but one never stopped to think on such occasions. Fortunately the church was not hit, otherwise I might have found my last resting place in that box. One day I called to pay my respects to a priest in one of these churches, a genial, white-haired, saintly man. "Let me show you my family," he said, and in walked three other priests who had lost their all. "Those wretched Germans even smashed my favourite pipe," said one, "and I have had to borrow this." He was smoking a churchwarden clay. I met one of these priests at six o'clock one morning in his white robes, preceded by two acolytes, on a road swept by shell fire. He had been to give extreme unction to a dying man. These men always impressed me as real heroes of the faith.

My duties covered a large area. I was the chaplain not only of the 38th Field Ambulance, but to a brigade of troops mainly from Kent – the Buffs and others. Transport was a prime necessity. At one time I had a bicycle and at other times a horse. I suppose this part of my story is reminiscent of the song 'The Galloping Major'. I had to learn to ride for I knew precious little about horse riding but knew that on active service at the Front it was absolutely necessary to become acquainted with this method of transport. In the instructions received from the War Office before departing, it was stated that 'horse and saddlery will be provided at the base overseas'. It was not mine to reason how or why, but, with a wonderful faith in the great possibilities of this marvellous organisation of ours, to accept the statement and be prepared for emergencies. That significant sentence thrilled me. I had visions of myself seated proudly on a real war-charger, riding with the men or galloping over the battlefield on some important errand. I even had the glorious thought that in some miraculous way I might dash through the enemy's lines on some great mission and win the coveted VC. I could already see myself at the picture papers, seated on a charger, with the title underneath – 'The Gallant VC Chaplain and his Horse on which he dashed through the German Lines!' But the vision was one thing, the actual experience another. I remember that as a lad I had ridden bareback on a bony wagon horse, much to my delight and much to my grievous pain afterwards. Then I had indulged occasionally in a thrilling donkey ride at the seaside or the village feast, so I felt ready for anything and could cry for sheer delight "A horse! A horse! My kingdom for a horse!" Oh, those days of anticipation but oh those days of realisation! Both are vivid and both will never be forgotten. Thrill upon thrill! Ache upon ache.

The day of all days soon arrived and the base overseas found me eager, if not ready, for the fray. After settling down, I inquired for the remount camp and on a certain bright sunny morning I found it. I had the warning of a brother chaplain ringing in my ears, "Be careful! The horses are terrors! Get a quiet mount." To back his warning he told me that when out riding one day he had been pitched clean over his horse's head, through the windscreen of a motor car and had had a narrow escape from death. On my way also, I had pointed out to me a certain dangerous spot where a groom had been thrown from his horse over a wall and had his legs broken. I was beginning to feel like a schoolboy waiting to be caned, but braced myself up, for it would never do to show the white feather. I shall never forget my first impressions of that camp. It seemed like a huge prairie ranch. Horses big and small, prancing chargers and mules. The men in charge were second to none, recruited from racing stables, farms and some even from the Wild West. I witnessed that morning some brilliant horsemanship and longed to acquire the same skill.

Going up the lines, I asked a sergeant if he could find me a quiet mount for practice. "Could I ride?" he asked. "I thought so," I replied. Should I require a man to assist me? No I thought I could manage. So a horse of fine proportions which looked amiable was saddled and soon I was riding proudly up the lines into the open field which I thought was a suitable place for a good gallop! It always seems to me that a horse knows full well when a novice is on his back. This one certainly knew; and, oh, the sly and wicked creature! It was as good as gold whilst I was riding it up the lines but once he escaped from the familiar surroundings and reached the open field, he did the 'Merry Widow' waltz with me. Round and round we went and I had soon lost my stirrups and was clasping him affectionately round his neck. My mind went back to the days when I played 'kiss-in-the-ring' as a boy. I could see the horse wanted to get rid of me but I stuck on like grim death. After the waltz came a plunge into the ditch but by a miracle

I still stuck on. I knew I looked ridiculous and the thought that several of the men were watching my antics did not make me feel very happy. I was too proud, however, to ask for assistance and so for a full hour the circus performance continued, until, spraining my thumb, I slipped off with a sigh of relief. Instead of riding proudly back to the stables, I led the horse and was glad to hand him over to the sergeant. "Come again tomorrow, sir," he said cheerfully. "You will feel very stiff but that will soon wear off." Well, I did feel stiff and it was with difficulty that I walked home; but I did not return on the morrow, nor for a few weeks but instead rode my good old iron steed.

One morning a chaplain, who happened to be a crack rider, called on me. Would I go out for a ride? he asked. "Certainly," I replied. I did not like to confess my inexperience and had a vague idea that somehow or other I should manage all right. So his groom, who was with him, dismounted, adjusted the stirrups for me and assisted me into the saddle. "I'm going to take you for a gallop along the banks of the canal," he said. I did not relish the prospect for this canal was frequently shelled. An Indian encampment was to be seen in the meadows on one side so I suggested we should ride slowly until we had passed the camp. This gave me a breathing space for the trial to come. "Oh, by the way," he said as we left the road for the canal-side, "you must be careful how you ride. A man was pitched into the canal the other day and drowned." This news was not distinctly cheering and I felt inclined to make excuses and return; but the sight of my accomplished friend sitting easily in the saddle and a desire not to look small in his eyes decided me. I would ride – even to death. I looked into the bright sun, at the canal, the camp and my mount which up to that moment had behaved like an angel, and wondered, if I were killed, what my friends would say when they read my obituary notice. We passed the Indians and then I suggested to my friend that he gallop ahead, so with a gentle prick of his spurs his horse leaped ahead and off he went. There was no need for spurs in my case; for no sooner did my horse see his fellow go, than off we went in chase! What strange creatures horses are! I would willingly have let my friend have the gallop to himself and jogged along behind but my horse willed otherwise. With a prayer for assistance, I stuck down my heels in the stirrups, grasped the reins in one hand and the pommel of my saddle with the other and off I unwillingly followed. How I stuck on during that whirlwind ride is a mystery. I had a vision of a streak of water and was vaguely wondering how I should feel if pitched in, when I came to a bridge and a dead stop. The next thing I remember is that I was on the ground, having somehow or other slipped off at the moment the horse stopped and there the docile animal stood looking slyly at me. "You look a bit white and blown, old chap!" said my companion, who came up at that moment. "I am," I replied "and am thankful to be alive." I then explained my inexperience and was proud to hear him say, "Plucky chap!" Nevertheless, I did not ride back again but returned the mount to my friend and wondered if ever the happy day would come when I could really ride with the same ease and freedom.

A few days after, I found a sergeant in the wagon lines who instructed the men of the gun teams and was a splendid instructor, too. I saw him training the men in jumping their horses in the field and asked him if he would give me a few lessons. He was only too willing and so, morning after morning, I went for my lessons at 6am; but my progress was only slow and I often wished that I had been blessed with longer legs.

"Press your heels well to the sides of your saddle."

"Make a lot of your horse."

"Grasp the reins in one hand, keeping them level with your horse's neck."

"Rise in your saddle when I say, 'one, two.'"

How well I remember his words of command but I found it difficult to practise them. One day he said, "I will take you out to visit the batteries at 5.30 in the morning if you care to come," so I gladly assented and the next morning found me there to time. My mount on this occasion was a good many hands high and its long legs and lanky body reminded me of a racehorse. Never shall I forget that early morning ride! At the very outset my horse chased after a column out exercising and only with difficulty was he persuaded to leave their companionship; but, at last, with the sergeant's assistance, we were able to proceed to the batteries a few miles off. On our return journey all went well until we met a man cycling. In passing us he rang his bell. My horse objected to bells, in fact hated anything that tinkled, so suddenly rearing, it got out of control and I had a vision of being carried over the trenches to the German lines and instead of the VC I dreamed of in days gone by, I thought of how I should fare as a prisoner. Just as I thought that nothing could save me, my friend the sergeant galloped up and headed the horse into a yard and so, as the story would put it, "saved my life." I shall never forget my genial friend the sergeant nor those horse riding experiences at the Front. I have ridden a good deal since, and often with men when exercising their horses, but for safety's sake give me the iron steed or the electrical horse that I and the other officers used to ride in the gymnasium of an old German liner, now used as a transport ship, when on our journey to the Near East.

One afternoon I paid a visit to the bivouacs of our Indian troops. I had ridden past the encampment in the unpleasant ride I have described. Most of the men were Gurkhas, Sikhs, Rajputs, Pathans and Mahrattas. It was a wonderful experience to meet those classes of fighting men of our Indian Army. Only one man could speak English and he acted as my interpreter. The camp itself was a remarkable one. In neat lines were quaint tents covered with mats, with the inside floor covered with straw. There were blacksmiths, shops, lines of kicking mules and store tents. Outside were wood fires covered over with iron plates and a number of men were engaged in roasting goats' flesh and making a kind of oatmeal cake. I was soon surrounded by a group of happy laughing men who squatted in a circle smoking from a huge pipe, passing it from man to man. It was the pipe of peace. Would I smoke it with them, I was asked. I did not wish to offend them. The stem had been in too many mouths for my liking but what could I do? I compromised by filling their pipe, much to their delight, with some tobacco sent to me by Sir William P. Hartley. I do not exaggerate when I say that it took two ounces to fill that bowl and soon the men were puffing out huge clouds of smoke. The conversation I entered into, through the interpreter, was the most amazing and yet interesting I have ever had. They all seemed greatly honoured to have an English officer in their midst and I shall always remember their eager faces and the merry laughter in their eyes. On leaving, they presented me with a number of their oatmeal cakes which they had prepared for me. I took these to the officers' mess for tea. Thinking I had had them sent to me as a present from home, they were eaten with a relish. When all were finished, I told them where I had got them from. During the next few minutes there was a pained expression on their faces and I will not repeat the remarks that were made. Strange how ungrateful some men can be!

It almost seemed as if we were doomed to operate in the Armentieres sector for the duration of the war but such was not the case. One day the whole division was thrown into a state of excitement and anticipation. We had, so it was rumoured, new fields to conquer. The order to move came quickly. In the hours of darkness the division began its move. It was one continual rumble of guns and tramp of marching feet. It was impossible to get much sleep, although my unit did not move until the morning at eight o'clock. At a very much earlier hour we had breakfast, we could not eat much and so we packed up a few sandwiches for the march. It amused me to see the pets the men had collected. I talked to the driver of one of our timber wagons and found him with a little monkey. He had dressed it in khaki with cap and even the badge of the regiment. Poor little mascot, he shivered in the early morning air. I gave him some chocolate and left him nestling in the man's greatcoat. Another man had a kitten and quite a number had dogs, big dogs, little dogs and puppies. Here they were, all taking their places in the ranks for the march. They went where we went, slept where we slept and had the best of the little tit-bits to eat.

Before we departed, the village priest and people gathered to cheer us on our way. We had chased the Germans out from their midst at the point of a bayonet and they were grateful, grateful because of the horrible outrages they had suffered before. There was that little farm by our wagon lines. In the centre of the yard opposite the house was the grave of a little lad of twelve. His brother, who had been dressed in khaki by our men and loved to be with them and to lead the horses to the pond, told me how he had died. The little chap had been collecting cartridges as souvenirs. Then the Germans swept through the village, they searched the houses for arms and even searched the women and children. They found the cartridges in the pockets of the boy and there in the presence of his own agonised mother, they shot him. And there he lay buried. There was no wonder that the people were glad to have us for our men had been kind to them, especially to the women and children. The people wept as we moved off.

It rained in torrents as we left and, splashed with mud and soaked to the skin, we arrived at a wayside station and entrained. We had already marched seven miles and the relief was great. We detrained at another wayside station. In the fields, waiting to begin the next stage of our march, were thousands of men. I found the shelter of a haystack and then went in search of food. In a back yard I found a man with an eye for business, helped by two stout women and a girl; he was cooking chips. I rushed excitedly among the men, crying, "Chips! Chips! Hurrah!" I wondered if they thought the Padre had gone mad. But no, there were the plates of rich, brown, crisp potatoes and all for the equivalent of two pence. Soon the stock was cleared and the little children, who had gathered round, cleared up the remnants of the feast. We moved on. As I reached the slope of the hill, I looked back. What a sight! The line extended for miles, as far as the eye could see; men, horses, wagons, guns, all moving along. There was one feature of the march that pleased me, we were all legging it. There were no mounted officers, the colonels, majors, captains, chaplains were all trudging side by side with their men and each was carrying his own pack. I was carrying, in addition to my pack, my Communion services in its leather attaché case. The colonel offered to give me a hand, then the adjutant. In front of me was a man who had fallen lame. At once I noticed that his pal took his pack, slung it across his shoulder and carried his double burden without a murmur.

We reached Verguin, where we spent the night. I was billeted for the night with two other officers in the house of an old couple. When we retired, we had to pass through their bedroom. They were both in bed at the time and looked so quaint as they sat up and wished us goodnight. The morning was bright, the rain had stopped and we stepped out briskly, singing as we marched. After a while we rested. The Roman Catholic Padre and myself turned aside into a farmyard and shared, with some men, in a pannikin of tea and slabs of bread and cheese. We all drank out of the same tin, facing us was a big heap of manure covered with swarms of flies.

It reminded me of the song I used to sing:

> Flies on the butter; flies on the ham,
> Flies on the bacon, and flies on the jam,
> Flies buzzing round my head and on my nose and eyes,
> But I am so much enjoying myself, I don't mind flies!

We were always troubled with flies and we certainly did not enjoy ourselves when they swarmed over everything we ate. On we went, passing through mining villages. There were trenches everywhere, under the houses, by the roadside, across the open fields. Five times the village we passed was lost and won. In the darkness we reached Vermelles. There was a huge pithead and near it a shattered brewery. The infantry were billeted in ruined buildings and dugouts. The advanced dressing station was in the huge rambling cellars of the brewery. I had sleeping quarters in another cellar, the floor was covered with straw and scampering everywhere were rats. In my sleep I had an awful nightmare, much to the terror of Father Owen Scully, the Roman Catholic Padre, who was sleeping next to me. I cannot tell what happened but he declared that I was standing up fighting the wall and in doing his I landed him a blow on the face!

Many strange coincidences occur in life and one is connected with Father Scully. After the Battle of Loos, he left the division and I never saw him again until a few years after the war. One day I went to Paddington Station to see my wife off on a journey to South Wales. I missed her in the crowd and wondered what had happened to her, so sent a telegram to Cardiff Station asking for news of her arrival. I walked up and down the platform whilst waiting for the reply. As I did this, who should I meet but Father Scully. The warmth of his greeting knew no bounds. He clasped me in his arms and we were both excited at meeting each other again. We went into the station refreshment room and had a long chat about our experiences together in France and we laughed again and again about the sleeping experience I have just described. He held his jaw and said, "That is where your fist landed!" He told me that he had been left a fortune and that he was going to Torquay for a holiday. I saw him off on his train and it was to be the last time I was to see him. After his holiday he returned to his church in Louth, Lincolnshire. One day he set out in his car to motor to Nottingham to meet his bishop. Whilst driving, the car skidded and overturned on the grass verge of the roadside and he was killed. He had passed through the perils of the Great War, had everything that he could desire in wealth and comfort, only to meet his death on a Lincolnshire country road. When I heard the news of this tragedy I was deeply grieved and thought of the old days when danger and privation had cemented a warm friendship.

The Battle of Loos had just begun and the men of my division were to take part in it. The next night I visited the men in the frontline trenches who were to attack at dawn. It was a dark night and the rain was failing in torrents. The shells were screaming overhead and the rattle of machine gun fire and the star shells shooting up into the sky made the scene like an inferno. I passed round the corner of one trench and heard one of the men say to his pal, "Everything points ter 'appiness, Bill." In another part I talked to two lieutenants who were Oxford undergraduates who had joined up with many more from the university. As is often the case, the conversation turned to religion: "Tell us, Padre, what will happen to us if we are killed in the attack? Will all the education we have received, all our plans for the future, all our hopes for a long and happy life have been in vain?" Then I remember those lovely words from the Book of Revelation and quoted them: "He that overcometh shall inherit all things; and I will be his God and he shall by my son … and they shall bring the glory and honour of the nations into it." They were both killed in the attack and I thought of the conversation which we had had together as I buried them. In my letter to their parents I told them of our last talk and quoted the same words which I am sure helped those splendid boys as they went over the top that morning. It is inspiring and comforting to know that their lives were not in vain and that 'He that overcometh shall inherit all things'.

The same day, I saw Major General Wing and his aide de camp killed just ahead of me. We laid them to rest in Vermelles. I was knocked over by the blast from the same shell. The next night, Father Scully and I received a wire from headquarters to go to take duty for a chaplain who was injured. The colonel lent us a flash lamp and we began our nerve-racking journey. The roads were crowded with horses and limber wagons and we had to wade through mud a foot deep. It was a weird experience and the greatest bombardment we had ever witnessed was taking place with us in the thick of it. It was indescribable. For an hour it seemed as if the whole place would be blown to atoms. That night will live in my memory – star shells, red light shells, guns of all calibres. We found the chaplain and a major in a dugout. The chaplain had been conducting a burial party in the afternoon along with the major and a number of men when the Germans opened fire on them. The major was wounded in the head and the chaplain jumped into the grave, spraining his ankle in the process. For a long time he had to lie with the dead soldiers he had gone to bury. The major said: "It is good and brave of you to come but we cannot send out any burying party in the midst of this inferno; not a man would return alive," so we had to postpone the sad task and cautiously return to our dugout. In this particular part of the line two chaplains were killed – a Roman Catholic whose bravery will never be forgotten, and a son of the Church of England.

During the height of the battle, I had one extraordinary escape. I was talking to an officer when I heard a voice: "Hello! Mr Kendall!" I crawled across to the man who had called. It was Scruby, the Guardsman I used to entertain in my home in Windsor. I had not seen him since I saw him off to the Front in 1914. The next moment the officer I had been talking to was wounded and the man who had taken my place at his side was killed. I was glad to meet Scruby under such circumstances and we were able to talk about old times. It was the last time I saw him because later he was killed.

After the battle we pulled out to rest and refit. We moved to the mining village of Labourse. There was a pit in full working order, although well within the range of shell fire. The workers were mostly old men and girls. There were some excellent hot baths in the charge of a woman. Our officers were glad to make use of them. I was billeted in a row of small miners' cottages. My home was spotlessly clean. The Prince of Wales, now the Duke of Windsor, occupied the next cottage to myself. He could have lived in a big chateau not far away but preferred the humble billet. I called and found he was sleeping on the red tiled floor, another officer sharing the room with him. There were no beds, just an ordinary mattress on the floor which was rolled up when I called. There were a few cheap pictures on the walls, two chairs and a table. I mentioned this once in a letter to his mother Queen Mary and she was delighted with my story. The Prince never let the HRH before his name get between him and the ordinary men. I had a marvellous bed with a canopy of white muslin tied with blue silk ribbon, also a lace bedspread – a contrast to the floor on which the Prince slept. It amused me to get into this dainty bed each night and the other officers used to tease me about it. In the room were various articles of female attire, also an old-fashioned bassinette and some children's toys.

All good things come to an end and this rest-out of the line was very good and most refreshing. It seemed that Army Headquarters were determined in my case that I should not rest long. I had been tried in battle and a new call awaited me. I was to succeed an elderly chaplain on the Somme, a man who was now too old for the Front and so had been posted to base. I, therefore, received my orders to depart and packed up, once more to continue the long, long trail.

12

The Somme and Salonica (22nd Division)

Foreword

Those who have served as Padres will recognise George Kendall's experiences as he describes them in this chapter. Rarely the most military of men, they so have often been given a map and then been told to meet their unit at a particular place. Travelling has formed a part of the experience of most Padres, and the travels described in this chapter will be echoed by many, from the Peninsula War to the deployments in Afghanistan and Iraq. The particular merit of this description is the insight it has provided to living, travelling and ministering in the time of great strife. It ends with that other potential problem for a Padre, as for everyone else on operations: the risk of contracting an illness which will remove you from the front line and your place of work.

What is also evident is his interest in the people of the places in which he finds himself. His descriptions might always be kind, but they have the merit of accuracy. Again, as with so many of his counterparts who have served the British Army as its chaplains, George found that he was also involved in the lives of the countries in which they were called to serve. If visiting a notorious nightclub might not have been part of the training of a Primitive Methodist minister, the need to do so in Marseilles did not appear to have frightened George Kendall.

There is one relationship which stands out in this chapter: that with his Catholic colleague, Father McGuinness. It seems unlikely that their paths would have crossed in civilian life, as this was a time long before such ecumenical contacts became commonplace. Ecclesiastically poles apart, they both recognise the shared element of their common ministry. Such colleagueship was to become normal among chaplains; it helped to develop the closer relations between Christians that began to be a feature of the post-war years.

The Rev Dr Peter Howson
Methodist Army Chaplain (1977-2002)
Author of *Muddling Through:*
The Organisation of British Army chaplaincy in World War One

My orders gave me no destination; instead, as was the usual practice, I had a map reference and this was supposed to be sufficient. I proceeded in a car to the nearest railhead and began my journey, again into the unknown. My companion for a few miles on that journey turned out to be Private Patrick MacGill of the London Irish, the famous navvy poet and the author of 'The Great Push' and other stories of the war. Fresh from the Battle of Loos, where he had many marvellous escapes from death, he had some hair-raising adventures to tell me of. On one occasion, he told me, he was sleeping in a house when the roof was blown off. His pals thought that poor Patrick's pen would be forever silenced, as they expected to find that he had been killed; but instead they found him asleep! We parted at the junction and I then waited for a train which started at midnight. This was necessary as the line was under observation by the enemy and was frequently shelled. Only one train was permitted in the twenty-four hours and that was under cover of darkness.

I travelled in the guard's van with a number of soldiers. They were taking supplies for the men in the line and the wagons were filled with all kinds of provisions. At a certain point all lights were extinguished and the engine itself was covered with a huge tarpaulin because we were travelling parallel with the German lines and within reach of their machine gun fire. It was a nerve-racking journey. Should a star shell illuminate the line and the train detected, we were doomed. I remember how I sang to myself the old song 'The little grey home in the West', and how I prayed: "Lighten our darkness, we beseech Thee, O Lord and by Thy great mercy defend us from all perils and dangers of this night." That journey seemed endless as we moved slowly along in order to lessen the noise. At last we reached our destination. It was Sunday morning, 10th October, my thirty-fourth birthday.

I found the railway transport officer and then found, to my dismay that I had been sent to the wrong place. The division I had been ordered to join were many miles south, so my midnight wanderings were not over. I found a Church of England Padre who kindly gave me food and lodgings for the night. After dinner in his mess, I saw an air fight. There was the rattle of machine guns. Would the German pilot escape? No! A great cheer went up from the men watching the fight as the German came down. In striking the ground, the plane bounced over a hedge and ploughed into a nearby field. I rushed across and found the pilot strapped to his seat but alive. I helped to release him and found that he had broken his legs in the crash. He was taken away by our men to the Field Ambulance.

I took the next train at seven in the morning. This was crowded with officers and men all the way to the Somme area. We passed through the loveliest of scenery, beautiful woods and dales, old chateaux and quaint towns. The journey seemed so restful after my weeks in Armentieres and Loos. The railhead, where we detrained, was eight miles from the firing line so the remainder of the journey was by car – to the headquarters of the 22nd Division. I met with great kindness there. Colonel Muir, the assistant adjutant and quartermaster general, took me back to the station in his car for the kit I had had to leave there. He also entertained me to lunch and introduced me to the commanding officer of the division, Major General The Hon F. Gordon, to Lieutenant Colonel W.J. Maxwell Scott, his chief of staff and to another staff officer

Major C.W. Pearless. The general told me of his brother, a Presbyterian minister and also said that his favourite book was 'The Psalms in Human Life' – a book I love. Colonel Maxwell Scott, afterwards knighted, was a descendant of Sir Walter Scott and lived at Abbotsford, Sir Walter's old home. He was a relation of the Marquis of Bute. All the officers became my great friends and were always anxious to help me. Later in the evening the general sent me, well supplied with comforts and magazines, to the line in a car driven by a staff captain. I was to serve the 67th Infantry Brigade and was attached to the 8th South Wales Borderers, then at Framerville. The trenches were just beyond the village but in 1915 it was a quiet place in the line. The enemy had only just been driven out and had set fire to some buildings but the magnificent cathedral-like church in the centre was only slightly damaged.

I was billeted in a big farmhouse at the corner of crossroads. It was a dirty old house and although practically in the front line, was still occupied by the farmer and his daughter. The daughter was by no means a beauty, and she only washed herself once a week. She had a vile temper and I must confess I was afraid of her. I remember the first Sunday I was there she washed herself and put on a clean blouse and, for once, went to Mass. Thinking a word of encouragement might do her good, I rashly complimented her on her appearance. How I regretted it afterwards! For she persisted in forcing her presence on me for the rest of the day and, in order to impress me still further, she kept her hat on too. At last, an officer who used the mess with me told her off in striking French and her vile temper was too much for words. I wished that the enemy had taken her when they left!

The room I occupied had a magnificent floor of ornamental wood blocks, caked with mud. It was also richly panelled. There were four big windows but all the panes had been smashed. My batman, Thomas, thoroughly cleaned the room for me but it took him a long time to scrape the mud off the floors. The old farmer used to get up at four each morning. His farm, in spite of the nearness of the enemy, was well stocked with cattle. When I asked him how he managed to save them from the Germans, he said that he had hidden them. In that particular part there are some curious underground caves where, in past generations, the farmers used to hide their cattle from robbers. I went to see them one day and could see how the farmer had been able to save his stock. The farmer had also a cellar of choice wines but, to his great anger, all were stolen. "The Huns took four hundred bottles," he told me and added, "I wish I had put poison in them."

It was whilst I was in this brigade that I began a very real friendship with the Roman Catholic Padre Father McGuinness. Before joining up he had been the professor of Latin and Mathematics at St Bede's College, Manchester near to my own Theological College. A real jolly man, he was a splendid athlete and we got on well together. We decided to mess together, as the brigade mess was too crowded, and our two batmen looked after us and saw to our rations and meals – excellent men and good cooks they were – we could leave everything to them.

Soon we were on the trek again as our division received orders to leave that sector. They were 'sealed orders' and we wondered where we were bound for. It is no easy task to move a division and for days our men were marching to a particular destination, known only to headquarters. I had a bicycle. This machine had caused a lot of trouble. I saw it one day and claimed it. The brigade major argued that I had no right to it. "Is this bicycle owned by the British Army?" I asked. "Yes!" he replied, "and we have to account for it."

"Am I not in the army?" I asked. He could not deny this so I added, "I have as much right to it as anyone else." That bicycle caused endless correspondence and I was ordered to give it up, so off I went to see the commanding officer of the division about it. I pointed out to him that the Brigade Staff had horses and that I must have some means of getting about. He agreed with me and promised to see that the machine remained in my hands. He did, much to the annoyance of the major!

On this march, we were billeted in a farm near to a village. It was occupied by two ladies. One had terrible physical deformities. When I went to the door to ask for a room, the old lady met me with a pitchfork in her hand. She was not going to have any English officers in her house! Well, there was no other billet available and it was getting late, so I tried to be as nice as possible. At last a happy thought occurred to me. I had, in my pocket, a coloured engraving of a charming old lady with snow-white hair, sitting in a lovely cottage. It had been sent to me along with a magazine. I pulled this out and presented it to her and told her that she bore a striking resemblance to the original. That did the trick! She eagerly seized it and took it inside the house to have a look at it, so I followed her in. So strategy won the day! I secured one room and six of us slept on the floor in our valises. I had one more passage of arms with the old lady when she refused to let the men draw water from her well. She locked the handle of the windlass to prevent us from drawing any water. This was a matter in which I had to exercise firmness and, at last, I managed to free the handle. One night we had the misfortune to break a chair but we paid so well for it that I think she would have been pleased if we had smashed all the furniture in the house!

Again on the march, column after column, to Gentelles. Father McGuiness was my constant companion. He, too, had managed to obtain a bicycle and as we went along he endeavoured to cheer me up by singing to me. One night we received orders: "Breakfast at 5am. Have all valises packed and placed on lorries." This we did and in due course we entrained at the railhead. On asking our destination, I was told Marseilles. Officers and men alike shared, not carriages, but cattle trucks and luggage vans. I was in a van with Father McGuiness and four other officers. We had our floor covered with straw and on top we placed our sleeping bags. In the centre we had a smoking oil lamp which, alas, fell down before we had been long on our journey. For two days and nights we rushed along through the most wonderful scenery in the world.

Here, let me record a remarkable coincidence. Up to a short time before the hour of departure, I had forgotten my rations and when my man (the best soldier-servant any officer could have wished to have) tried to secure some, he found that they had all been given out. Strange are the ways of providence for, just as the train was on the point of departing, the battalion postman brought me three parcels. I found the parcels, which came from my wife and friends, contained large cakes, apple turnovers, with a supply of sugar, apples, sweets, tea and all kinds of sundries. My man, a sergeant major and the officers in my van all had a share, so we had cake for lunch, cake for tea and cake for supper, along with apple tart and apples. On our way we were able to get a drink of tea made with water from the engine. Each morning we shaved with the water from our bottles. The nights were very cold but we slept fully dressed and had our blankets and valises.

Passing the outskirts of Paris, we travelled through the heart of France and made brief halts at Chalons, Macon and Lyons. During the day we opened our sliding doors and sat on the steps. Never shall I forget the Valley of the Rhone with its vineyards, old chateaux, quaint villages and magnificent range of the Cevennes. The majority of the men were Welsh and how they sang. More than once you could hear the strains of 'Land of my Fathers', and 'Jesu, Lover of my Soul' sung to the tune 'Aberystwyth'.

But, I think the hymn that moved me most and which vibrated through the whole of my being because of the circumstances and the uncertainty of the future, was 'Lead Kindly Light' which that haunting verse:

> So long Thy power hath blest me, sure it still will lead me on
> O'er moor and fen, o'er crag and torrent, till the night is gone.

So, on we sped with new scenes opening out before us. When we left the North, the nights were cold but farther south we found warmer weather and, one morning as we rushed through a tunnel, we emerged into glorious sunshine and there, in the distance, we could see the spires and houses of Marseilles and the blue waters of the Mediterranean. As we entered the sidings, the Welshmen sang an old song, so touching, so appropriate: "Farewell, farewell my native land." To many it would be a real farewell, for they would never again see the shores of France, of Wales or of England.

Our next move was to the docks and there we found our transport The Huntsend. In peacetime she was a famous German liner. This was to be our home for the next two weeks. Some two thousand five hundred officers and men then began the long process of embarkation. It took many hours to settle down. We wondered at what hour we should sail, but it was two days before orders came and so we took advantage of the waiting period to obtain leave and see something of Marseilles.

I noticed that in the great sheds the whole of the Indian Division was waiting for transport to Mesopotamia. In going through the sheds I found the men sleeping in rows on the floor and many of them were coughing. I remembered my visit to their camp in the Armentieres sector. It was wise to send them to a warmer climate for it would have been difficult for them to endure any further the bitter cold of Flanders. How long they had to wait for transport I do not know, as all the available shipping was taken up with the embarkation of our division. I was able during our waiting period to give them cigarettes and other comforts as I had a plentiful supply sent by many kind friends from home.

On our last night in dock some of our officers decided to go to a theatre. I was asked if orders came to sail, to go at once and inform them, otherwise there would be serious trouble if they were missing when the roll was called. I was on deck when the orders came and so true to my promise I got a car and along with my colleague the Roman

Catholic chaplain, went in search of them. We called at the theatre but they were not present so I asked the commissionaire if he had seen them and he said "Yes" – telling me where he thought they had gone. After a still more extensive search I found them in a rather notorious nightclub in a big cellar. With my colleague I descended the steps and there we found them surrounded by a bevy of Marseilles beauties. They were richly dressed and powdered but in my opinion they were far from beautiful. We were not greeted with enthusiasm by these ladies but the officers said they must depart with us. What happened then I have only a dim recollection of, for a fight took place. I remember one officer being knocked down by something – for Marseilles was notorious in those days and a hive of some of the worst criminals on earth – in any case we fought our way through and up the stone steps to the street outside and eventually arrived back in time for the roll call. The officers expressed their sincere gratitude for our help.

We thought that the transport would be leaving in the course of the next hour or two but there was, as was often the case in those days, a further delay and we did not leave until the following afternoon at four o'clock; the date was Saturday 30th October 1915. That night I lay fully dressed in my bunk with my lifebelt by my side for there were submarines about, and to sink our transport would have been a great achievement. Two officers sat talking to me in my cabin until 2am. All was in darkness and the men were all on the alert. It was a time of intense excitement but there was no panic. The transport's captain, a clear-headed Scot noted for his seamanship, was on the bridge.

I was up at the break of day on my first Sunday at sea and I could not help singing Harry Lauder's song:

> Oh, it's nice to get up in the morning,
> When the sun begins to shine,
> At four o'clock, at five o'clock,
> In the good old summer time.

I had two parade services on board in the morning. They were attended by nearly all the officers and men and the transport's company led by the captain. The general read the lessons at both the services and we sang the old hymns with great fervour. Father McGuiness, at the same time, celebrated Mass for some one hundred and fifty members of his church.

I noticed that we were being escorted by two French destroyers and their presence gave one an added sense of security. We were not taking a direct course but hugging the shores of Italy. We sailed past Corsica and so on to Malta and the Mediterranean. I was thrilled when we entered the glorious waters of the Aegean Sea. The sunrise with its liquid lights, its purified air, and its tremulous silver on the sea, was all too beautiful for words. I feasted my eyes on the enchanted islands we passed, perfect little gems set in the midst of blue waters. In the west I would see the fair and romantic land of Greece, with the memories of Byron. I wondered if it was still inhabited by that picturesque and high-souled race for which he died. I caught the first glimpse of

Mount Olympus with its snow-capped peak rising 10,000 feet into the clouds beyond. We sailed near the mainland. I could see the coastline with its rose-red rocks, the sloping mountain sides with their cypress and olive trees, and the picturesque villages with white-washed houses standing out clearly against the background of rocks. I looked long and earnestly through my glasses for objects of interest, a monastery surrounded by a high wall and built on a rocky headland jutting out into the sea – Mount Athos, the Holy, rising 6,300 feet on the East.

We soon made out the lines of the Bay of Salonica. There was great excitement on board and we were thrilled by this first sight of the ancient city, with its busy port, its mosques and minarets, its palaces and the mighty range of mountains which closed in the background. This was the great gateway through which we should pass to the grim and desolate Balkans. We anchored some distance from the harbour, and we were in the midst of a forest of masts and funnels. They bay was studded with the craft of all ages. There were monitors of the most recent type and feluccas with their striped sails of the exact pattern in which St Paul came to Salonica in the year AD 53, transports, store ships and supply ships, great hospital ships with their white-painted sides and red crosses, huge grey warships of all kinds flying British, French, Russian and Italian flags. We were soon surrounded by a crown of boats manned by swarthy Greeks, who were anxious to sell their wares – oranges, Turkish Delight and souvenirs.

Evening came with its gorgeous sunset, a huge crimson ball softly disappearing behind purple mountains, all shades of colours blended in wonderful streaks of light flashing out to sea. We had orders not to land until the next day, so I arranged a farewell concert on board. Two thousand five hundred officers and men, including the general and his staff, gathered on the deck. We were packed like sardines in a tin. Some were perched on ladders, others in the rigging, the general and his staff on the bridge. The covered hatchway was the platform and the Marconi operator the pianist.

How the men sang and recited. I remember one lad gave a recitation of a tragic order and we roared with laughter as he ended each verse with this couplet:

> For I am to hang by the neck, mother,
> Hang until I am dead.

The last verse describing the dramatic reprieve was greeted with great cheers. Another man gave a parody on 'O, Alice, Where art thou?' and the men greeted this with: "Where, where is she, we want Alice." Other songs followed and a Welsh choir sang 'The comrades song of hope'. Amid great cheers I asked them for an encore and a solemn hush came over all as they sang the old Sankey hymn, with the oft repeated refrain:

> In the sweet bye and bye
> We shall meet on that beautiful shore.

The men were not thinking of the shore on which they were landing on the next day, but of home and the happy meeting bye and bye, and, if death came, of the hope of meeting in Heaven. The general and the transport's captain said a few words and with the singing of 'Land of my fathers' and 'God save the King' our concert ended and the long day closed. We marched to our camps by the River Vardar the next day, a long march, passing under an ancient arch that St Paul passed through as he too travelled the same road on his missionary journeys. All was in a hopeless muddle. The slow, cumbrous bullock wagons were mixed up with motor lorries, and the lorries skidded, the bullocks floundered knee-deep in mud. The kicking pack mules of the Greek Army and the despatch rider on his motorcycle made things worse.

What a motley crowd of wayfarers we met on our march! Native women, some with bare feet, like children in their picturesque dress, so like our gipsy children at home and quite as anxious to obtain our Tommies' pennies, money-changers, native vendors selling oranges and sticky pastry, groups of jugglers, native bands with drums, cymbals and a sort of bagpipe; stalwart French soldiers in their sky-blue uniform, Zouaves and Greek and Serbian soldiers – it was a wonderful picture and full of romance.

We were covered with dust and felt almost scorched with the fierce sun, and yet it was a November day. At last we came to the British camp and we were thankful to rest. How different all this was to the battlefields we had left in France, but it seemed a naked wilderness, and as barren and untamed as it was in the Middle Ages. There were no walls, fences or trees, just a broad expanse of desolate land, broken by shallow ravines and by the tumuli that were the tombs of men who lived ages ago, or even the survivals of the mounds on which prehistoric villages were built.

The camp was only just established, a large hospital tent and a number of bell tents. The general and his staff occupied these and I was fortunate in getting one. The night came quickly and darkness made the rugged plains drearier still. In the distance I could hear the jackals howling, and the barking of the fierce wolf dogs which I was told were the lineal descendants of the war dogs of Alexander the Great. I slept that night with a fully loaded rifle by my side – a wise precaution for we were in the midst of many dangers.

The night had been very stormy with a torrential downpour of rain and when I opened the flaps of my tent the sun was shining. The men had a very trying night and were now drying their clothes. I saw a number bathing in the river and then a rather amusing sight – a native woman hiding in the rushes stole out and was just making off with the Tommies' uniforms when she was seen by one of the men and like a deer, jumping out of the water, he bounded along chasing the woman and recovered his precious belongings. The woman sought safety in the marshes. There were a lot of natives prowling about around the camp, ready to steal anything. They were particularly fond of empty bully beef tins and jam tins. I noticed one very old woman had collected a large number and as I approached she promptly sat on the lot – a most uncomfortable seat.

I called our brigade camp 'the city of a thousand candles'. There were no tents for the men but they made the best of things and were very ingenious. There were huge beds of bamboo with big leaves by the river and they were soon cut down and carried to the camp, and made into wigwams, and there they stood, hundreds of them in neat rows, a triumph of inventive genius. It was like fairyland of which we dreamed as boys, and to see the candles at night shining through the leaves was a sight never to be forgotten, a city, indeed, of a thousand candles.

We revelled in strange experiences. There were long snakes to be killed, lizards which darted away at our approach, jackals which prowled around at night, tortoises by the hundred. The latter proved a source of great amusement when tied together and matched for a tug of war, for they generally decided to go in opposite ways, and the ancient and heavier ones dragged those of a younger generation in the direction of the best cover, where a quick snooze was preferable to the strain of warfare. All day long on the Monastir Road, near the camp, there was a continuous procession of strange, homemade bullock carts, of donkeys and mules. On some donkeys we could see women riding with babies on their laps, exactly as they did a thousand years ago. Great herds of goats and sheep could also be seen, led by shepherds with crooks and dogs of wolf breed. The men looked fierce and had knives in their belts. There were many refugees fleeing from the mountains to Salonica, carrying with them their belongings. Then could be seen the Greek irregular cavalry, passing along to the frontier, riding emaciated donkeys and mules with bridles of string and a rifle slung over their shoulders. They sat sideways on the first mule, leading a second bearing a heavy load of hay and provisions. And so day by day, we witnessed this moving picture, romantic and ever-changing, meanwhile training in the valley for the stern mountain warfare to come.

We got very tired of our monotonous fare, it consisted of bully beef and biscuits for breakfast, biscuits and stewed bully beef for lunch, biscuits and canned butter for tea, and bully beef and biscuits for the evening meal. That was the fare in the first week or two before our supplies came. We were fed up with the hard biscuits of those days and the bully beef. I took the long journey into the city one day just to have lunch at the motel Mount Olympus, but what a lunch! Fish in oil, beef in oil, pudding in oil! I was well lubricated but sick with all the oil. It was a journey in vain – a long way to go for oil!

Soon our men had to move into the grim and desolate mountains to help the French. The area of operations extended as far as the confluence of the Tcherna, and the right wing as far as Lake Doiran. The operations at that stage were confined to three or four gorges, through which the Bulgarians were bound to pass if they attacked. I had the sorrowful task of burying the first of our men. We reverently carried him to the plains south of the Monastir Road and I laid him to rest within sight of the blue waters of the Aegean Sea. Many more, alas, travelled the same pathway. Dysentery, enteric and malaria were rife largely due to the lack of fresh food and the pest of flies. In this land pestilence walked in the darkness, and destruction wasted at noonday.

I seemed one day to have caught a double dose of both dysentery and malaria. I was desperately ill and after a few days of intense suffering was taken by ambulance to Salonica and transferred to the hospital ship the Carisbrook Castle, and so ended my service with the 22nd Division.

13

The Hospital Ship 1916

Foreword

First-hand accounts of momentous events bring history to life. George Kendall served in the Mediterranean about the same time as my grandfather, and will have been familiar with similar sights.

George describes in touching terms his experience on the hospital ship *Carisbrook Castle* – a converted liner that clearly impressed him, and one of many that were needed to cope with the casualties from a theatre of the Great War that tends to be overlooked.

Dr Andrew Murrison MP
The British Prime Minister's Representative
for the Commemoration of World War One

I have only a dim recollection for the hospital ship the Carisbrook Castle to which I was transferred. I felt so ill at the time, but I do remember the kindly sister in charge, who did her best to chase away dull care and pains, and I remember too one of the greatest surprises that I had, and that was when the medical officer came to examine me – his name was Captain Kendall, my own name. What a coincidence! Captain Kendall came from New Zealand and after training in a London hospital he had joined the RAMC and here he was in command of the medical services on the Carisbrook Castle. Naturally he took a special interest in me and tried to see if he could claim any relationship. I was on this ship for several days and then we sailed to Mudros, at the entrance to the Dardanelles. I remember how we sailed from Salonica in the midst of a gorgeous sunset and the next thing that fixed itself in my memory was seeing the rock-bound coast of the island of Lemnos, with its bay. There were no less than ten great hospital ships lying offshore and we joined them.

The Britannic was there, soon to be sunk after her sixth voyage, in fifty fathoms of water off the Isle of Zea. The torpedoing of this great ship which, according to the laws of war and humanity was immune from attack, was one of the most diabolical crimes of the war. I little thought as I gazed upon her that it would be for the last time and that so many would perish in her. These hospital ships, with their white painted sides, red crosses, green bands and yellow funnels were huge palaces of mercy. At night they were all illuminated with rows of green lights from stern to stern, with three red illuminated crosses on either side, the centre one being exceptionally large. The mixture of red, green and white lights of the ten ships produced a rainbow-like effect on the water, making an entrancingly beautiful picture.

The next day another great ship anchored with the others – the Aquitania, to which owing to complications in my illness, I was transferred by lighter, along with a great number of others, from Gallipoli and Salonica. I was told afterwards all about this great ship – a floating palace of 47,000 tons and a horsepower of 450,000. She consumed 1,000 tons of coal a day in her 150 furnaces and her length and breadth was such that I was told that Cheapside could be placed inside her. There were electric elevators, a gymnasium, theatre, library, huge dining and drawing rooms, laundry, cold storage and wonderful suites of millionaires' private rooms. The crew numbered six hundred and there were forty medical officers, one hundred nurses and four hundred orderlies. These facts relating to this splendid old ship are worthy of record. I was only one of four thousand patients. The Carisbrook Castle and the other smaller hospital ships had transferred their patients to the Aquitania and then proceeded to their bases to collect other sick and wounded.

We sailed the next day. The great rooms were filled with beds. I occupied a luxurious cabin fitted up with radiators, electric light, wardrobes, mahogany bedsteads, dressing table with oval mirror, rich red carpet on the floor and a lovely bathroom. My companion was a young lieutenant, nineteen years of age, who was longing to be back in dear old Scotland. He had suffered a good deal in the fighting in the Balkans. What a change all this was from that grim and desolate land and what a change too in our food, from bully beef and hard biscuits to the best food that could be provided to help us back to health and strength. No wonder that after a few days on board we began to feel better. There was no snobbishness on board, the officers and men all mixed together freely, for had they not all received their wounds in the service of their country? The sisters were wonderfully kind and seemed like angels of mercy, and the doctors gave their best attention, and were every sympathetic. Nothing was too good for the suffering ones; burdens were lifted from weary shoulders and we all thought that we had reached Heaven.

How can one describe that glorious voyage through the blue waters of the Aegean and Mediterranean Seas? We were homeward bound, and when well enough we sat on the boat deck and basked in the glorious sunshine and let the breezes from Heaven clear the disease from our bodies. How we feasted our eyes on the islands we passed. We were not aware of the course our ship was taking, but one evening we arrived in the Bay of Naples. Naples of classical antiquity, hoary, and worn with the storms of ages, lay before us. To the right, towering up to a great height, stood Vesuvius, its sides covered with lava and its summit lost in a dense cloud of smoke issuing from the crater. It was a moving sight. In the background were the mighty mountain ranges lost almost in the clouds. The setting sun changed the hue of the ocean from blue to purple. The bay was studded with craft of every description, from the great Italian warship and liner to the little felucca with its red and yellow lateen sails. It was a scene to be remembered, and we retired to rest feeling it was good to be alive and see God's beautiful world.

The Sunday morning was one of the most beautiful ever beheld. As the bright beams of the sun lighted up the landscape, one could see luxuriant gardens, with olive trees, feudal castles, waving woods, and cathedral spires, and to crown all, gaunt and mighty Vesuvius still smoking. The clearness of the atmosphere acted like a tonic. Soon all-round the ship were a crowd of bumboats with Italian sightseers and traders. None were allowed on board, but they managed to sell the men a few curios, handing them up with the aid of long poles with a bag attached to the end, at the same time keeping a wary eye on the harbour police, who were constantly driving them away.

We had our service on board at ten o'clock. A time of tears and yet a time of joy, for as we sang the old hymns and listened to the message, all the hardships of the past were forgotten and heaven seemed very near; our aching bodies were forgotten in a soul-thrilling peace. Once again Jesus walked the seas, and into our troubled souls the old, old message came: 'Peace, be still, and there was a great calm'. We spent the weekend in the bay and shipped sufficient coal to carry us home. This huge vessel consumed one thousand tons a day, we were told, so a large supply was necessary.

On Monday we weighed our anchor, and sailed to our next stopping place, Gibraltar, a distance of one thousand miles or more. Our hearts ached more than once during that portion of the journey, for some of our lads 'crossed the bar' and were buried at sea. On these occasions the flag of the ship flew at half-mast, and we used to gather on the lee side of the ship and commit our comrades to the deep, thinking of those desolate hearts, those loved ones at home, who would never see their lads on earth again. At these services we generally sang the old hymn 'Jesu, Lover of my soul' but with added meaning. And so our lads 'met their Pilot face to face' at sea, and now rest beneath the blue waters of the Mediterranean 'until the sea gives up its dead'.

We arrived at Gibraltar in about three days from leaving Naples, and the grim, rocky fortress was an impressive sight. It stands there as a mighty sentinel guarding the approaches to the Mediterranean. How proud we were as we saw its huge guns pointing in every direction across the Straits. Across the narrow stretch of water we could see the northern shores of Africa, and all around were ships of every description. Passing on through the Straits we soon entered the Bay of Biscay, and there we encountered heavy seas, and the rolling and pitching of the great vessel made it impossible for one to stand, and the crockery was smashed in all directions. The men, however, bore it wonderfully well. They did not mind the ordeal in the least, for they were going home.

So we sailed onwards, and one Friday evening we saw the lights of the Isle of Wight and anchored for the night in the Solent, and the next morning the tugs came out to meet us and we were towed safely into Southampton Harbour, where about twenty-four hospital trains were waiting to convey us to various towns. And so our dream ship arrived home.

14

Sinn Féin Rising (59th Division)

Foreword

In 2016, the centenary of the Easter Rising – the events of a week which ended in abject military failure, but which would shift the course of 20th century history – were endlessly debated in Ireland. Overwhelmingly, the voices – whether of 21st century commentators and historians, or of those who lived through the events – came from the Irish side. Kendall's typically calm, measured account of his experiences, and his sharp and largely sympathetic observations of the aftermath of what people he met in the ruined city called 'The Mad Rising', are a rare first-hand account from the other side.

In Dublin, he encountered many figures who would have major roles to play in the decades to come – including Éamon de Valera – and an unforgettable vignette of Countess Markievicz, once W.B. Yeats' gazelle-like girl in a silk kimono, who appeared to Kendall 'a tall slender nervous kind of woman'. In 1918, she would become the first woman elected as an MP at Westminster, but refused to take her seat.

His most poignant meeting was with another of the 1916 leaders, the Scottish-born socialist and trade unionist James Connolly, on the eve of his execution. By then, Connolly – badly wounded in the leg in the fighting – was so ill that he was taken to Kilmainham Gaol by ambulance and shot tied to a chair. Kendall recorded that he prayed for his executioners: 'I will say a prayer for all brave men who do their duty'.

Maev Kennedy
The Guardian Newspaper

The hospital train I boarded at Southampton took me to the military hospital at Whitworth Street, Manchester and there I was nursed back to health. After my recovery I was glad to be able to visit my old college and live over again those days when I studied there. I had a chat with some of the professors and the students who had remained – just a mere forty or so because all the others had joined the ranks of the fighting services. Then came a period of sick leave, which I spent with my family, followed by the usual Medical Boards and then the inevitable posting.

For the first two weeks I was sent to a camp near Mansfield and then to the 59th Division, then at St Albans. In Divisional Orders I was posted to the 177th Brigade commanded by Brigadier C.G. Blackader DSO. I mention his name now because of the long arm of coincidence which brings many surprising incidents in the journey of life, particularly in wartime. I went with General Blackader and the Brigade Headquarters Staff to Dublin during the Easter Rising in the troubled Ireland of those days. I little thought when I left the brigade and division and returned to France, that I should ever meet him again and yet I did in a very strange way. I was out at rest with my unit at a village named Toutencourt, near the valley of the Ancre, when I came across him in the street. He was then a major general in command of the 38th Welsh Division, who were also at rest in the same village. That night we attended a boxing match together in a wood on the outskirts of the village. The next morning the village was intensely shelled, and there were many casualties. I had one of the narrowest escapes, being in bed in a farm when a shell struck it and the beam of the ceiling of the room where I was sleeping came down and missed me by a fraction. I went afterwards to enquire about many officers and men I knew and also General Blackader. "Where was the general?" I asked. "Taken to the Field Hospital," was the reply. "What has happened to him?" I asked again. "He was bitten by a mad dog." This dog, like others, terrified with the bombing, had rushed through the streets with foaming mouth biting all it came across before it was shot, and it had bitten the general. It was the last time I saw the general. I was told afterwards that before any serum could be obtained to fight the condition, he had died of hydrophobia.

To return to my experiences with the 177th Brigade – the men in this brigade were mostly from Lincolnshire and Leicestershire; in fact, I knew many of the Lincolns and their parents, and I looked forward to a period of happy service with them in that delightful part of the country around St Albans and Harpenden, but it was not to be. Easter Monday came with the shock which shook England. The *Sinn Féin* had risen against us in Dublin. It had been rumoured that our division was going overseas to join the Expeditionary Force; instead we were ordered to Dublin. I left with the Brigade Headquarters, and the four battalions of the brigade, by train to Liverpool and then through the night to Kingstown. After a meal at the Royal St George Yacht Club, we proceeded by road to Dublin and established our headquarters at Ballsbridge. I was wondering about looking for a billet when I met Mr George Byrne JP, who enquired if he could help me. I told him I was looking for a billet and he at once suggested that I should be his guest at 36, Elgin Road. I found that Mr Byrne was the chairman of the Dublin Harbour Trustees and had big shipping interests in the city, also in Cork, Belfast and London. Some of his ships had been torpedoed. His son, who I met and admired, was an officer in the Royal Irish Rifles. I shall never forget his kindness to me, and that of his family, whilst I stayed in his beautiful residence. How strange it is that you meet someone in the street and through that person's kindness all one's troubles vanish.

Personally I was fond of the Irish people and therefore overwhelmed by this tragedy caused by the misguidance of the leaders who led the rebellion. There was also another cause. Many loyal and devoted men told me it was their considered opinion that the outbreak would have been impossible, but for the gross and unpardonable laxity, long continued, of the Irish Government at that time, and they wanted those responsible for this to be removed from office.

'The Mad Rising', as it was called, even by the Irish people, was a black one, not only for Dublin and Ireland, but for the whole of our Empire of those days and our Allies. Fire and destruction blazed through the heart of Dublin, leaving a track of death and sorrow. The casualty list of all concerned was very heavy and the city was a shambles. I stood in the midst of blazing streets with snipers' bullets whizzing around. I entered Liberty Hall when it was captured. I found it a perfect warren of rooms, rifles, crowbars, printing presses and documents were all scattered about. I visited Dublin Castle and talked to our wounded, and the wounded *Sinn Féiners* – they were lying in the same wards and were receiving the same treatment. I witnessed the capture of the Countess Markievicz, a tall slender nervous kind of woman. She had been fighting, dressed in a brilliant green male uniform, at the Royal College of Surgeons. For years I had the fur rug she used until it perished with moth! I also saw De Valera, captured, and I had a chat with him. I do not suppose he remembers our conversation but I have watched his career as Prime Minister of the Irish Republic. Before the Rising he was a professor at the Blackrock College. He has mellowed since those days.

James Connolly – who was the commandant general of the forces operating against us – was badly wounded in the leg at the General Post Office, and surrounded on 29th April. I saw him twice whilst he was in hospital, the second time being on the eve of his execution. Speaking to me on the first visit he said in answer to a question of mine about his attitude – "You know the saying."

"What saying?" I asked – and he replied, "The price of liberty is eternal vigilance." This too was the saying I heard as I spoke to his men in the Dublin Castle Hospital. Listening I felt it was not my duty to condemn, or argue. Connolly was, for years, a professed agnostic, but at the hour of death, he returned to the faith of his fathers. That night a Roman Catholic priest was admitted to the hospital and he administered Holy Communion to Connolly and gave him Absolution. Asked to pray, at the end, for the soldiers about to shoot him, he said, "I will say a prayer for all brave men who do their duty." And so he died, the last of the *Sinn Féiners* to be executed. Patrick Pearse, Thomas MacDonagh, Major John McBride, Thomas Clarke, Edward Daly, Joseph Plunkett and the other leaders I had visited were all shot on various dates. Plunkett was married at midnight to a sister of MacDonagh, at Kilmainham, just before his execution. His brothers George and John being sentenced to ten years' penal servitude.

I had the sad task of burying civilians and soldiers, in their clothes and just as they were killed, in gardens or fields. I remember the shock I had when I laid a woman in a grave with her hat and dress on and repeated the burial service. After the rebellion I had charge of the exhumation of all those I had buried, for I had kept a record of places, and dates, and names, and in the hours of darkness – midnight to the early morning – they were reverently placed in coffins and after I had identified them, re-buried in consecrated ground. The last sad task took me from 9pm to 2am when I superintended the exhumation of Lieutenant Daffen, Colour Sergeant Major Rogers and Private Dixey. I re-buried them in the churchyard of St Bartholomew's.

There were some amusing incidents to chase away the gloom. I saw a woman in Sackville Street, proceeding slowly across O'Connell Bridge. She was wearing a shawl over her head. The noise of firing was deafening at the time but she seemed quite unconcerned. In the crowd, watching from a safe point a man said, "Faith, mebbe she's insured." She arrived safely across and entered a side street. She was quite young and good looking, but I am afraid slightly under the influence of drink. As she turned to the excited group of those watching she calmly said, "Women aren't such cowards as men."

Mr H.H. Asquith, then the Prime Minister, came in the afternoon after the execution of Connolly. There was a review of the troops in the grounds of Trinity College, under our divisional general, Major General A.S. Sandbach CB DSO KCB, commander-in-chief of the Forces in Ireland. The two generals spoke to me and I was introduced to the Prime Minister who said that he had been told that I knew a good deal about the events in Dublin; would I give him some information? I told him that the *Sinn Féiners* respected the chaplains and that I had worn my white clerical collar and they had allowed me to move about freely, so that I could minister to the dying and the wounded. I answered all his questions and he thanked me most warmly.

Years afterwards I remembered our meeting as I attended his funeral in Westminster Abbey. After the rebellion I was able to relax for a few days and through the kindness of warm-hearted Dublin friends, I was driven to the Vale of Avoca, a place I had often wanted to visit because I loved the poems of Thomas Moore, who lived there. The journey was through some of the loveliest scenery of Ireland. I sat under the same tree that the poet sat under, and my soul was at peace. I was also invited to the Vice-Regal Lodge, the home of the then Viceroy. A visit to Kilarney's lakes, so fair, with everything laid on for my comfort, also to Cork, Waterford, Tipperary and other places. I was also honoured by giving a lecture in the Town Hall at Lismore. This was attended by the deputy lieutenant of the county, parties from the Duke of Devonshire Castle and the Earl of Waterford's, the dean of the cathedral, and a crowd of residents and officers and men. A collection which realised a big sum, was taken on behalf of the YMCA.

I may shock some by also saying that I actually attended a race meeting. I had never been to one and wanted to see an Irish crowd. There was every conceivable kind of gambling, three-card trick, roulette tables, as well as on the horses. I was not ashamed to wear my white clerical collar although another Padre dispensed with his. I like to see the horses and enjoyed the good-natured shouts of the crowd. I did not have even the proverbial shilling on any horse. A gipsy operating a three-card table saw my uniform and collar and whispered, "Put ten shillings on the lady, Father, and

I'll see you win." And so he would, but had I done so, he would have shouted: "Come and have a try – it is all above board. See how His Reverence has won – come along and try your luck," and so on. What a big advertisement it would have been for him.

I moved with the brigade to Fermoy, and ministered to the officers and men. Whilst there, the River Blackwater overflowed its banks. The roads were covered to the depth of eight feet, homes were ruined and many people rendered destitute. Our Brigade Headquarters had water up to the top of the first floor and we had to evacuate the premises. Two of the Leicesters, a corporal and a private, were driving a transport wagon over the bridge when they and the horses were washed away. Even coffins from the graves of the churchyard were washed down the river. We found the bodies of the soldiers later on and I buried them. The soldiers helped to clear up the wreckage after the floods subsided.

15

Ypres Salient (38th Welsh Division)

Orders came for me to depart once again to join the Expeditionary Force. Lovely Ireland, with all its tragedies was left behind. The journey over the Irish Sea was the worst I have ever suffered. The boat put out at 2am and I went to sleep. At 4am we were nearly stranded on the breakwater and a tug was required to release us. We shipped heavy seas.

I was concerned at the condition of a crowd of soldiers, one had a fit and many were suffering from seasickness. Entirely on my own authority I went below deck to them and said, "Come and have breakfast with me boys." I was just about to pay the steward the bill when an officer came up and said, "I will not allow you to pay Padre." He then paid, bought a lot of cigarettes for them and later on paid for all their lunches. I was deeply moved by his generosity. I then asked the saloon passengers if they would mind if I brought the Tommies to share it with them and they willingly agreed. We got up a sing-song and I had them all at it from 9am to 3pm with short intervals. And so we sailed away and duly landed. The inconveniences had vanished in a rich fellowship – saloon passengers and Tommies.

After a short embarkation leave I proceeded once again to Boulogne and reported. I stayed the night at the officers' club and then entrained for the Ypres Salient railhead at Poperinghe. A new officers' club had been opened just a little way from the station. I stayed there for the night and slept on the floor. It was fortunate for me that I did not stay the following night for the club was shelled and destroyed and the officers staying there were killed. The next day I was posted to the 113th Brigade, of the 38th Welsh Division, and attached to the 15th Royal Welsh Fusiliers. The senior chaplain of the division, The Rev Peris Williams, who ranked as a major, kindly took me to the headquarters of the battalion and introduced me to the commanding officer and the other officers. There is no chaplain I have ever met that I liked more than Peris Williams. He was greatly beloved by all in the division in which there were nine Free Church chaplains, seeing it was a strong Free Church division, and three of the Church of England.

My brigade were then occupying the trenches in the Ypres Salient and had suffered a good many casualties. It was the depth of winter, snow and ice, bitter winds and all kinds of discomforts. We had a camp in a wood behind our lines. My companions were the transport officer, the quartermaster and the French interpreter. Our mess room was a little wooden hut and our sleeping quarters were canvas tents. I shall never forget the intense cold. The snow was piled all around our quarters and this helped to keep the wind from our tents. Each night there was a terrific bombardment and the shells played havoc with the trees and our nerves.

My batman at this time was a cultured man, in private life a London lawyer. He had joined the ranks and had seen a great deal of fighting, and was one of the most gentle and kind men I have ever met. If a man asked him to lend him a few francs he would say, "I'll give you five francs if you promise me not to spend it on drink." He had a soft musical voice and I always felt like apologising to him when asking him to do anything for me. There is a rather amusing story told concerning him. On one occasion he was on sentry duty, and was bending down, when an officer of high rank approached him. The officer was most indignant because he did not get the customary salute, and asked the reason why. "Well, sir," my batman answered, standing to attention, "you see I had a slight irritation in my leg and I felt I must scratch it. Please excuse my apparent negligence in the circumstances." He then gave the salute. The officer laughingly told the story afterwards and said, "What could I do with a man with such a soft voice, and slowly answering me with such a collection of words?"

I had some good services with the troops in this wood. I remember, too, the day I made an exciting journey from the wood to the trenches. The afternoon I arrived another chaplain called for me and with two orderlies we mounted our horses and trooped off. We arrived safely at the trenches and left the horses with the orderlies under the shelter of a bank, and had tea in a cosy dugout with the colonel of a certain regiment and his staff. That dugout, I remember, was lined with fancy canvas on which were pinned all kinds of papers. There was also a little stove in the corner, and a table down the centre, on which was a tablecloth and even white crockery. We had buttered toast for tea that day, which was a real treat. It was rather late when we left the trenches, and the return journey was made in the light of the moon shining over the snow-covered battlefield. The roads were crowded with all kinds of transport and I soon lost my companions, and lost my way too. I shall remember that ride to my dying day. A keen east wind was blowing across the shell-swept plain, and I experienced all the sensations possible for a man to experience. I first of all perspired a good deal with the trotting, and then soon after I was frozen to the saddle. I felt that each step the horse took was chafing my skin and I suffered great pain. My feet and hands becoming numb with the cold, I tried to trot my horse faster, but had to give it up. I had toothache and many other kinds of aches, and felt I was wandering through every by-lane in the famous Ypres Salient. I at last struck the main road and found I had made a circle, and was only a short distance from where I started, but I could now find my way home by the aid of our field signal poles. But I had more discomforts to suffer as my horse took it into its head to shy at all the passing motor lights and stationary red lights marking danger spots. At one point it dashed off into a wood, and as I could get no assistance, with difficulty I slipped off its back, breaking a few straps in the attempt, and then I painfully led it the rest of the way to the camp. I was thankful to reach the shelter of my little hut in the wood. The next morning, I was too stiff to walk and I bore the marks of that journey for many a day, as the skin came off my legs and they were very much inflamed and swollen. It was not by any means a life of ease.

There is another incident which occurred about this time which is stamped indelibly upon my memory. Two privates and a corporal of a famous Welsh regiment had been granted a well-earned leave, and so with joyful hearts they cleaned their equipment and left the trenches, making their way to the railhead some ten miles away. Alas! On arrival at the station it was found that the leave train had been postponed, and so these men, keenly disappointed, returned to the trenches. They had no sooner reached a certain dangerous place on the canal bank than a chance shell came over, killing them on the spot, and so three little homes in a Welsh village nestling among the hills were desolate. Had these boys known it, they could have stayed the night at the railhead in a rest billet, and proceeded on leave the next day, but with a keen sense of duty they plodded their weary way back again into the jaws of death and there they were called to enter upon their eternal leave, and three simple crosses near Bard Cottage (the name given by these Welsh troops to a heap of stones) mark their last resting place.

I received a message early the next morning to conduct the burial service of these three men, and mounting my horse, with an orderly for company, I trotted off. It was a bitterly cold morning in the depth of winter; the ground was covered with snow and as hard as iron. I had the greatest difficulty at times to keep my horse on its legs. There was a terrific bombardment on and all along the roads I could see the flashes of our guns and hear the shells screaming through the air. The enemy were replying vigorously and I knew I was in for a hot time. It was too dangerous to take my horse up to the trenches on the canal bank, so I left it in charge of the orderly at a ruined chateau and borrowed a cycle for the rest of the journey. Arriving at the trenches I found a number of men trying to dig the graves, but it was a fearful task as the ground was frozen to the depth of several feet owing to the long frost and the marshy nature of the soil. They were engaged in this task when the familiar scream of a shell was heard, and the whole party rushed for a dugout just in time to see the high-explosive tear up the earth a few yards beyond; another came and buried itself deep in the earth at the side of the dugout. Thank God it was a dud, and so did not explode. Then shrapnel began to burst overhead and we heard the pieces falling all around. This was all the result of a Boche plane sighting our working party and giving the signal to their batteries. Our guns now began to retaliate and for a long time we had to keep under cover. During the waiting period I went through a deep gap which was covered with ice and crossed by a narrow wooden bridge over the frozen canal between the two lines of trenches, and had lunch in another dugout with some officers. Two of them I found, were ministers' sons, and all were men of religious conviction, so it was a real joy to talk with them. The adjutant furnished me with the details respecting the three boys I had to bury, and gave me their home addresses. They also gave me a warm invitation to take up my abode with them – the major offering to share his dugout with me. I accepted this, promising to return in two days. I shall never forget how they all said, "We like to have a Padre living with us."

In the meantime, during a lull in the bombardment, the graves had been completed and we laid the boys to rest, but owing to the exposed position I was only able to repeat the opening sentences of the burial service, the committal and a short prayer. It is a solemn moment when engaged in such a task, for one never knew whether a chance shell would come and scatter further death. The burial had been fixed for 11am but it was 3pm before we could complete the sad task. In the distance the leave train these boys should have travelled in was steaming out of the station, but what mattered it? For these lads the strife was over.

Occasionally we made the journey to Poperinghe, and it was here that I met Tubby Clayton for the first time. I had heard in the line all about Talbot House and so I paid it a visit. It was all that I had expected – a home from home. There were crowds of Tommies and it was good to join them. Upstairs Tubby had formed a Holy of Holies – his chapel – for quiet times and prayers. As you sat there you felt that peace within, when all around was tumultuous.

The 55th Divisional Concert Party was cheering the boys with a revue called 'Cheer-Oh'. The Divisional Theatre, in spite of shelling, was packed. I noticed the amusing skits on a printed programme:

The Management will not hold themselves responsible for any shells that may arrive during the performance.

Any property found in the theatre will be kept by the finder. Hence the saying 'Findings keepings'.

The audience is requested to refrain from discussing digging parties as this has a tendency to put the wind up the artistes.

In the event of fire the orchestra will play 'Keep the home fires burning' with all effects.

It was all good fun and gave the men, who had been through a gruelling time in the trenches, a chance to forget all their troubles in the riotous laughter of one of the funniest revues ever given on the Western Front. I suppose, when out at rest, I arranged more concerts than most men. Memory is flooded with thoughts of some of these – the circumstances and, above all, the talent of the men who were always ready to take part.

I have a vivid recollection of one old and tried warrior reciting a poem that must have been his own composition and inspired too by his experiences. It is too good not to be recorded by someone, and here it is – the title he gave me was 'The Dead Mule Tree', and there were four vivid verses:

It's a long step round by the crucifix for a man with a mighty load,
But there's hell to pay where the dead mule lies if you go by the Baileul Road,
Where the great shells sport like an angry child with a little of broken bricks,
So we don't go down by the Dead Mule Tree but round by the crucifix.
But the wild young men come bubbling out and look for an early grave,
They light their pipes on the parapet edge and think they're being brave.

They take no heed of the golden rules the long, long years have taught,
And they will go down by the Dead Mule Tree when they know that nobody ought.
And some of us old 'uns feel some days that life is a tiring thing,
And we show our heads in the same place twice, we stand in the trench and sing;
But we never go down by the dead mule tree, we aren't such perfect fools.
And the war goes on, and men go down, and, be he young or old,
An Englishman with an English gun is worth his weight in gold.
And I hate to think of the fine young lads who laughed at you and me,
Who wouldn't go round by the crucifix, but died at Dead Mule Tree.

Somme and Arras (50th Division) 1917

Foreword

Chapter 16 finds George Kendall joining 50th (Northumbrian) Division. The Battle of the Somme has come to an end, and with it a distinct phase of Britain's war. The hoped-for breakthrough had not materialised. Instead, four months of heavy fighting had pushed the Germans back some seven miles, at the price of extraordinary casualties: 420,000 British, 200,000 French and probably 500-600,000 Germans. This was total war with a vengeance. Total warriors were already in the ascendant in the army: Douglas Haig (created a field marshal after the Somme) remained firmly in post as commander-in-chief of the BEF, and General Sir William Robertson had served in the key position of chief of the Imperial General Staff since the end of 1915. Now Britain also had a prime minister dedicated to mobilising the nation for total war, for Kendall's friend, David Lloyd George, replaced H.H. Asquith in December 1916. This set the scene for one of the most serious civil-military clashes in British history. Lloyd George refused to accept that the logic of total war led to attrition on the Western Front, and the new PM thought little of Haig's abilities. He worked to undermine the c-in-c's position – notably by conspiring in February 1917 with French generals to get the BEF placed under French command, with Haig being sidelined. The failure of this gambit had serious consequences. Relations between the prime minister and Britain's most senior soldier were poisoned, and Lloyd George's credibility was weakened, which reduced his ability to impose his will on the generals.

In contrast to Lloyd George, Padre Kendall admired Douglas Haig – preaching at two memorial services for the former c-in-c in 1929 and 1930. His admiration was reciprocated: Kendall was mentioned in Haig's final despatch. Haig was a Christian, whose faith and devotion to his church (the Church of Scotland) flowered under the pressure of High Command. He saw effective chaplains as important for maintaining troop morale – a critical factor in total war. Haig recognised in George Kendall just that sort of Padre of whom he approved. Kendall's well-written and highly readable memoir gives a flavour of the sort of chaplain he was: able to communicate with ordinary soldiers en masse, and with individuals too.

It is well worth pondering upon Kendall's account in this chapter of the impromptu service he held on Easter Sunday 1917 – the day before the Arras offensive began – and his story of subsequently meeting a wounded soldier who had been there that Easter Day. Padres in the First World War have a bad press – often undeservedly so – but as historians have increasingly come to realise, men such as George Kendall had a significant role in tending to the material and spiritual needs of the men of the BEF.

Gary Sheffield
Professor of War Studies University of Wolverhampton

I was hoping that I might be able to stay with the Welsh Division but the principal chaplain, at General Headquarters, decided otherwise, and so an urgent wire was sent ordering me to proceed to a certain map reference number which I shall always remember because of my difficulty in finding it. The number was A 19 A 9 2 and is firmly fixed in my memory. The facts were these – an old chaplain friend of mine had suffered a serious injury and was sent to hospital. Another chaplain had been sent to succeed him but he only lasted one week. He was of a very nervous type and the shelling upset him so much that he had a nervous breakdown and was sent back to the base where he remained for the rest of the war. The principal said that I was well-seasoned and he wanted someone who could stick it for some months. It was not mine to reason why, so I packed up, first taking my successor to the trenches and then, later in the afternoon, proceeding to the railhead at Poperinghe to begin my long journey to find the mysterious number where my new division was fighting.

That journey took me several days, in the course of which I met with many adventures and a good deal of inconvenience. The railway transport officer put me on the train at 10pm, and through the night I travelled in an unheated carriage. It was four degrees below zero and everything was frozen. At one point, when the train had stopped, I got out and had a walk to increase my circulation. I then, to my horror, saw a train coming down the line and thinking it was mine I jumped on the step. A man in the carriage opened the window and saw me clinging to the handles of the door. "What's the matter, chum?" he asked. I said, "Is this the troop train?" He replied, "No, it is the Paris Express." He opened the door for me. "What shall I do?" I wondered. Here I am in the Paris Express and my train is somewhere a mile or two back. Providence was at work for me that night. For some reason or other the train stopped at the next station. I hastily jumped off and ran back on the line to find my train. It was a race I can never forget. I had left all my baggage in the train and I wondered if it had gone and should I be left alone on a desolate railway line to be frozen to death – as some men were I found out later, that very night.

At last I found the train and it had been shunted into a siding, probably to allow the passage of the Express. There were some Australian soldiers on board and I found them smashing floorboards to make a fire. They said, "We are not going to freeze to death in this God-forsaken hole." I was determined not to go into my cold and dismal first-class compartment, so I wandered up the length of the train and found a van. In it was an officer and three men of the Royal Engineers, and they had a glowing brazier in the centre and a stock of coal they had taken from a wagon in the siding. I breathed a prayer of thankfulness and got in, and they made me a cup of tea. The time was 4am and the cup of tea and some bread they toasted for me was the only food I had tested for over ten hours. I was warm for the first time since I began my journey, thanks to that brazier in what to me seemed a heavenly van. There was a pet dog with us and he too enjoyed the warmth. At 8am we got some hot water from the engine and washed the soot from our blackened faces. We all shared the same water and towel and the dirty water was also used to wash out the frying pan and mess tin, and these were wiped dry with a sack. Then the men produced a ration of tinned stew, fried it, and boiled some tea and we had a real feast around the brazier.

I arrived at Romescamps at midnight. Here I found shelter in a small hut. At 4am a military policeman came and told me that the train was ready. I rushed along a siding a mile away, clinging to one tin helmet, one haversack, kit bag, box respirator, overcoat, waterproof and stick. I slipped down on the ice, shook myself and my scattered belongings. I collected my goods and reached a long line of wagons, to find that I was to travel in the guard's van. In the van were three Frenchmen and myself. We had a small charcoal brazier which smoked us out. For nearly three hours we sat in that van waiting to depart. At last off it went and we reached another railhead at 11am and still was miles away from my new division at A 19 A 9 2 wherever that was. I had not eaten since 4pm the previous day and I had a three days' growth of beard and my face was covered with soot. We reached another station and got out.

The RTO (railway transport officer) allowed me to sit in his hut by the fire and gave me a cup of tea and two slices of toast, for which I was thankful. I then got a lift in a lorry to Corbie, some ten miles away. My valise was dumped on the pavement and there I was, a lost chaplain.

Two Australian soldiers came along and asked me if they could help me. They picked up my valise and other things and carried them to a monastery; I expect they thought that was the right place for me. I then went to a restaurant for a meal, and there I had the fortune to meet Lieutenant Parsons, a real good Samaritan. I told him of my troubles and he said, "I have a billet in the town, come and share it with me." I had a wash and shave and a general clean-up. I spent two nights with him and made up for my lost meals and sleep. I left Corbie on the Monday by lorry to Villers-Bretonneux, and there I found the headquarters of the III Corps. I told the lieutenant general in command of my adventures and he entertained me in his mess until the next day, and told me where A 19 A 9 2 was and the name of the division I was to join. So for the first time I was told that it was the 50th Northumbrian Division.

My adventures were not over. The lorry driver who was to take me to the division, got lost, and in the dark he dumped me at a ruined chateau at Fontaine Le Capay. I made my way to the cellars and found they were occupied by the officers of the 141st Field Ambulance of the 1st Division. There was a Canadian doctor in the cellar, a splendid man who took a lot of trouble to make enquiries for me, then the colonel and other officers came in. The chateau was an advanced dressing station and only one thousand yards from the trenches. No one could take me to where my division was, and at last the colonel said, "We cannot have you wandering about all night. You had better stay with us." I slept in a very deep cellar, covered with straw and full of rats. I was glad to have the company of another officer and before we slept we had a rat hunt and he shot several.

The next day they took me about three miles and then left me and I trudged along a desolate shell-swept road. I then came to some trenches. A man jumped out and said, "Keep your head down, you are in the front line. We have been watching you and were fearful that you might be sniped." An officer came along and I said, "Have you a map?" He produced one. "Now," I asked, "can you direct me to A 19 A 9 2?" He replied, "Yes. Go along that trench where you can see some tree stumps and there, in a very deep dugout, you will find our Brigade Headquarters." I went as directed, entered the dugout, saw a staff captain and said, "Is this A 19 A 9 2?" He replied, "Yes." I then said, "Thank God I have found you at last." I told him my story. I had been ten days trying to find the division. The staff captain sent me to stay with the 2/2 Northumbrian Field Ambulance at Estrées. It was in a labyrinth of former German dugouts. I met the colonel and a major and had tea and dinner with them. I slept in a horrible dugout the first night. I was alone, and all night long shells were falling around and there were several hundred rats which I fought with a bayonet. The French had left the place full of straw, rifles, old boots and bread covered with mildew. The doors and windows had all blown in and I had four torn and dirty blankets, as my own kit was miles away and waiting to be collected. It was like a bottomless pit and during the sleepless night the horror of a great darkness seized me.

The next night I slept in a dugout along with the sergeant major and a sergeant, and I slept like a top, feeling safe in their company. The next day I was posted to the 5th Northumbrian Fusiliers, the 'Fighting Fifth', as they were called, of the 149th Brigade, consisting of the 4th, 5th 6th and 7th Northumbrian Fusiliers. I called on the 50th Divisional Headquarters and the staff were very kind to me and gave me tea. I then went in search of Father Flanagan, the Roman Catholic chaplain, and thus began a very happy fellowship and co-operation which lasted for several months. We took a dugout in the Valley of Bois St Martin and were looked after by our batsmen. Each day we made a round of the trenches and had many narrow escapes. We felt at times that even our dugout would be blown in, but it was no use worrying.

We had one amusing experience, not so amusing perhaps for Father Flanagan. I was walking along a road near the Front with him when all at once a salvo of shells dropped near the road. The next minute all was a scene of confusion. I saw my comrade knocked on one side by a mule which took fright, and several men dive into a ditch. It seemed as if an earthquake had occurred. When the smoke cleared away I looked across the road to the spot where the shells had fallen, expecting to see several casualties, for a number of men were working somewhere in that direction. What was my astonishment to see one of our lads rush from the midst of the shell-holes, covered with dust and clasping tightly a tin of salmon. He had been to a little dugout to get this dainty for tea. I said, "Are you hurt?"

"No, sir," he replied, "but my word, the Boche nearly got my salmon that time." Such was the spirit of our lads; they laughed and made the best of all their dangers.

We pulled out from this sector of the Somme and trekked through many towns and villages to our training centre, there to refit and await drafts from home. The longest stay we had was in the village of Warfusee, a few miles from Amiens. Along with Father Flanagan we had a rather strange billet in a big farmhouse. We occupied a bedroom in a loft, and there we also had our mess. The farmer was a socialist and a great debater. He never wore socks, but wrapped his feet round with pieces of rag. As there was no fire in our room we used to sit in the big kitchen with the servants. Madame, the farmer's wife, would arrange her toilet, no matter who happened to be in the kitchen. She had a pretty daughter, strong and vigorous, who milked the cows and did most of the work indoors, as well as on the farm. We had to pass through the bedroom where she slept to our loft, but she did not mind this in the least, and her young brother had a bed in the same room. Everything here was of a primitive description. Outside the door was a big heap of manure. They had a weird-looking old man, who was a servant. He was very short and a hunchback, and fearfully jealous of Madame. Why, I do not know, and the whole family used to tease him about it, including the farmer. He could not talk and used to make strange noises. He would eat anything you gave him and keep on eating all the day, and used to make himself ill. One night someone gave him a huge chunk of cheese and a big tot of rum, and he danced about, making weird noises and shaking a huge knife he always carried. He seemed just like a character out of the pages of 'Deadwood Dick'. He slept in a cellar on the floor, and the weather was fearfully cold. I shall always remember the weird-looking hunchback of Warfusee.

One day we tried to smuggle an oil-drum stove into the loft, intending to put a stove-pipe stove into the place, and so have a fire. The daughter, who ruled the house and was a little vixen caught us in the act, and there was a big row. "A fire in the loft! The very idea! No! No! We shall not have it!" she screamed. "If you are cold you can sit in the kitchen." The kitchen bored us stiff, what with the hunchback, Madame and her toilet, the socialist farmer and an aggressive daughter. Matters came to a crisis, so we decided to leave the wretched billet that night. Madame and her family were wild and tried to keep our saddles and valises; but, to use the language of the hymn, 'We fought our way through', with the assistance of our two batmen, and obtained another billet in the same village. This billet was inhabited by an old lady of eighty and her mute daughter. They did all the work on their small farm and the house was full of priceless, antique furniture. I have often wondered what became of the two, for later on their house and the house of the farmer in our previous billet were destroyed when the Germans took possession.

On the Good Friday, Father Flanagan was taken to hospital suffering from dysentery. I missed his companionship for he had been a splendid friend. On Easter Sunday we arrived at the old chateau near Arras. The march from our last stopping place had been long, yet full of interest, for all nature was waking from the sleep of winter, and the breezes and golden sunshine cheered and refreshed us. We passed through several quaint villages, each with its grey old pile of buildings dedicated to the worship of God. Never was there such a building as this old chateau, which was to be our resting place for a few hours. It was approached by a long striking avenue of trees, and the magnificent front, with its flight of stone steps leading to the house's huge entrance hall, impressed on immediately. Connected with the main building were extensive stables and outbuildings in the form of a square. There was, in fact, sufficient accommodation for the whole battalion, including officers, men and horses.

After a well-earned rest and refreshment, I wandered into the courtyard, wondering whether it would be possible to hold any kind of service. I noticed a great crowd of men who were shouting and cheering, and soon I understood the reason. A boxing match was in progress. Of the two opponents one was a celebrated army boxer, the other a novice and a mere lad. The men were cheering the youngster on, and the elder man was allowing himself to be punished a good deal in the face. "Give me another," and the boy obliged. "That's right, it's good for hardening my skin, I'm getting out of practice. Come on, youngster, let me have it." The men were laughing at his good-humoured remarks. Just as I approached, the boy had finished, and a challenge was issued to the ring for a fresh opponent to face the expert. In a flash I realised that here was the opportunity. I stepped forward, rolling up my sleeves and taking my stand on a manure heap, faced the men. "What!" they exclaimed with surprise, "Is the Padre going to fight? Just fancy, and on a Sunday too." I shall never forget the scene, nor the smell of the manure.

The courtyard resounded with the laughter of the men, and the sun lighted up their faces. There was a movement of intense excitement when I said:

> Boys, I am not much of a boxer, but I am a fighter. How do the great words run? Listen. Fight the good fight of faith. That is it, and what a great warfare. Hear the advice of a man of long ago, who had witnessed such scenes in the arena: 'So fight I, not as one that beateth the air, but I keep under my body and bring it into subjection; lest that by any means, when I have preached to other, I myself should be a castaway.' We need to keep in training just as our friend here, who has given you so much amusement. But there is a time for everything; you have had your turn, now I want mine. It is Easter Sunday, and our loved ones at home are singing praises to God for the greatest victory of all. We are soon to enter into action, and before another Sunday comes we may have fought our last fight. Just let us sing a few hymns and be at one with those at home on this day of all days. Come along; who will join me?

The idea appealed strongly to the men; not one moved, and reverently they uncovered their heads and we sang, with an added meaning the old sweet hymns. Easter Sunday. Yes. And up to that moment, in the midst of the constant moving about, it had almost been forgotten. Thank God, it was recalled, and the opportunity seized. And what a message for those men, who faced death every day, and had to face it once more in a few hours 'Death is swallowed up in victory. O Death, where is Thy sting? O grave, where is Thy victory? … Thanks be to God, which giveth us the victory through our Lord Jesus Christ'. That service brought the men into close contact with God. It awakened thought and feeling; it brought back memories of other days; it brought infinite comfort, and strengthened the bond of friendship between the men and the chaplain.

Here is the sequel. We had suffered fearful losses at Wancourt Towers, near Mons and I was with the battalion doctor, helping with the wounded. It was in a deep cellar, protected by layers of sandbags and lit with acetylene gas lamps. In the centre was the operating table and along the passages leading off, the men were lying on stretchers. A man was brought in suffering with a gaping wound in the back, and was placed on the table. I spoke to him, and said, "Can I do anything for you?" The eyes of the man lit up as he recognised my voice. "I was at your service, sir, on Easter Sunday afternoon. It did me good and helped me out yonder; thank God for it – 'death is swallowed up in victory.' Write and tell my poor old mother about it." The man, after receiving all the attention that could possibly be given, passed out to the casualty clearing station. Whether he recovered from his wounds I know not; but I wrote to his mother, and rejoiced that I had seized the opportunity that Easter Sunday afternoon. To many it was their last service on earth.

My brigade moved into the trenches at Tilloy. The day before I had marched with the men some nine miles, and I had spent the night in a vast underground cavern in the citadel at Arras. It was bitterly cold and I broke up many ammunition boxes and made a fire and the men lay around it for warmth. I sat up to keep the fire going, covering myself with a filthy blanket, and at dawn we moved off. We were soon wet through as it rained heavily and we were worn out with lack of sleep. We manned the trenches and awaited our call to renew the attack. The Battle of Arras continued throughout the week and all the four battalions I ministered to were thrown in, one after the other. We suffered many casualties. I frequently visited the aid post in the trenches and the advanced dressing station, to help with the wounded. The communication trenches were long and many stretcher-bearers lost their lives carrying the wounded. One day I went back into Arras and climbed to an observation post at the top of the cathedral. It was a dizzy climb. I also visited the caves just beyond the station. These were so large that a whole brigade could shelter safely in them. In crossing the station yard and railway lines, I was blown down by a shell which exploded nearby, and a man crossing with me was wounded. Another shell came and caught the bridge, blowing up a lorry full of men passing over – nothing was left, the men or the lorry. At last we were relieved and moved back into Arras where our billets were. However, there was not much rest as the city was continuously shelled. The whole place seemed a veritable death trap. My billet was in a large house, but half had been destroyed by shell-fire. The old woman caretaker still stuck to her post and lived in the cellar. She was wonderfully plucky and calmly went about her work. I slept upstairs, and one night a shell struck the house, and we all had a marvellous escape.

On the Sunday morning I held services for the officers and men, in a huge building which had formerly been used as a college, but now was partly in ruins. We were again and again interrupted by shells falling around. In the afternoon I had another service in the large room of a factory. We were singing the hymn 'O God, our help in ages past', when a shell fell a few yards away, bringing down loose bits of mortar on our heads. For a moment we looked anxiously at each other, wondering whether to try to seek a safer place, but we continued the services. On leaving the building we saw the crater the shell had made, and also the ambulance at work, for several men passing by had been caught. At last orders were received for us to leave Arras. We had lost so many men that it was necessary for us to refit and await reinforcements.

It was springtime and nature was awakening into newness of life. The sap was even rising in the shell-torn trees. What a difference the sunshine makes! As I mounted my horse I felt how good it was to be alive, after the mud and blood of the trenches. After lunch, in the first little town I came to, I wondered into the village square and to my joy the band of a Yorkshire regiment came down the street and began playing selections. It was the first time I had heard a band at the Front. What thrilled and moved me, however, was when they played an old hymn so beloved in Yorkshire: 'Praise ye the Lord. 'Tis good to raise our hearts and voices in His praise'. What memories the tune Ombersley awakened. A crowd of men gathered around and I could see how greatly they enjoyed the music.

We moved to various parts of the line from time to time – from Arras to the Cojeul Valley and further south. In my diary I have the record of dozens of towns and villages, at which we stayed, and the long marches we endured. Often we rose at 4am to begin these marches before the heat of the day. I sent home for a supply of mouth-organs and I formed a mouth-organ band and it became famous. How often the men stepped out to the strains of the 'Colonel Bogey March', and to the popular tunes of 'Pack up your troubles in your old kit bag' and 'It's a long way to Tipperary'. The long marches were all the better for this mouth-organ bank of the 'Fighting Fifth', as they were called.

Strange and sometimes weird places were our lot to shelter in. I remember a graveyard where the tombs had been used by the Germans, before we cleared them out, as dugouts. I entered one such tomb. It was very deep. In it was a coffin and the Germans had knifed open the lid and exposed the remains of the occupant – the village priest. His features were quite clear and the body complete. I think it had been embalmed.

I read the inscription on the broken lid:

Le Curé of this village
(with his name which I forget)
Died January 22nd 1913
Aged 93 years

He little thought that his bones would be disturbed. I could visualise his long life of service in that village and all that he had endured. I reverently closed the coffin and prayed that he might rest in peace. I then got the men to close down the tomb and remove all signs of its desecration by the Germans.

My next story can be better described in the style of Bunyan's 'Pilgrim's Progress'. It was published, much to the amusement of our men, in one of our trench magazines and was called 'A Page from Padre's Diary':

As I passed through the wilderness of this shell-battered region, in company with numerous men wearing clothes of a drab colour and carrying on their shoulders strange looking packs, I came to a certain sunken road in the side of which was a den. I noticed there were other dens and cubby holes on either side of the road into which the men were already creeping, to rest their weary heads in safety. The heavens were full of winged monsters which continually dropped deadly looking objects; these on reaching the earth made a great noise whereat the men burrowed more deeply and cried with loud voices:

"Where did that one drop?

"Is that theirs or ours?"

In the front of my den was a tin plate on which the Leader of the Hosts of Khaki had chalked this strange inscription.

"The Vestry"

Burials at any time.

Open Day and Night.

Marriages and Births arranged.

Whereas, seeing I was the prophet of the Band and wearing this white collar of my office, my heart rejoiced. It appeared to me that I should be able to exercise the functions of my office. Alas! On creeping into this den on my hands and knees I found I was in a tight place, for the vestry, so called, was the shape of a grave and looking up I could see that it would be open day and night, and should one of those heavenly objects drop, my own burial might take place at any time. The earthy smell, the slimy crawlers and the rumbling noises were a burden to me and at times my heart quailed.

And it came to pass that at eventide I lay upon my back, meditating upon my condition. I waited for I knew not what. In my distress I chanted the Psalm composed long years ago by one named John Wesley, whose prophetic eye must have seen my miseries and that of my poor afflicted flock:

"Plunged in a gulf of dark despair

We wretched sinners lay."

Whereat the thought gripped my soul that the many wretched sinners I had to minister to were glad to even despair in a dark gulf, than to despair out of it, for were not those grievous messengers of affliction – rum-jars and whizz-bangs flying about?

I abode in that den three days and nights. At times I had visits from the men in khaki and certain others who wore red tabs, thereby showing clearly their superior rank, enquiring diligently concerning the last line of the legend over my den, but as there was 'nothing doing' they departed with sad countenances, bemoaning their unhappy lot.

And it came to pass, on the third day, I lifted up mine eyes and behold a messenger approached and entered the den where certain valiant warriors who Commanded the Companies lived and agonised. In his hands he carried a pink form on which were inscribed the commands of the Chief of the Armies in these words:

"Flee from the City of Destruction and take your rest."

Which being interpreted means – "March back to billets and there eat, drink and be merry."

So I girded up my loins and marched forth with the mighty hosts, leaving the gulf of despair far behind. Then the men in khaki sang this strange song:

"Oh, we'll have some fun, etc., etc., etc.,

Beer and Rum, etc., etc., etc.,

Ham, Lamb, Beef and Jam, etc., etc., etc.,

So come! Come! Come!"

And in all the land there were none so happy.

We went into the trenches again at Heniel. My battalion was sent up the line to occupy the Foster Avenue trench – another veritable death trap with snipers always on the watch. The first day I arrived the trench was blown in and I was trapped in the mud and debris to the waist. My batman, who was with me, was wounded and two other men, one a sergeant, were killed. I was set free by the men but several yards of the trench had disappeared and so, after my man was taken away and those killed put on one side to await burial, I crawled on my stomach over the remains of the parapet.

It was a frightening crawl because of the snipers, who were having a pot shot at me and the other men. I was glad when we reached the colonel's dugout. He soon had the men out repairing the damage and filling in the breach.

I found the front line safer that afternoon. I was so fed up that when I left the trench I sat for a long time at the entrance much to the surprise of the men who were going in with the rations which had arrived.

My companion, Father Looby, who succeeded Father Flanagan, was a brave young chaplain. We often visited the men in the trenches together. Much to my grief, one day he had a direct hit with a shell and was killed. This shook me up and made one think more than ever of the sentence we so often repeated when burying our men – 'In the midst of life we are in death'.

It was on the same road to the trenches that I first noticed a little white wooden cross erected to Captain R.A. Field MC of a Yorkshire regiment. He was killed there in April 1917, and on the cross was written a testimony to his devoted life:

> He feared death so little
> Because he feared God so much.

Thousands of men read that message as they entered the trenches, and who can say what courage and inspiration came to them as they passed, many of them never more to return.

I had been many months with the Northumbrian Fusiliers, and had previously served in the Ypres Salient, at the Battle of Loos, in the Armentieres area, and the Somme and the Battle of Arras. I expect my chief at Earl Haig's headquarters thought I needed a change, so one day I received orders to depart, and take up duty for a time at the No.6 Stationary Hospital, Frevent, twenty miles from the Front.

It was with real regret that I left the brigade and the 5th Northumbrian Fusiliers. Colonel Wright, and his second in command, Major Irwin, had always been very helpful, especially in their efforts to solve many of the problems that the men brought to me. They were only too anxious for the welfare and happiness of the men. I remember two incidents, amongst many: A boy came to me in the trenches one night, and he was crying bitterly. I said, "What is the trouble?" He replied, "I am frightened." I asked, "When did you arrive?" and he again answered, "Only yesterday, sir."

"How old are you?" I asked him. "I am only sixteen, sir."

"Did you give your wrong age when you joined up?" again I asked. "Yes, sir, I told the sergeant I was eighteen." I went at once and told the colonel about the boy, and he sent for him and the regimental sergeant major. The result was that he gave immediate orders for the boy to be sent off to the Details Camp to await his transfer to a base camp where there were many other boys who had given their wrong ages, and where they were kept in safety and well looked after.

The other case was of a boy who had deserted and had been arrested. The colonel asked me to see him and get all the facts of his life. He was, in my opinion, a fine type of boy who had absolutely lost his nerve in a moment of panic. The colonel said, "If I am spared to return home I shall have to live where this lad lives, and I want to save him." I prepared the case for the boy, beginning with his early life, school days, working days and his period in the army. I found that when a boy he had suffered a rather serious accident which brought on concussion, and I stated that this was probably the cause of his panic and desertion. I visited the boy a good many times. At last he was brought to trial but was not shot, as many were. He had, instead, a period of detention, and he made good. After treatment he came back, in due course, to the battalion, and maintained the traditions of this famous 'Fighting Fifth' until, one day, he was killed.

The Rev J.O. Aglionby, who before he joined up was the vicar of The Venerable Bede Church, Sunderland, was the Church of England chaplain to my brigade. He was afterwards appointed the Bishop of Accra. I found him willing to co-operate with me in every way, and he showed his broadmindedness by his willingness when we were out at rest, to hold united services. A very fine type of chaplain, he was careless of danger and I always remembered his impressive six-foot-three figure walking around the trenches, encouraging the men and giving them, as I did, cigarettes.

The time came for my departure and all the officers and men wished me, as they said, "The best of luck." I had been with them in battle, on the march, and in the rest billets, and I felt the parting. The 50th Division was always in the thick of the fighting. These hardy men of the North were great soldiers and as the Epistle to the Hebrews puts it, they 'Waxed valiant in fight, turned to flight the armies of the aliens'.

17

Interlude (Frevent Stationary Hospital)

Although only some twenty miles from the Front, one could still hear the guns booking, yet Frevent seemed to me, after the Somme, like a peaceful town at home. True we had the enemy planes over a good deal. It was in a lovely wooded countryside and the town with its cobbled streets, was very quaint. I had a billet with some delightful French people and I shared it first of all with Father Paul Rafter and later with his successor, Father Doyle, the Roman Catholic Padre. I seemed, all through the war, to have as my close companions, Roman Catholic Padres, and I found them men of sterling qualities and very brave. They were always ready to co-operate with me. We would argue about our different views but always with sympathy and understanding.

The hospital was one of long wooden huts used as wards, and they contained over one thousand beds, which were always full of the sick and wounded brought from the casualty clearing stations. The wards were airy and bright; in one all the beds were covered with red blankets in another with blue and in another with grey, and the effect was pleasing to the eye. Everywhere there was a profusion of flowers placed in brightly polished shall cases. The men were from all regiments and countries – Australia, Canada, South Africa with occasional French and Portuguese, as well as our own.

The extensive grounds were well laid out. The huts were surrounded with lawns and beds containing a wonderful variety of flowers. In one corner you could see the cleverness and ingenuity of the men from a series of large regimental crests – a tiger, or St Andrew's Cross, or medieval castle, harp or whatnot. These were worked out in thousands of pieces of coloured glass, red brick, lumps of chalk, tiles and clay. A new passion for the picturesque had seized our soldiers. Wherever you went in hospital, base or even at the Front, you would find artists at work. It was a new school of decoration, and the dingy ground was made vivid by man-sized devices in all the colours of the rainbow. Everywhere too were rustic seats for the patients to rest on when out. There they could bask in the sunshine and drink in the life-giving breezes from the countryside.

In the grounds were all kinds of buildings, nurses' quarters, officers' mess, quartermasters' stores, and a very large recreation hut. At one end was a large stage tastefully decorated, and there were numerous tables, cosy chairs, and all kinds of games. In this hut our concert parties gave wonderful performances, showing the wealth of talent we had. We had an officers' troupe which I took charge of. It was composed of seven doctors and two Padres; our pianist was a nurse.

I remember an amusing incident during a performance we gave. I was singing my favourite song – 'Come under the old umbrella' – the umbrella itself was a marvellous creation – when I knocked the quartermaster off the stage. A swipe by the umbrella caused the tragedy. The men raised the roof with their cheers as the quartermaster disappeared, and shouted "Encore!"

There is always in my mind, in thinking of the experiences I had in the First Great War – the amazing cheerfulness of our men, even in the midst of the most discouraging and frightful conditions. There was the laughter that ran with death. A sergeant said to me one day, "If we had no sense of humour we should almost go mad." So there was laughter in hospital, and laughter at the Front.

In the recreation hut we held our religious services, which were always well attended, for the men loved to sing the old hymns, and how they could sing! It was wonderful, too, how the men liked to gather for discussions with me on all kinds of social, industrial and religious problems. What an insight one got into the workings of the human mind and heart at such times. I felt it wise to let the boys talk, to encourage them to give their views and opinions. These were the men who had, in the school of experience, and in the presence of death, endured and suffered, and they would not tolerate show and hypocrisy in any form.

I remember most vividly one such discussion that we had on religion. It has lived with me ever since. Said one man:

> We are not theologians, and at the same time we are not fools. We don't kid ourselves that we are atheists and imagine that this wonderful world in which we live was the result of some freak and chance – and it is wonderful. We have good enough sense to know that our universe, created and controlled, must have had some mastermind behind it, and that men haven't given their lives in times past for something that is nothing at all. We know that a faith which has lasted and grown for nigh two thousand years must have something mighty good in it. Give us a pure unvarnished religion that we can believe and hold fast to. Give us the religion of the Man who went about doing good, untrammelled by ecclesiastical additions. Give us a practical, living faith, that will make us better men and the world a better place to live in. And we don't forget that there are such things as different denominations, but we cannot quite understand how that came about. Men have their own opinions on every subject, and so different people worship God in different ways, but it's all the same religion and we would like to see a stronger unity in the spirit of the cause, neither the maker of this universe nor the Nazarene, was narrow-minded. We know that you cannot feed us on heavy theology, any more than you can feed a baby on beefsteak. We want to believe. We think that our pals who went down beside us are better off than we are, and we want to look forward to more than six feet of earth ourselves. We have had a dose of Hell, give us a dose of Heaven.

Every inch of the ground around the hospital was utilised. We had a vegetable garden, growing potatoes, beans, carrots, cabbages, and other varieties; we even had glass frames for growing cucumbers. Our lads, when recovering, loved to cultivate these plots; and took great pride in them. There was no lack of volunteers. The exercise was beneficial, and they had a natural desire to be producers. There we had livestock to care for – hens and chickens, ducks and rabbits, also pet dogs and kittens. There were also our cricket and football pitches, and our tennis courts – all so very beneficial to patients, orderlies, nurses and doctors.

Near the hospital was the railway line, and a great event was the evacuation of the sick and wounded by well-appointed and easy-running hospital trains. These trains, I think, were one of the wonders of the war. In the early days the predominant type was made up mainly of goods vans fitted to racks to support stretchers, and supplemented by straw-strewn vans for the more lightly wounded; but these were displaced by the magnificent corridor-car 'coaches' for patients able to sit up, and specially constructed cards, with tiers of berths down each side and a passageway between them. These berths had both wire and ordinary mattresses and blankets and sheets. The carriages were placed in the following order, working from engine backwards: a carriage used as an isolation ward; a coach with its compartments arranged as sleeping quarter for the medical and nursing staff; a kitchen coach, four or five ward carriages; an administrative carriage, providing an office, a room for the performance of operations, and a dispensary; four or five coaches for sitting-up patients; a carriage for general cooking purposes; a coach to serve as sleeping quarters for the orderlies; a van for store, and a guard's van. About four hundred patients was the average load for such a train. So our boys travelled in luxury to the base, the train going at a speed of about twelve miles an hour.

I remember the great kindness and help I received from the commanding officer, Colonel Harding, from the doctors who were unceasing in their administrations. Captains Carruthers, Wood, Stuart, Fox and Clegg-Newton, and also the Church of England chaplain, Padre Rodgers. There were many others whose names I have forgotten. The matron and large staff of sisters and nurses all made up an ideal staff. The principal chaplain, Dr Simms, and the assisting principal chaplain, The Rev Owen Spencer Watkins, both paid me welcome visits from time to time.

We had an amusing magazine called 'The Croakers Journal', to which I and others contributed. Some of the contributions were very amusing. I am reminded of many other such publications issued by all units everywhere in the line, in hospitals and at the base. I think two verses in one of these journals should be handed down to posterity. We all remember those tins of jam – so numerous and so sickening to many.

This was the subject of the verse and the poem's title was 'Jam':

> We love a hundred, we hate but one
> And that we'll hate till our race is done.
> It's known to you all, it's known to you all.
> It cast a gloom and it cast a pall.
> By whatso name they make the mess
> You take one taste and you give one guess,
> Come, let us stand in the waiting place,

A vow to register face to face
We will never forego our hate
Of the tasteless fodder we execrate – Jam
But we hate with a lasting hate,
Hate of the tooth and hate of the gum,
Hate of the millions who choked it down
In frozen trench and camp in town,
We love a thousand, we hate but one
With a hate more hot than the hate of Hun – JAM

And was added – 'The brand of jam shall be nameless'.

In addition to my duties at the hospital, there were surrounding units I ministered to. The German prisoners of war camp was one. I think it was a very wise precaution to have this camp in the same area as the hospital, as it prevented the bombing that surely must have come, both to the hospital and the town, and the reinforcement camp. The prisoners were humanely treated and I never remember one trying to escape. I am sure they felt that they were far better off with us than with their army. I used to take on service a week for them, and they welcomed this. I had the help of an interpreter and I was allowed to move amongst the men and talk freely to them. Then the cavalry were in the grounds of a big chateau. I loved to visit these men with their splendid horses. On one occasion we had a horse show.

I also served the men in the Canadian lumber camp. It was situated in a glorious wood lying in a fruitful valley with a river running through the centre. There was an old French water mill and an up-to-date sawing mill erected by the enemy. The wood was on either bank of the river. The huge trees were cut down and dragged along the stream to the mill to be sawn into planks and beams for huts, shelters and dugout. The men were bronzed and stalwart, with big muscles and broad shoulders. These were lumber men from British Columbia. To see them use the cant-hook in handling the huge trunks was a never-failing source of delight, and some twenty-six thousand feet a day of timber was sawn. This proved a harvest to the natives for you could see crowds of women and children collecting the chips and branches for winter use.

The YMCA had a splendid and well-served hut in the town. Here I visited the men of various units and held regular services for them. Later on I was the guest of the YMCA in Paris for three days' leave. Mr Worthington, who was in charge, arranged for my hotel accommodation, a car and courier. I had every comfort and saw all the principal places of note. At the Palace of Versailles, I was met by the Governor, who personally conducted me round.

18

Artillery (17th Brigade, RGA) 1917–18

Foreword

It may be appropriate if I begin this foreword by quoting the words of the then Prime Minister, David Lloyd George: 'The war was won by the incredible valour and endurance of the men who braved – actually and physically – death in every element for the honour of their native land'. Nor was this some politician's glib choice of emotive words, since he had two sons serving at the Front. The younger, my father Gwilym, was a gunner – and it may perhaps not be stretching a point too far that he was aware of the 17th Brigade, RGA and indeed, might have even met George Kendall.

Modern generations may find it hard to imagine the privations and intolerable conditions of life in the trenches, but throughout this personal and self-effacing record of understated courage and service lies the true pastoral commitment of George Kendall to his ever-changing flock. Service in the Dardanelles, during which he caught malaria, and later on the Somme, where he was gassed, this quiet minister/ chaplain took it in his stride – merely observing wryly on one occasion: 'I am afraid I got the reputation for bravery, which I did not merit, at one point that night'.

Two other remarkable facts should be made about this out-of-the-ordinary chaplain: first, he was charged with the task of educating and preparing the men for life after demobilisation at the end of the war, and he chose and selected a formidable group of men to carry out this task – thus the Army Education Corps was created; secondly, amidst all the heart-rending re-interments to military cemeteries in Belgium and Northern France, in which he was so active after the Armistice, it fell to him to pick the six anonymous bodies from which one – 'The Unknown Warrior' – was selected by a general for burial in Westminster Abbey with all the panoply of the State.

It is pleasing to record that he visited Lloyd George at his home on more than one occasion in both war and peace – and this writer, for one, would have been delighted to have been a fly on the wall at these meetings, for George Kendall was an exceptional human being and a man of God.

Lord William Lloyd George
Grandson of the Prime Minister David Lloyd George

My year in the artillery was to be not only exciting, but eventful. The officers and men, matron and nurses of the stationary hospital gave me a good send-off and probably wondered what would happen to me.

Both in war and peace one had to submit to the inevitable – obey orders and ask no questions, and I often quoted the lines of an old hymn:

> Keep Thou my feet; I do not ask to see
> The distant scene; one step enough for me.

My first stopping place in my journey to find my brigade was Fremicourt, where the railway transport officer, Lieutenant Turner, helped me a great deal, providing me with sleeping accommodation in his hut for the night. The search next day took a long time but later in the afternoon I found the V Corps Headquarters where I had tea. I was sent on by lorry to the little village of Matz. It was then 10pm and a bitterly cold winter night. Neither the driver nor I had the slightest idea where the location was. We went on through the village and seeing some green flashes in a valley, we proceeded in that direction. I saw a faint light in a ruined cottage some distance from the road and I asked my driver to dump my kit on the roadside whilst I went to make enquiries. I made my way over barbed wire entanglements to the cottage and found an officer, surrounded by sandbags directing the fire of his battery. "Where in the world have you come from, Padre, at this time of night and in such bitter weather?" he asked. I told him that I was in search of the 17th Brigade, and the 135 Heavy Battery to which I was to be attached. "Where is your kit?" he asked. I told him and he added, "You are lucky tonight Padre, there were several killed on that spot last night during a heavy spell of enemy shelling – it is a death trap." He immediately did all he could for me, sending two men for my kit and as it was so late he took me to the officers' mess, which was in another ruined building near to a derelict tank. I shall never forget the warm welcome I received from this battery's officers. I was famished, frozen and miserable. One officer gave me a mug, which I thought was cocoa and as I drank it I gasped – it was rum! The first I had ever tasted. The effect, so far as I was concerned, was electric. I was then helped to a shanty between a battery of eight-inch howitzers, and lay down between two guns, and was soon lost to the world. They told me in the morning that there had been a good deal of shelling of the position during the night, and they were amazed to see me calmly sleeping through it all. I am afraid I got the reputation for bravery which I did not merit, that night. It was the rum that did it – my first and last dose.

I found the battery the next morning. It was in a deep gulley with high banks. The dugouts were in the sides of the banks. I had one at the corner of the road entering the gulley and all the men going up the line to the trenches passed it. I found it a very hot corner, for the gulley was subject to a good deal of retaliatory shelling by the Germans. The officers' mess was a large dugout lined with timber. I had a very thick head after my night's adventures, and it was a bitterly cold morning. Major McCrae, a son of Sir George McCrae MP was in command of the battery, and he welcomed me and did all in his power to help me. He was a fine type of officer, immaculately dressed, and a strict disciplinarian. He won the admiration and respect of all the officers and men. My batman, Moulder, had been the Duke of Marlborough's valet before he joined up. He was with me for several months and later on Fowler took his place. What a lot we owed to our batmen. I had quite a number during the six and a half years I served on the battle fronts and in the army of occupation, and all were excellent men.

The other units I had to serve were the 13th, 56th and 248 Siege Batteries. I was particularly happy with the 135 – a battery of sixty-pounder guns. I loved the great horses which pulled the guns, especially when we went on trek, into new positions. They were like the old shire horses. The officers were also mounted, and I was pleased to have a horse allotted to me. There was no more thrilling sight than to see our battery when on the move, with the guns and their crews, the horses pulling the guns and the mounted officers. My diary has a record of fifteen miles and more in the day, a long night's journey finishing in the early hours of the morning.

The gulley, however, sticks in my memory. Often we were shelled by day and bombed by night. I remember one shell landed in front of one of our officers, but did not explode. Another went right through a tree into a shanty, and landed between two sergeants; one was kneeling, the other was lying down. They were blown up but by some great miracle neither was actually wounded. I had a similar experience. A shell came through my shanty, missed me and buried itself in the floor without exploding. I suffered for a time with shock.

The officers were a grand lot of fellows – in fact, the best it had been my pride and privilege to live with. There were the two horse-masters, Captain E.A.V. Stanley and Captain W. Murland. I rode many miles with them. Captain Stanley had two of his own horses with his initials 'E.A.V.S.' marked on them. He had brought them over from his own stud and they were placed on the strength of the battery. When he left us for home he said to me, "You can have my horses, Padre, as a gift." I was glad and proud to possess two fine horses. Alas, both were killed and I was nearly killed with them in the crossing of the Canal du Nord.

Captain Murland was with me one dreadful night as we were advancing. We reached a deep ravine by the canal about dusk. The Germans had been in that position, until driven out, a few hours before. We occupied a shanty of corrugated iron set into the bank – Captain Wilkins, Murland and myself. A thunderstorm came with a torrential downpour which nearly washed us away. This was followed by high-explosive and gas shells. A shell fell on the bank just above the shanty and brought down the whole of it on or heads. I heard a voice asking, "Are your safe, Padre?" I said, "Yes. Are you Wilkins?"

"I am, apart from the dust and gas which is almost choking me," he replied. Then I heard Murland: "Padre. This place smells like a house of ill fame." His bottle of hair restorer had been smashed, and the perfume was mingling with the other smells. I did not know, myself, what a 'house of ill fame' smelled like, but this shanty was certainly full of 'ill fame'. Alas, in the next shanty our cook, Vance, was killed, and Tedder, a batman, wounded. Two sergeants were also killed and seventeen horses, along with six officers' horses, and all this during the Battle of Epehy.

Captain Wilkins went later on to become a major and commanded the battery. I had many exciting adventures with him. One afternoon, when we were in the Foret-de-Mormal, I went reconnoitring with him for a new gun position. We had just left the fringe of the wood when the Germans almost surrounded us. Wilkins was about to defend both of us with his revolver, when I stopped him. I said, "Let's lie low." He was not too keen about doing that. To our relief a company of our men, the Lincolns, appeared on the scene, then I saw a bayonet charge and the routing of the Germans. After the war I met Wilkins frequently and visited his home.

Then there was Captain L.A. Elmer, who afterwards took up farming in Kenya. He was with me once in a billet when a shell brought down the beam of the roof of a farmhouse, and it was right over the bed where we were sleeping. "Look out, Elmer!" I called as I jumped out of the bed. The next moment we were both in the farmyard clutching our breeches and tunics – only just in time.

There was also Lieutenant Ewart Vallis, our youngest officer – a fine lad. He was out with me one afternoon when my horse stumbled into a shell hole and threw me. I landed head first into the hold, but my steel helmet saved me from serious injury, although my neck was still for some days. I was with Vallis too when he was wounded, and as I carried him out and was putting him on a stretcher to be carried to the dressing post he said, "When I get married Padre, I want you to officiate." Years afterwards I had a letter from him, via the War Office. 'Would I go up to Congleton to marry him?' I went, and found that he was the manager of the largest coal mine in the area. He had qualified as a manager and was also qualifying as an inspector of mines. I stayed the night with him and married him the next morning at 8am. At the wedding luncheon his bride kissed me, his mother-in-law and mother both kissed me, and thanked me also for the care I had taken of Vallis whilst with the battery. It was a kissing time for me but also a time of precious memories. Vallis was my guest in London on another occasion.

Lieutenant George Steel Morrison, who hailed from Edinburgh, was also often with me as I rode with the battery, and as I was in charge of the messing for both officers and men, I often took him with me to buy goods. On one occasion I bought a small field of cabbages, on another a large quantity of vegetable marrows, to add variety to the diet. Then I managed to buy eggs from time to time. I then launched out and got livestock. I bought rabbits and they quickly increased, ducks, and soon a good-sized pig. These were purchased with gifts of money I received, including four pounds from a missionary in West Africa. I had a wagon allotted to me to carry my farmyard and as time went on, and especially on one occasion when our rations were missing, my rabbits, ducks and pig saved the situation. Morrison, if he is alive, will be glad to be reminded of those hectic times and all we did together.

There was also an old Etonian, Lieutenant A.W. Richards. We shared the same tent when on trek, and also many dugouts and dangers. It was a real joy to have an invitation from him, long after the war, to meet and have lunch with him in Piccadilly.

Our brigade commander was known by the name of 'Tiger'. He was a colonel with a long record of service, and although over fifty, was a striking example of energy, pluck, and bravery. Although of a stern exterior, he had a most sympathetic heart, and was always anxious for the welfare of the men. He regularly attended my services.

I remember one Sunday morning I had a service under the shelter of a bank, and referred, in the course of my address, to the work of the Salvation Army.

Afterwards, as we were sitting on the grass, engaged in conversation, he said:

Padre, I want to tell you a story. You referred this morning to the Salvation Army. When I was in India I admired the work of the Salvation Army officer. He lived with the natives, and never left them to go to the hills, like others, during the hot season. I used to see him walking about with bare feet, helping the natives. One day a knock came to my door and my orderly announced a visitor. It was the Salvation Army man. I said, 'What can I do for you?' thinking he had come for financial assistance. To my astonishment, he replied, 'I should be grateful to have a bath, sir.' Here was the good old British desire for cleanliness! The reply so pleased me that I invited him, then and there, to be my guest for a few days, and he consented. My friends were astonished at my action, but I was proud to have this man of God, who was doing such good work, in my house.

One day we went for a walk and we came to a lovely expanse of country. The Salvation officer suddenly stopped and pointing to the scenery said, 'I feel I must pray. Let us pray' – and before I knew what had happened I was down on my knees by the man's side, and he was pouring forth his soul to God. I was deeply impressed, and have never forgotten it.

Yes! 'Tiger', otherwise Colonel Phillips, was a good name for him. I remember that one afternoon overlooking the valley of the Ancre, he said to me, "I want to reconnoitre a new position for my brigade. Come with me Padre." So we went on. After a while he said, "Keep your head down and don't talk." I could see the reason why. Not far away were the German trenches. He quietly surveyed them, and the whole area, right and left, and then we crept away. I thought of that afternoon, and of all that he had been to me, when I saw in *The Times* that my 'Tiger' colonel had passed away in hospital, his death being due to the effects of the hard life and exposure at the Front.

At this time, it was realised by the Government and Higher Command that the men overseas should be given the fullest opportunities of mental and practical preparation for their lives as citizens after the war. With this object in view, Active Service Army Schools were to be organised and I counted it a very great privilege to be appointed as the 17th Brigade educational officer. I suppose that I was one of the first to be selected for this work, which became the foundation, eventually, of the Army Educational Corps. For this appointment I received the sum of two shillings and sixpence extra per day.

My work then became of a threefold character – spiritual, mental and moral. The aims we had in view were two – 'mental and practical' preparation for civilian life. The authorities knew right well that the war would result in a complete re-organisation and re-adjustment of industrial life, and the strongest force in the future, for good or evil, would be the temper of the army on its return home. My first task – the headmaster's task – was to appoint an education officer to each of the batteries of the brigade, and I was astonished at the wealth of talent I found. Some of the men appointed were university dons, some science masters and schoolteachers in private life. It was an eye-opener to me to find really brilliant talent amongst the officers and non-commissioned officers, so I completed my organisation and arranged classes and lectures in Citizenship, Business Training, Languages, History, with practical and theoretical courses in Science, Agriculture, Engineering and kindred subjects.

I can only give a brief example of how we set about our task: I was in a ruined village one night near the line, and there in one of the very few remaining rooms of a house left standing, I saw a classroom. The windows were all broken, a damaged bar from a café served as the tutor's desk, and the men sat at some old-fashioned desks which had been rescued from the demolished village school. The blackboard was being used to illustrate a lesson, and all the time there was the booming of the guns. The men, covered with dust and wearing steel helmets, had walked three miles from their batteries along one of the most dangerous roads in the area, such was their keenness to equip their minds. One of my battery officer-tutors told me how the chance came to him to do a little educational work.

In his report to me he said:

> My chance came when I went on duty twenty-four hours in a position open to the view of the enemy, when there was little to do but keep under cover. A ruined village, bricks, iron girders, shelter, exploded guns, dud shells – not a very inviting spot. Time passed slowly. I proposed classes in French. I was greatly surprised at the keenness shown. My classroom was the men's cellar, their seats were wire-netting bed frames, my blackboard was the side of a cartridge box, my chalk – bits of chalk from a trench. In two turns of duty I gave six lessons in French.

I might add that any man who attended a course of study and satisfied me was given the certificate of the Active Service Army Schools.

Great strides have been made since those early days, but it is of historical interest for me to record the beginnings, and how we made the best of our opportunities under almost despairing conditions. I had voluntary services of all kinds and in many strange places: under the camouflage in the gun positions, in ruined buildings, under the shelter of a bank, and in dugouts. More than once I have preached kneeling down, with about thirty men kneeling around me, a few candles lighting up the dugout, and all the time the incessant noise of guns. I also administered Holy Communion under similar circumstances, using my field Communion service, a lovely set with fair linen cloth, cups and bottles in an attaché case, supplied by the army.

I remember one Sunday afternoon, holding a service in a dugout on the Somme. We were all kneeling, as the dugout's roof was very low. I was just saying a prayer when I stopped and cried out, "Clear out for your lives, boys!" We rushed out round a traverse in the trench and that moment a shell whizzed over and demolished the dugout we had left. Some instinct of danger came to me in the middle of that prayer, but I am sure it was a providential warning. I had more than one such warning and other men had the same experience.

It was a real joy, one day, to come across the first American troops. They came from Virginia and seemed a strong-limbed and fine type of soldier. They had a band and were in an orchard. I had dinner with the officers and received a warm welcome. They asked me to speak to their men, and I told them of the experiences in the trenches. They were marching up next day to take over a sector.

On 9th March, Major McCrae was thrown from his horse and broke his collarbone. I went to the casualty clearing station to see him. He was succeeded by Major W.G. Forbes MC, a very efficient officer, whom I rode and lived with for some months, until he was killed.

The great German offensive came and we were in the thick of it. They sent over forty divisions against our 3rd and 4th Armies. They were favoured, I remember, by a heavy mist and they effected a surprise and got through our lines at points west of St Quentin. Then began a fighting retreat on a wide scale.

Dramatic and sometimes amusing incidents were not lacking. There was the stray cow, left by some farmer, which our men adopted, and I am afraid milked rather frequently. It seemed only too ready to follow us and was well fed with all kinds of eatables. There was the story of one of our siege-gun officers. The gully where our position was, was overrun, and our men retreated to the crest of a hill near the village of Metz. The enemy was on the next crest and still advancing. The officer in question had that morning left his dentures in a biscuit tin which was left in the side of his dugout. On the hill crest a colonel and the officer collected some seventy Army Service Corps men, cooks and stragglers, and the colonel said, "Now men, we must defend this crest to death – if any man runs I'll shoot him." Still the enemy advanced, and the German officer, now enrolled as an infantryman, said, "If my teeth had been in, they would have chattered." Still on and on came the enemy and again the officer said, "O God, this is the end." When all seemed hopeless, salvation came. Suddenly, through Metz, came the Grenadiers. They marched, he said, as if on parade, to within forty yards of the Germans and then routed them with a bayonet charge. The Germans fled and retreated. The gunner officer returned to the gun position and to his dugout. In the entrance was a dead German officer and two soldiers who had been bayoneted. He removed the bodies, entered the dugout, put his hand inside the biscuit tin, retrieved his teeth and put them back in his mouth. All this happened in a few hours. All the guns were pulled out that night and in the retreat not one was lost.

We passed through the old desolate battlefields and on through Albert, and finished up on a ridge overlooking the valley of the Ancre. Our headquarters were then established at Toutencourt which was, at first, intact. I was surrounded with a pleasant countryside of farms and woodland. We, at any rate, were glad that the Germans were fixed in the desert of shell holes and trenches, whilst we were in a lovely spot still inhabited by farmers. It was a fresh change, and we had the chance to build up our gun teams and once again fix new gun sites to harass the enemy, before we in our turn advanced once more.

A good many divisions were in and around Toutencourt, and we arranged concerts, boxing matches, football and other games. I remember a big boxing match when Bombardier Wells, the famous gunner boxer, came and gave an exhibition. There was an enormous crown of officers and men, including several generals. I was so fired with this show that I began to box, and I had several contests from time to time. My boxing career, however, finished one night when I found a giant of a gunner. I whispered to him, "Give me a chance, do not hit me too hard, I am only doing this to encourage other men to take part." He nodded his head and I noticed a rather wicked look in his eyes. I suppose he had never, in his wildest dreams, anticipated fighting a parson. We put on the gloves – "Seconds out of the ring" – and they left. I faced a sixteen-stone giant. I was then five feet eight inches and weighed thirteen stone. We sparred – I retreated – he advanced. Up went his big fist at the end of his long arm. Up, up to the point of my jaw – a stinging uppercut. Down I went and bit the dust, and I am sorry to say the men around cheered. I was seeing all the colours of the rainbow. "One, two, three," and so on to the bitter end of the referee's count, and although dazed and shaken to the very depths, I was thankful to hear his loud voice shout "Out!" and out I was, and for the last time. I never entered the ring again. Of course, I shook the gunner by the hand, but there were some thoughts I could not speak. "Give me a chance," I had asked him – a chance to carry on for a little while, I meant. I suppose he interpreted it to mean 'a chance to knock the Padre out'. He, alas to my pain and anguish, took the chance. It was a real grief to me when my opponent was killed as he was two days later, and I had to lay him to rest.

Toutencourt was bombed heavily, and suffered much destruction from high-explosive shells. There were many killed, including civilians. I spent several days making a dugout in a hillside. The digging and clearing of the earth was a back-aching task, but at last it was finished. I had lined it with timber and made tier beds, and it became ship-shape. We used this dugout for several weeks and then handed it over to the officers. I like to think that I had contributed something of permanent value and no doubt, after the war, it was used by some farmer who would be able to make it his home whilst his own house was rebuilt.

The turn of the tide came in the August of 1918, with the attack of the French 1st Army and our own 4th Army in the Somme sector. This was destined to wreck the whole German scheme and shatter their power for good. Our brigade took part in this advance and the 135 Battery of sixty-pounders became field artillery. All the well-known places we had left were recaptured. No one, looking back, could possibly describe the horrors and the hardships from August to November. It was a nerve-racking time. All along the roads during the advance we came across dead horses and men. I buried as many of our boys as I could. We passed once more through the wretched Somme area. I remember at Miremont we pitched our tent in the darkness, and a heavy storm came on and nearly blew it down. I got out to tighten the tent pegs and fell into a shell hole, where there were the remains of a horse and a German. In the morning we found that we had been sleeping near a German cemetery which had been blown about a good deal by shell-fire. The next day we were subjected to intense shelling.

We advanced steadily right across the main Albert Road to Seven Elms. This obtained its name from the stumps of seven elm trees by the roadside. Here we pitched our tent for shelter in a deep shell hole. The first night was one of intense bombardment, and we were thankful for the shelter. About midnight, I heard someone trying to get into the tent, and then a voice called, "Padre." I recognised the voice as that of our last battery commander, who had been sent home to England gassed, and had found us after a fearful search at that uncanny hour! This major, alas, was killed the last time his guns were in action, on the morning of the Armistice. At the place I buried some of our lads, also a German, and I made rough crosses for their graves out of box wood and inscribed them with indelible pencil. From there we passed through Le Transloy, right across the Canal-du-Nord. At the latter place we sheltered for a few days and nights in a deep cutting.

I called the place:

> The abomination of desolation. The Gothes came over at night.
> I saw two come down in flames – an awe inspiring sight.

I was waiting for our post orderly to bring the mail one afternoon when a shell killed him, and scattered the contents of the mailbag. I buried the man and tried to pick up the hundreds of letters lying about.

Many of our men were killed during those few days and we were glad when we pulled out and advanceed further. It would take an article sufficient to fill a book if I were to describe the successive stages of the advance – the crossing of the Hindenburg line and our great welcome from the people of the various villages we passed through. They hailed us as their deliverers, for they had been held in bondage by the enemy for four years. I shall never forget the death of Major Forbes. He was due to go to England the day after he was killed, but stayed one more night with the guns in order to give a brother officer a rest. At 3am the battery was in action, and he left the chart-room in a trench to stand by the side of the men firing the guns, in response to an SOS signal, when a shell exploded and a big splinter went through his shoulder into his spine. He was wonderfully patient, but died in the field casualty clearing station the next morning, about the time he should have been in the train going to Boulogne. The matron and sisters in the ward wept in speaking of his death. He was only twenty-eight, and his only brother had been killed in action, and I had the sorrowful task of writing to his widowed mother and settling his affairs.

I can see his grave now, as I write, and the cross we erected with the words painted on it:

He hath prepared for them a better city.

Some years afterwards I visited his mother in Stokesley. Time had softened the blow and so she could calmly sit as I told her of her son's bravery and his last hour on earth. I slept in his room and my thoughts went back to the night when he saved another through putting off his own leave – but himself he could not save.

A day or two after this I came across, quite unexpectedly, a Methodist minister friend of mine who was an officer in a nine-inch battery in action by a railway embankment. Whilst here, the whole embankment was blown up by a delayed-action mine, just after a big supply train had passed safely over. My friend's dugout escaped. I was riding past on horseback at the time and received a shock. It was a weird experience. A man was killed on the road by a flying stone. About this time our Roman Catholic chaplain was killed by a shell as he was walking along a road. The closing week of the great drama had its lighter side, just as we had found humour at the darkest times. Who will ever forget the struggle with the transport over the mined roads and temporary plank bridges that took place of the structures blown up by the retreating Huns? The obstacle race went on all day, and often all night, until even the mules grew weary of it and the Indian drivers fell asleep in their saddles. And what a cheery welcome awaited us in the French and Belgian villages where oftimes the people stayed up all night to give us coffee as we passed through. When there was an opportunity of staying anywhere, real homes were at our disposal and it was no unusual thing to 'scrounge' a piano. The problem was how to decide who should be first to play it in case it happened to be a booby trap.

We passed our last few days in the grim and dark Forêt-de-Mormal. This forest covered an area of fifty square miles. It rained in torrents and the roads were blown up by mines. In the centre of the forest we came across a village the Germans had only left a few hours previously. I found a billet with a family who had been sleeping, for protection, in the cellar, which was entered by a trap door. They looked pale and famished, but I cheered them up and shared my rations with them. I slept that night on a wooden bed, covered with straw. The night before it had been occupied by a German officer. I had cause to regret it – for the little insects which I collected as I slept. It was a long time before I cleared myself of them. All through the forest we had white tape stretching from tree to tree to guide us. We all felt like a lot of Red Indians stalking their enemies, for we were actually on the heels of ours. At last the forest was cleared of them and we arrived at Berlamont-sur-Sambre. A crowd of women greeted us. We were kissed as their deliverers and given coffee. It was 8th November. The 38th Welsh Division had fought their way over the Sambre, and we were blasting the German troops with our sixty-pounders. Fighting went on for the next few days, and we suffered casualties, but the Germans were on the run.

The morning of 11th November came, and at the eleventh hour all the 17th Brigade officers were waiting together. We did not speak much. The end of the titanic struggle that had extended over so many weary months and years was greeted by the same quiet stoicism that had characterised all our most hazardous operations. If a single cheer was raised in the whole of the brigade I did not hear it. Probably our hearts were too full for words – but more probably still it was a matter of temperament: the same undemonstrative British spirit that accepts all great crises with apparent indifference and entire lack of emotion.

In the hour of deliverance, we were not only thankful, but sorrowful. We thought of our pals who had gone West and were lying, as we left them in some spot forever England.

I have often told the story of the lad who died in one of the early battles. He was a Scotch laddie and a great lover of poetry. In his last moments of life, he recited a poem that he must have loved dearly. It was written by J.B. Selkirk, and his only grandson, Lieutenant Douglas Burn Buchan Brown of the Royal Navy, died gloriously for England at the Battle of Jutland on 31st May 1916.

I thought of the poem, and recited it on that Armistice morning, and so I quote it here:

At the Fall of the Curtain

The curtain's falling, and the lights burn low;
So, with God's help, I'm ready now to go –
I've seen life's melodrama, paid the price,
Have known its love and losses, hopes and fears,
The laughter and the tears;
And now, God knows, I would not see it twice.
I've crossed life's ocean, faced its blinding foam,
But now Heaven whispers, I am nearing home;
And though a storm-tossed hull I reach the shore,
A think of tattered sails and broken spars,
Naked against the stars,
I soon shall be at rest for ever more.
For if again I pass these waters through,
I know the kingdom I am sailing to.
What boots it where I lie? – beneath the sod,
Or down the dark impenetrable deep.
Where way-worn seamen sleep?
All gates are good through which we pass to God.

The mother of Lieutenant Brown, and daughter of the author, had thousands of copies of this poem printed for me and I give the words that accompanied the poem:

> Lieutenant Buchan Brown was the only grandson of the author of this poem, which is reprinted by his mother for the Rev. George Kendall, Chaplain to the Forces, to distribute among the troops.
> This poem has been a comfort and a blessing to thousands of our men who in quiet confidence face the dangers of the battlefield and the perils of the ocean, realising "That all gates are good through which we pass to God."

Field Marshal Earl Haig wrote me a letter of thanks for having the poem printed and distributed to the men. He also added that he was, as a Scotsman, deeply moved by it. I had also many other letters from all sources.

19

63rd Royal Naval Division 1918–19

It was a great surprise to me to have a wire from General Headquarters informing me that I had been promoted to senior chaplain, with the equivalent rank of major, to the 63rd Royal Naval Division. On receiving this news, I paid a round of farewell visits to the officers and men of the 17th Brigade. I had been with them in many battles and I had got to know them intimately. I was the only chaplain in the brigade for a long period, and at my last parade service some eight hundred officers and men attended. This was held at Quievy.

On my last night the brigade commander, Colonel Phillips, gave a farewell dinner in my honour, and the next day he kindly sent me in his car to the headquarters of my new division at Roisin.

During the advance our brigade had supported the division in covering fire, and preparing the way for the infantry to advance. I remember that at Grandcourt and Miramont, we were so close together that I invited the general and some officers to dine with us in a sunken road. The reason was this. I had my last three ducks killed to supplement our rations. Our cook had made a fire in the side of the bank and with the aid of biscuit tins had made a good job of the cooking. We sat under the bank that August evening – gunners and naval division officers – and feasted on my well-fed and well-prepared ducks. They all congratulated me as mess president of our mess, for my foresight in bringing along my livestock, of which the ducks were part. Arriving at headquarters I duly reported and was kindly welcomed by Major General C.A. Blacklock CMG DSO, who was then commanding the division. Afterwards I had the honour and pleasure of dining with him and his staff. I was then made a member of one of the headquarter messes, and later became president of this mess.

One of the first requests I had was to contribute an article for the famous journal of the division, called the 'Mudhook'. The editor said that it must be amusing and it was to be the 'Peace Number' and the final issue. I cannot do better than to give this article, entitled: 'Peace at Last'. That I succeeded in making it amusing was proved by the laughter it caused throughout the division.

I insert it in the hope that it may amuse my readers, especially the survivors of the division.

And it came to pass at the eleventh hour on the eleventh day of the eleventh month, in the year of Our Lord nineteen hundred and eighteen, that the command rang forth in the midst of the mighty men of the Empire that is called 'British', "Cease Fire", "Unfix bayonets". Whereat my heart greatly rejoiced, yea, verily, as the bridegroom rejoices when he goeth forth to meet his bride.

And a mighty should went up from the host of the men called the Anchor Host, for verily they were in front of the battle, and had sorely discomforted the hosts of the Huns.

And it came to pass that the Chief Captain of the men of the Anchor Host called together his wise men, his soothsayers and astrologers, and he enquired of them diligently concerning this thing which had come to pass.

And they said with one voice: "Verily it is thus" and all the men replied: "Yea, thus it is."

Then the Captain said: "Call me the Quarter bloke."

And when the man that is called Quarter bloke appeared, the Chief Captain said: "Bring hither the wine which maketh glad the heart of man and bring forth the unconsumed portion of every man's ration that I may make merry with my men."

And he with the three stripes and the crown upon his arm sent forth his servants to do his bidding, and behold they returned wringing their hands and saying:

"Alas! Alas! Woe is unto us for we are undone, the wine and the rations are no more, verily they have been destroyed by gun fire." Whereat there was most disturbance in the ranks of the mighty men of Anchor and the Chief Captain was filled with wrathful indignation.

They said one of the men standing near to the Chief Captain: "Let us drink of the water that remaineth in our bottles and eat of the rations that remaineth in our haversacks, called iron rations."

So they did eat and drink and the water was bitter and the rations verily were like iron, whereat many had strange pains.

And it came to pass after this that the men of the Anchor Host wandered from village to village for many moons, and the wise men did instruct them in the way they should go, and certain fair damsels and young men called the Follies did delight their hearts by their dances and songs.

And it came to pass that when the Feat of Christmas came near, the command went forth to demobilise which, being interrupted, means: "Buzz off."

And certain men who had aforetime worked in the bowels of the earth, did buzz off, and they crossed to the land that is called Blighty. Whereat those who remained were envious of their brethren and groaned exceedingly.

And they said: "How long shall we tarry in this strange land?"

And the Chief of the Demobilisation said: "Ye shall tarry but for a season, eat, drink and be merry."

And lo! It came to pass that after many moons they all buzzed off and departed to their homes, some to their wives and some to get them wives. And they begat many children and there was PEACE.

Now the rest of the doings of the Anchor men, are they not written in the book that is called 'MUDHOOK?'

I found my life, at this stage, full of interest. One had to act as welfare officer, educational officer and in all other sorts of ways. There was also the administration of my department. The parade services were at all times exceptionally well attended. The division carried a large area, and I made my way about on horseback.

Christmas came, and I was determined to make it a memorable one for the children. I had my parade service with the divisional artillery in the morning at Ancre, and had lunch with Colonel Sykes and his officers. Late in the afternoon I called at a convent. Our Tommies had been making a collection throughout the division to give the French kiddies of the area a treat. Toys had been sent for from Paris, and a huge and gorgeous Christmas tree provided. There in the huge, but sadly damaged, convent hall it stood in all its glory. The candles on it were lighted, and it was weighed down with dolls, crackers, trumpets and toys of all description. Oh! Those generous Tommies had given well; they had kiddies at home, and the poor little children of the devastated area appealed to their big, loving hearts. Where they came from is a mystery to me, but they came from the East and West, North and South, in charge of the pale-faced, blacked-robed nuns – and those nuns earned our gratitude by their devotion to our lads, devotion which had cost suffering and scars. A lump came to my throat as I heard the shouts of joy of those kiddies as they danced wildly round the Christmas tree. We fed them, sang to them, jumped with them. It was a time to be remembered by all who were there.

Thrilled with the moving scenes in the convent, I remounted my horse. It was dark and raining. I was tired and anticipating the dinner in our little mess. Trot. Trot. How dismal was the ruined village through which I was riding! The cobbles were very greasy through the rain after the frost. All at once I was thrown from my horse into the mud and had a miraculous escape from breaking my neck. I limped the rest of my way, leading the horse to my billet, scraped off the mud, and went to the mess. There, gathered round the festive board, were six dejected-looking officers. "What's the matter?" I asked. "You look a gloomy lot for Christmas night."

"Matter!? We're in the soup, Padre, the Christmas turkey has not turned up."

We dined that Christmas night off bully beef. I have hated the stuff ever since.

> The best laid schemes o' mice an' men
> Gang aft a-gley.
> And leave us nought but grief and pain
> For promised joy.

The kiddies always appealed to me. They were the veritable waifs and strays of the area and had suffered many hardships. The nuns of the various convents were very kind to them, as they were to our wounded soldiers, during the advance. I was out walking one day when I saw a little lad carrying a huge sack of turnips, much too heavy for him. He was a bright lad and bravely struggling with his load, so I got hold of his sack and carried it on my own shoulders. Who should come along at that moment but General Montgomery – just as famous as the present Field Marshal of that name. He smiled, stopped his car and got out. Shaking me warmly by the hand he said, "I see you are taking the load, Padre, from weary shoulders." He had a few moments of conversation and passed on his way. I once more shouldered the sack, and the lad took me to his ramshackle house. I went in and deposited the sack on the floor of a rather squalid kitchen. I shall never forget the look of amazement on the face of the lad's mother, or the lad's smile. "Would I have some coffee?" the mother asked. "No," I replied, "I must be going." They both came to the door and followed me with their eyes until I passed out of sight. So there was this combination – a dirty sack, a ragged boy, a Padre – but who expected to meet a general! But the general was one of the kindest of men and was always kind to me. He had motored twenty-five miles when he came up to me. I knew his son, the general never gave him any preference and, like his father, he was always in the thick of the fighting.

I have found in life, and in all circumstance, that the milk of human kindness is the best milk in the world. All the differences by which men are divided would vanish if this milk were freely used. 'Kind hearts are more than coronets' – and that is true the whole world over. My billet was a quaint white-washed house. Madame, her husband, and two fine sons made a happy family. The husband had been imprisoned by the Germans during the occupation of the village, his crime being that he had neglected to take off his cap to a military policeman. Madame was very industrious and her two sons walked nearly twenty kilometres each day to attend Technical College. There was a great shortage of clothing, and Madame had darned the stockings and socks of the family until they were one mass of patches. She had made one of her sons a good suit out of a brown blanket. For a long time, the family had lived in the cellar, and they were suffering from the effects of gas. Madame used to bake her own bread in the big brick over in the outbuilding and I noticed that each cottage had an oven of this description. I was very sorry for all that they had lost and I was able to give Madame a good bale of clothing sent by my wife, and friends at home. It was a God-send to her, and she was very grateful. The local doctor died during my stay there, and the whole village turned out to his funeral which, I was told, cost a thousand francs.

In the villages of Ancre and Audregnies, the troops were billeted in the big rooms placed at their disposal by the nuns of the convents. In every village there seemed to be both a convent and a theatre and both were used for concerts, plays and recreation. As part of our educational scheme we used both for lectures to the men on all kinds of subjects. I myself gave lectures on 'Citizenship' and kindred subjects. The general, officers and men would fill the hall selected. On one occasion I thought I would give the men a change, and I announced as the subject of my lecture: 'Men we know, and wish we didn't'. When I asked headquarters to put it in orders, I was told to change the subject of my lecture. I wanted to give it, for it was amusing and at the same time, instructive. I changed the title, but I delivered the same lecture that I had planned, so it made no difference. Even the general had a good laugh and the men cheered me and cried, "Encore!" The moral is – be careful with your lecture titles.

The high-water mark of my experiences in the dvision was the Consecration and Presentation of the Colours on 14th February 1919. This was held at Dour. I got up early and went by car, with General Blacklock and the staff. It was snowing and very cold. Assembled in a large field were the Anson, Drake, Hawke, Hood and the 14th

Worcestershire Battalions.

In the centre of the parade ground were five drums, and on them, five new silk standards in their covers; opposite to them were the officers who were to receive the standards along with their attendant officers. In the front of the square was the saluting point – raised platform with the Union Jack flying proudly. There was a huge crowd of spectators from all parts, officers and men and civilians. Bishop Gwynne, the deputy chaplain general, myself and seven other chaplains were in attendance and we took up our positions in front of the drums. General Blacklock, his ADC and attendant officers and the army commander, General Sir Henry S. Horne KCB KCMG, took up their positions. The hymn – 'Onward Christian Soldiers' – was sung, accompanied by the massed bands of the battalions. The standards were then unfurled and held aloft by five chaplains. Bishop Gwynne afterwards conducted prayers, including the prayer for the Consecration of the Colours. After the Consecration of the Colours, they were laid on the drums and the army commander, in the name of the King, presented each one to the officer standard-bearer, who received it kneeling.

General Horne then gave a moving address, some extracts of which I give here, because of the great tribute to the division which played such an important part in the ultimate victory of our arms:

> It is my proud duty today to present to each of the battalions now on parade, the King's Colour. I do so in the name of His Majesty the King, and I charge you to guard and honour these Colours in accordance with the high traditions of the Royal Navy and the British Army.
>
> When the Royal Naval Division was raised, four and a half years ago, the battalions received distinguished titles and inherited with these titles great traditions. What a proud story; what a glamour of romance; what wealth of tradition is connected with the names of Anson, Drake, Hawke and Hood, and with the old 29th and 36th Foot.
>
> Past history had been written for you, but it remained with you to write history for the last four and a half years. This you have done; the Royal Naval Division has proved itself worthy of its inheritance on many a battlefield and during many an hour of weary watching in the trenches.
>
> You must remember that your Colour represents the spirit of the battalion. Men change, and new faces appear in the ranks, but the Colour remains, the embodiment of the 'esprit' and of the tradition of the battalion. I have no doubt that these Colours will always be guarded by you in war, but I wish you also to realise that you must uphold the spirit of the Colours in peace. We have gained a great victory over the Germans. Hostilities have ceased; but peace is not yet assured. Europe is in a state of great unrest, and this unrest had spread to a minor degree to our own country at home. As the British Army has been victorious in this war, so it must set itself to work to ensure a proper and lasting peace.
>
> Remember that the Army now represents all that is best of the British Nation, that they have the power, and that therefore the responsibility rests with them, and it is our duty to do what we can to ensure for England and for the British Empire the fruits of Victory and the blessings of peace.

Let me tell you, as an old soldier, one who has spent his life amongst the troops and loves the British soldier with all his heart, that I wish to warn you that when you go home you will meet perhaps with influences which will not be either for your good or for the good of the country. You have learned loyalty and discipline out here; when you go home help properly constituted authorities to maintain law and order at home. If you can help in this direction you will have done your duty not only on the field of battle, but also in the pursuits of peace.

I wish to thank you for the great efforts which have been made by the Royal Naval Division, for its fine fighting throughout the whole of this war, and especially during the last few months whilst with the First Army. I felt perfect confidence that any task which I should call upon the Royal Naval Division to perform would be carried out to the full, I have not been disappointed.

After the ceremony General Horne had a chat with me, and then Bishop Gwynne and myself entertained the chaplains to coffee. It was a time of rich fellowship and good humour. The Bishop invited me to visit him as his guest when he returned to Khartoum. I always regret that I was not able to do so. I never saw him until thirty-three years afterwards. One night I was on the platform of Billy Graham's mission at Harringay, and to my joy Bishop Gwynne arrived to lead the great audience in prayer – he was then ninety years of age, and died a year or two afterwards. I had a chat with him after the meeting – thirty-three years had passed – years which had witnessed world-shaking events, and another Great War. We little realised that morning at Dour all that was to happen to us and that our next meeting would be at Harringay.

The Bishop believed very strongly in working for the unity of the Christian churches, in fact he told me that morning so long ago that he himself had founded a Free Church mission to support his own Anglican work, and that he ran it for some weeks in Khartoum, because he wanted the help of the Free Churches as a barrier against Islam. After leaving the Bishop I called at the headquarters of the Drake Battalion and met Commander Buckle of the Ansons, who had won the DSO three times. Commander Beak of the Drakes entertained us. Commander Beak had won the VC, and had been wounded. Both, before the war, were London County Council schoolteachers and neither had earned, in those days, more than two hundred pounds a year. They were just civilian soldiers who had done very brave deeds and, on demobilisation, were going back to civilian life, unconcerned about the future. I have often wondered what happened to them.

I lectured one afternoon in the Theatre Royale at Audregnies, and in the evening at Montignies. I mention this day, because between the lectures I paid a visit to the Countess Jeanne de Belleville, who helped Nurse Cavell in Brussels, and did so much for her before her execution. The Countess was condemned to death at the same time as the nurse, but the Pope and the King of Spain interceded for her to the Kaiser and he, no doubt wishing that he could turn back the pages of history, ordered her reprieve. If only he could have also saved Edith Cavell! That afternoon will be long remembered by me as over a cup of tea together she told me of the work of Nurse Cavell, her trial and death, and how much she was beloved, and honoured in Belgium. Every time I pass Nurse Cavell's monument near Trafalgar Square I think of the afternoon I spent with the Countess, who herself did so much in helping our own soldiers and those of the allies to escape.

We had, from time to time, many distinguished visitors. The Archbishop of Canterbury, Dr Davidson, afterwards Lord Davidson, and Sir Alfred Pearce Gould, the brilliant surgeon arrived one day. I had a parade service on the Sunday morning for the whole of the divisional artillery. Brigadier General W.A.M. Thompson CB CMG, with his staff, attended, also Sir Alfred. After the service we had lunch with the general and in the afternoon Sir Alfred asked me a lot of questions. He was a strict teetotaller and wanted my opinion about the 'rum ration'. I gave him an honest one and spoke of its value to the men in the trenches before an attack at dawn. I wanted to correct the idea that the men were under the influence of drink, as was so often stated by those at home who were so ignorant of the facts. The tot, I told him, was only a small one taken as a tonic to steady the nerves of the men and help them in the greatest ordeal of their lives. If the critics, who were living in comparative comfort at home, could have seen the fearful condition of the trenches and the horror of the bombardment, they would have understood. It needed supermen to endure all this. I also said that the rum was used just as a doctor at home would order brandy to be given to a patient in dire physical straits. I had known some men, I added, who had refused it. It was impossible to supply hot drinks or any substitute. Sir Alfred thanked me for my frankness and said that was the kind of information he wanted, all too often he had been deceived by others when asking these questions. Sir Alfred made a great impression on me and was not the tyrannical man some had tried to make me believe; in fact, he showed at least on this occasion, what I call 'sweet reasonableness'.

Demobilisation at this time was proceeding smoothly and the divisional numbers were decreasing. We moved from Roisin to Saint-Ghislain. This was a great coal-mining centre. The pits were in working order and the miners were planning strikes, and so keeping up the fashion. I was billeted with a dear old lady who was the mother of a prominent minister of the Belgian Government, and also a delegate to the Peace Conference – a very sweet and gracious lady. She had no servant and did her own work – keeping the house spotlessly clean! All our men had nice billets. One was in the home of a pottery manufacturer. His works I visited and there was a wonderful collection of vases and all kinds of beautiful examples of the potter's art. He told me that he imported his best clay from Devonshire. All the villages had electric light and were connected by light railways. I had an attack of influenza whilst I was there, but Madame looked after me in my billet, and soon cured me. When our mess was disbanded after the demobilisation of its members I lived in the billet, and Madame did all the cooking for me.

There are two lines of a hymn which I often quoted:

> We've no abiding city here,
> We seek a city out of sight.

This was my experience. Orders came again to depart to a 'city out of sight'. Where was it? I soon knew. My orders were to proceed to join the Rhine Occupation Forces, and the city was Cologne.

20

The Army on the Rhine 1919

The Rev Ronald Priestly MC, one of my colleagues who had been a great help to me during my time in the Naval Division, went with me to Mons Station. I left at 6.30am and arrived in Cologne at 5pm. To my joy I found on my arrival that I had been posted to the 2nd Northern Brigade, which included the 11th and 16th West Yorks and the Hallamshire Regiment (York and Lancs). There was also a Field Ambulance and other units. As all these batteries were from Sheffield, Bradford, Leeds and other parts of the West Riding, and being from the Riding myself, I felt perfectly at home with the men.

My attachment was with the 1/6th West Yorks (Prince of Wales' Own). The commanding officer, who became a great and helpful friend of mine, was Colonel T.N. Scott-Moncrieff Howard DSO. He came of a distinguished family and nobly maintained its traditions. There were forty-two officers in all, including Major W. Henry Hill MC, who strange to say was a member of my home church – a coincidence which to me was a very happy one. I soon met the commanding officer, officers and men of the two other battalions. My nominal roll was a very large one.

I found that our occupied area extended inland to a depth of about seventy miles, including a bridgehead over the Rhine with a thirty-mile radius. There was also a small bridgehead at Bonn. Bonn, the Oxford of Germany, had at that time some seven thousand students attending the university, trying by hard study to make up for the wasted years. We had an Agricultural Science College there where our young officers were given a six-week course to equipment them for farming when they returned home. We had courses on other subjects in the university and a General and Commercial College in Cologne, for business training, banking, accountancy and arts.

The schools in Cologne where our men were billeted were to me a revelation of modern architecture. Each one had a museum, with glass cases full of all kinds of animals, birds, fishes and skeletons; also a chemical laboratory, gymnasium, concert hall, with pipe organ and grand piano, library, a kitchen fitted with all kinds of stoves for cooking lessons, and numerous classrooms, and all this in 1919. They were greatly in advance of us at home and I am glad that now we have caught up with them in our school planning. Our men appreciated the atmosphere of these school billets, where they slept and lived, and where also we held each morning an educational lesson. I had continued as an educational officer and on the Rhine I was also amusement and recreation officer as well as a chaplain. My work was endless, from early morning until late at night.

I ran a cinema with first-class films in the evenings, and then I equipped and trained a jazz band, and also a concert party group which I called 'The Merry Blue Boys'. All this meant buying clothing and instruments. The purchase of instruments was not difficult, but the clothing was otherwise. At last I found a store and for the sum of five hundred marks I purchased twelve fancy costumes; one a Chinese robe, another a Turkish dress which formerly had adorned some fair maiden in a harem; two wonderful German uniforms and several clowns' pantaloons in all the colours of the rainbow. I also got wigs, caps, hoses, a jester's rig-out and a red and white and blue drum major's staff. In addition to all I have described, we had our own canteen.

At the request of the editor of the Army-on-the-Rhine paper 'The Cologne Post' I wrote numerous descriptive articles on places and events, and with the full approval of General Headquarters, I became the special correspondent of the *Sheffield Daily Telegraph* to keep the people of the West Riding in touch with the men of their regiments. I often burned the midnight oil but I had every assistance from the editor, and a sergeant who could speak and write German perfectly, was detailed to be my full-time assistant.

There were numerous organisations of a social and religious nature at work in the occupied area, including the YMCA, the Scottish Churches, the Church of England and Salvation Army, and Miss Decima Moore and her fifty ladies who ran the British Empire Leave Club. The latter had a magnificent place, a real Palace Beautiful, with its huge cinema hall, library, writing room and restaurant. From there river trips in the splendid Rhine steamers, and drives round the town and country were all organised at the expense of the generous supporters of the club. The Central YMCA had a magnificent place. In it they had a beautiful hall called the 'Loreley' after a famous Rhine legend. There was also a music room called the 'Elgra' where men could practise all kinds of instruments and receive free instruction from Professor Jones, the musical director. There was a yard where men could play cricket under the guidance of a real wizard of the game, and a splendid dining hall with rustic seats and tables, the walls of which were painted with mountain scenery. There was also a splendid library in charge of the famous writer, Mr Hornung.

In the great hall, lectures were given by the most famous men of the age on all kinds of subjects, also by great religious leaders. I had the honour of addressing two meetings there, along with the Bishop of Lichfield and Archdeacon Jones, of Sheffield. Dr Hugh Black was also a visitor on another occasion. On a Sunday I saw as many as two thousand men at the evening service, a most inspiring sight. Dr Francis was the life and soul of the great work carried on in this centre.

One day I had a message to say that Herr Hagenbeck had made an application to bring his circus and numerous animals to Cologne – would I see him and inform him that he could come on the condition that each afternoon a free show was given to the men, but that he could charge his usual prices for admission for officers, men and civilians in the evening? Herr Hagenbeck, who told me that he had great difficulty in feeding his animals in unoccupied territory, was only too anxious to agree. His first circus duly arrived with the biggest top I had ever seen. If I remember rightly he had some fourteen lions, twelve polar bears, nine or ten tigers, dozens of elephants, horses, camels, black bears and dogs. I had never seen such a collection, not even in a zoo. He had, too, a great staff, many acrobats and animal trainers. I got to know him well and I used to go in the mornings, with my sergeant, to arrange the programmes for the day. On one morning he asked me if I would like to see the animals at close quarters and I said "Yes," and so with a couple of trainers to act as guards, he took me down the runways at the back of the cages and opened some of the iron gates. The lions and tigers, at least those selected, seemed quiet enough. I asked him what would have happened if one had attacked me. He replied with a smile, "Sir, they were all doped before you came along." Years afterwards, when Herr Hagenbeck brought two shiploads of animals and his circus to the Royal Agricultural Hall, he sent me some tickets for my wife and family, and placed us in special chairs in front of the arena, near the circular cage where the lions and tigers were giving their turn. He also provided chocolates for my wife and cigars for me and afterwards took me around, as he did in Cologne.

The great circus of the American First Division came to give us a show, and some seven thousand officers and men were present at the performance in Cologne. The three hundred-odd performers, all American soldiers, together with a hundred specially trained horses, cages of lions, tigers and bears, an elephant and many clowns, paraded the streets of the city with their two jazz bands, followed by the inevitable stream of excited children. The brightly coloured costumes and the gaily decorated vans, and the cages of animals formed a vivid spectacle. The side shows and menagerie were housed in two huge aeroplane hangars, whilst the main performance was witnessed in a huge open arena.

The show opened with the customary grand entry of a 'galaxy of circus stars gathered from the four corners of the earth', as my programme put it. Then followed twenty amazingly clever acts, which were reminiscent of Barnum and Bailey, Bostock's and Buffalo Bill's great productions. There were comedy jugglers, trapeze artistes, acrobats, performing dogs, bears, lion tamers, Wild West scenes with Red Indians, stagecoach, cowboys and forty clowns, to provide irresistible merriment. The programme concluded with a concert. We gave the kiddies many treats. They always came in crowds to watch our sports in Blucher Park. We had open-air teas there and kiddies would be waiting for the remnants, and generally got a good feed. One afternoon I lined about twenty children up and, much to their huge delight, I dropped a spoonful of jam into each opened mouth. They wanted more and got it. It was so amusing to watch them and they were a happy, sticky lot of youngsters.

Christmas came and I wanted to do something for the German kiddies in Cologne – our men had taken these kiddies to their hearts. We had a record collection and bought a wonderful selection of toys and sweets. I dressed myself up as Father Christmas on Christmas Eve, and accompanied by a mighty company of lads carrying parcels, I knocked at the doors of the houses and was at once admitted – not one refusal – and walked into the bedroom where the German kiddies were sleeping and filled their stockings, receiving the blessing of their fathers and mothers. "Blessed be the hand that prepares a pleasure for a child, for there is no saying when and where it may bloom afresh again," said Douglas Jerrold, and the Christmas spirit of peace and goodwill will bloom forth in the hearts of those kiddies of Rhineland.

Let this also be said to the world at large, in these days, when there is so much suspicion and hatred: that first Christmas, in Rhineland, when the Germans were short of food, the British Army went on half rations so that the near starving people could have food. Did not St Paul say to the Romans, so long ago: 'If thine enemy hunger, feed him; if he thirst, give him drink; for in so doing thou shalt heap coals of fire on his head. Be not overcome of evil, but overcome evil with good'.

The Duke of Connaught, accompanied by General Sir William Robertson (afterwards Field Marshal Lord Robertson), the commander-in-chief on the Rhine, came to inspect our division. It was a great occasion. The Duke was greatly impressed with the work carried on there and all our work to keep the troops interested and happy. Afterwards I went with the Duke and the Field Marshal to visit the YMCA.

Later on it was a great treat for us to leave Cologne for two weeks in order to enforce the Peace Terms if the necessity arose. We were up at 5am on the morning of our departure and moved the same day to Dunwald, over the Rhine. The next day we began at 4.30am and moved on to Hilgen. The country was exceedingly beautiful, and very fertile and prosperous. I saw fine herds of cattle everywhere. The cottages were splendidly furnished and all lighted with electricity. A great many roads flanked by avenues of fruit trees. I was told that the fruit was sold, and the proceeds went towards the expense of keeping the roads in repair. It was considered a great crime to rob these public trees. There were mighty forests full of deer, and delightful trout streams. The scenery reminded me a great deal of some parts of Scotland. At Debringhausen you rose to a height of one thousand feet, and had a gorgeous view. Our men were billeted in a huge auditorium in exquisite grounds, where German workpeople, employed in the dye works at Cologne, came to recuperate.

Whilst in this area, I used the village church for my services. I went to see the pastor one day. I found him in his fields in shirt sleeves, mowing his grass and smoking a huge pipe. He was a fine big man and was very fortunate in some respects, for he owned two splendid cows and several acres. He had a fine-looking Manse near the church. The State paid his stipend and was supposed to keep his church in repair, but it was in a wretched condition. The pastor's wife acted as caretaker, and their little son tolled the bell three times a day, not for services but to tell the people the time to rise, have dinner and go to bed. His duties were very light, for he only held a service on Sunday mornings.

I enjoyed a visit, one afternoon with some officers, to Altenburg Cathedral. The setting of this magnificent building, was a lovely glen, and the scenery all around was very beautiful. During these two weeks I held my services in churches and in orchards. We had concerts each evening in various halls and my concert party and jazz band were in great demand.

We returned to Cologne and had all kinds of events to celebrate the signing of the Peace Treaty. On the Saturday we had sports and a tea in Blucher Park and a Thanksgiving service for the whole brigade, at which I preached in the garrison church, the colonel reading the lessons. Later on we had a Torchlight Tattoo in the Linoenthal Park.

On 18th August, Winston Churchill, the members of the Army Council, and many distinguished guests came for a great review of the Army on the Rhine. Winston Churchill motored round the ranks as the lines extended a great distance. In the evening I was with Lord Askwith and Sir Arthur Yapp, for further celebrations at the YMCA.

One outstanding event for the men was the river trip I organised. The band of my battalion came with us and meals were served on board. In that enchanted hour even demobilisation had lost its charm; a soft mist gave way to a flood of sunshine overflowing the hills; the breezes sand their hymn of praise; the wooded slopes, the vineyards, nestling under their crags, the ancient castles and pretty Rhineland towns and villages, were all too lovely for words. Our journey upstream, past the Seven Mountains, and other places of interest, ended within sight of the famous 'Little Willie's Bridge', an hour's run from Coblenz. On the return journey a dance was held for all ranks on the lower deck. The strains of the band and the sight of the happy faces of our men as they waltzed around, made a perfect picture, a fitting end to a glorious day.

The final, and I think outstanding Victory celebration was at the IV Corps Tattoo at Nideggen Amphitheatre. From out the trees, some five hundred feet above, there stood steep bluffs of brown basalt, crowned with the ruins of the 12th century Schloss of the Dukes of Julich. 'First Post' rang out, and as its echoes died away, rockets and star lights rose from all the hills and woods, and covered the field below with a cascade of light, while the meadow was lined with green and scarlet lights along the river and the woods. At the same time searchlights met to form a vaulted arch over the meadow, under which 'boys' dressed as prehistoric men and animals indulged in a struggle for existence. When 'man' had vanquished, all the mammoths removed their carcases from the field. The scene changed, and the outlines of the cliff and ancient castle were picked out with coloured lamps, while from half a dozen points, 'serpents' of gold and scarlet lights emerged from the woods, drawn by the music of the massed pied-pipers of the Scottish regiments. After meeting, they performed wonderful revolutions.

Presently a fanfare of trumpets summoned from the woods a column of blue and red lights. They passed round the flanks of the torch-bearers, and when they met again the arch of searchlights dropped onto them, and revealed a troop of cavalry. For twenty minutes they did musical rides, canters, and sabre exercise. Again a signal rocket, and the torch-bearers formed an evolution revealing 'God save the King' picked out in lights of flaring torches and massed bands played the National Anthem. Then another evolution revealed the phrase 'good-night' and the torches vanished one after another, while the bands played 'Abide with Me'. It was a thrilling event not likely to be forgotten.

In the course of my duties in another part of the city, I visited a convent which was used as a home for crippled children. I asked the Mother Superior if I could use the chapel for some Sunday afternoon services. I was perfectly frank with her – and told her that I was a Free Church chaplain. She said she understood, others had been to ask for the same privilege but had not told her of their church associations. She would let me use the convent chapel but would put a screen in front of the altar. I had the use of the chapel many times, and to the joy of the Mother Superior, I devoted the collections for the benefit of her crippled little ones. In addition, our generous men brought many offerings of fruit, sweets and toys. 'The quality of mercy is not strained' – as Shakespeare said in his 'Merchant of Venice'. Our gifts 'dropped like the gentle rain of Heaven upon the earth beneath, and were twice blessed – to those who gave, and to those who received'. These incidents are worth remembering.

There was one interlude in the midst of my busy life. I was asked to represent the services, especially the army, at one of our big meetings in London. The meeting was held in the historic Metropolitan Tabernacle and I was given leave to attend. Some three thousand people packed the tabernacle and at the beginning of my address I read letters which I had received from Dr Simms, the principal chaplain, Bishop Gwynne, the deputy chaplain general in France, and Field Marshal Earl Haig. These letters awakened great enthusiasm and set the tone to the great meeting, which was presided over by Sir William F. Hartley.

The letter of the Field Marshal is of especial interest. There has been published a war book called 'Retreat', written by an artillery officer who had become a naval officer, Lieutenant Commander C.R. Benstead. In it he described a Padre, spiritually-minded, but lacking in human understanding. He is a tragic figure in the novel. Readers of the *Evening Standard* gave their views on this question, following an article by Dean Inge, on the book. I wrote a reply, as Dean Inge suggested some chaplain who had seen a good deal of active service should take the matter up. I said in my reply that the Field Marshal's letter, which I gave, should silence the critics of army chaplains, especially as represented in the book.

Here then I give the letter, as I think future generations should know the truth. It was sent from the Field Marshal's GHQ in France, on 20th February 1919 and was as follows:

Dear Mr Kendall, I am glad to have been given this unique opportunity to express for myself and many thousands who have served under my command our appreciation of the wonderful work which ministers of religion of all churches have carried out with so much steadfastness and courage through four and a half years of war.

To the chaplains of all denominations serving with our Forces the war was a crusade, and the inspiration of their teaching has been felt through all ranks of the Army.

They taught our soldiers what they were fighting for, strengthened their resolution in time of trial, comforted the stricken and at all times set an example which had a powerful influence for good upon the daily life of all.

No man can lightly estimate how much they have contributed to the triumph of our cause.

Yours very truly, D Haig FM

This letter shows that the Field Marshal was a deeply religious man. I was told that every Sunday he attended the Church of Scotland's service at his headquarters. His chaplain was The Rev George S. Duncan. In his 'Private Papers' edited by Robert Blake there are many references to the sermons that Mr Duncan preached, and in writing to him after the war, he makes one of his rare references to his religious feelings.

'Yes, he wrote, 'it was very difficult to keep going all the time of the long war, and I am frequently asked now how I managed to do it. Well, I can truly say that you were a great help to me when I was C in C in putting things into proper perspective on Sundays'. I think that Blake is right when he writes: 'His faith sustained him through long years of strain and anxiety. It gave him that rock-like quality, that imperturbable calm with which he met disaster and triumph alike'.

The Field Marshal also had strong views on church unity. In these days when there is so much talk of the re-union of the churches it is refreshing to hear the Field Marshal's views. He was a Presbyterian, but not narrow-minded. A friend and inspirer of the chaplain, he was anxious for them to sink denominational difference. When the Archbishop of York (Dr Lang) who afterwards became the Archbishop of Canterbury, visited his headquarters and had spoken to him about the necessity for opening the doors of the Church of England wider, he records: 'I agreed and said we ought to aim at organizing a great Imperial Church to which all honest citizens of the Empire could belong'. Two years afterwards, when in conversation with the King, he urged him to press for the formation of a great-minded Imperial Church, to embrace all churches, except the Roman Catholics, and he added that Empires of the past had disappeared because there was no church or religion to bind them together. To prevent this, all must unite in the service of God.

The letter I quoted was the second that the Field Marshal sent me. In the midst of all his tremendous tasks he could spare time to write to an ordinary chaplain like myself. It was a very great sorrow to all of us when, on 29th January 1928, the Field Marshal died suddenly. This was especially the case as regards the British Legion, which he had founded and had done so much for. I attended the official funeral service in Westminster Abbey on 3rd February. It was accompanied by all the pomp and pageantry that the obsequies of the Field Marshal demand. The King's three eldest sons walked behind the gun carriage that bore the coffin. The Marshals of France, Foch and Pertain, were among the pall-bearers. I, myself, marched in the procession in my khaki uniform. It was a moving service and one full of memories.

I like to think of the last scene in his beloved Scotland, on a plain farm cart drawn by four horses, the coffin was carried from the station of St Boshells to the Abbey of Dryburgh – five miles through the country that he knew so well, the Valley of the Tweed. Finally, he was laid to rest in the earth that covers Sir Walter Scott.

I was privileged and honoured to preach for two years in succession the Field Marshal's memorial sermon to a great gathering of ex-servicemen in the North of England. There were many standards of the British Legion in the Parade. It was held in Saltburn and all the hotels were filled for the weekend.

I am sure the Field Marshal would have been glad to join us as we sang Kipling's great hymn 'God of our fathers, known of old', with the verse:

The tumult and the shouting dies,
The captains and kings depart.
Still stand thine ancient sacrifice,
A humble and a contrite heart.
Lord God of Hosts, be with us yet,
Lest we forget – lest we forget.

To return to the metropolitan meeting – I read the letters to which I have referred and I spoke of the courage shown by our men, of their amazing cheerfulness under the most discouraging conditions, of their love for home, of their wonderful spirit of comradeship, of all their sacrifices. I told many stories of the brave deeds and of how the men had endured hardships as good soldiers. I had the great audience with me as I told this plain straightforward story.

After the meeting I left with Sir William, to stay with The Rev J.T. Barkby, a lifelong friend, who was then one of the secretaries of the Royal Navy, Army and Air Force United Board, and then followed a seaside holiday with my wife at Seaton in Devon.

On my return I found that Colonel Howard had been transferred to the staff at GHQ and had been succeeded by Colonel Barwell. Colonel Barwell one day had an original and I think, unique idea of having a battalion picnic. The novelty almost took our breath away and when orders appeared in which it was decreed that the battalion would proceed by road in full marching order to Rodenkirchen on the Rhine, and bivouac, the excitement knew no bounds. We left shortly after dawn, with the band playing, on through Lindenwall, Bonnerwall and the outer defences of Cologne. The natives were awakened by our martial music and the tramp of many feet and soon every window was crowded. I rode with the colonel at the head of the battalion. At 8am we had breakfast on the line of march and arrived at Rodenkirchen at 10am and proceeded to bivouac amongst the bushes and trees next to the famous bathing pavilion. The day was spent in bathing and games.

We had one tragedy. A young lieutenant, who had become a great friend of mine, was drowned whilst bathing. It was my sad task to bury him, after the Court of Enquiry, and to write to his widow in Scotland. We slept that night in the woods, and all slept soundly, and marched back to Cologne the next day.

One of the last services I held was a Brigade Harvest Festival. I always felt we should keep up with those at home. We held it in the Nusebaumer Strasse School, and the officers and men brought fruit and flowers. We sang the old hymns and Colonel Barwell read the lesson. My text was: 'Cast thy bread upon the waters, for thou shalt find it after many days'. After the service we took the bunches of grapes and other fruit to our sick lads in the hospital. Many officers and men came to me with their personal problems, which were often concerned with family matters. I like to think that I saved many a home from being wrecked.

Civilians also came to me from time to time to ask for help. I remember a German asked to see me one morning about the sergeant who was billeted in his home. He said that his wife had got too fond of the sergeant and that he himself was being neglected. I shall never forget the plaintive way in which he said, "The sergeant he gives me bully beef. I do not want his bully beef. I want my wife." Now I knew the sergeant was a decent sort of man. I sent for him and told him about the husband's fears. He said he was not very happy in the billet and so he was given another one.

Once again I received my marching orders. I was to take duty as chaplain, educational and recreation officer at the General Hospital some miles from Cologne. The 1/6th West Yorks gave me a farewell dinner at which the colonel proposed my toast and the officers sang 'For he's a jolly good fellow'. I had enjoyed my service with the battalion and the brigade and it had been the more enjoyable because we were all from the West Riding.

About this time, I had an unexpected honour conferred upon me. I was awarded the Order of the British Empire (Military Division). I was one of the first to receive this Order. In addition, I was mentioned in despatches.

21

The Rhine General Hospital

The General Hospital was some miles from Cologne and was reserved for those men who were suffering from venereal disease. For obvious reasons I do not wish to give the number or the location of this hospital. It covered a large area and was surrounded with barbed wire to the height of several feet. There were a lot of very long huts which were used as wards, and other huts for officers. We also had schoolrooms, reading rooms, a large hall for concerts and a YMCA where we held our religious services and which had a splendid canteen. The doctors lived in a little cluster of villas a few hundred yards away, and the officers' mess was in a big house in the centre.

At the entrance to the hospital compound was the guardroom. There were one thousand beds and alas, they were always occupied. Here you could see the sin, shame, misery and often despair; others treated the matter lightly, forgetting the serious nature of the disease and all that it implied. The temptations in the city of Cologne, in particular, were tremendous. There were many prostitutes whose ranks were swelled by numerous amateurs. It should be remembered that soldiers of all nations had lived in Cologne and the prostitutes were not all of German nationality. We kept a book – a very large one – with the photographs and dossiers of most of the women who had passed on this disease. When a man had contracted it he was asked all particulars as to its source and shown the photographs. These women, from time to time, were rounded up and given compulsory hospital treatment, and many were deported.

It was not my task, nor desire, to condemn these men. There were plenty outside who were just as guilty but had not been 'caught' – the sin was in being 'caught' and so was the punishment. My task was to win these men back to self-respect and to urge them to exercise self-reverence and self-control, to keep the mind pure, and the body healthy. Always borne in upon my mind were those wise words of St Paul, uttered so long ago, and which I have tried to make my standard in my treatment of others: 'Brethren, if a man be overtaken in a fault, ye which are spiritual restore such a one in the spirit of meekness; considering thyself, lest thou also be tempted'. I met with many tragedies, but it is not my wish to reveal them. You had to win the confidence of these men and make them feel that you could be relied upon to keep their confidence and problems inviolate. I think I managed this, for when I left the hospital, after a long period of service, I received a book – a big exercise book – with the signatures of many men thanking me for all the help I had been able to give them.

I began my educational work with my staff of six sergeant majors and one lieutenant instructor. Classes were arranged in all kinds of subjects – History, Geography, Grammar, Writing, Mathematics, Languages, and also for various trades. I had all the help I needed from the head of the Educational Corps at General Headquarters – all the books and materials and the classrooms necessary to work and study in. I myself took the men who could neither read nor write and I trained them to do so, in what I think was an original way. This was the class where much patience was needed, and whilst I had the whole of the administration of the school in my hands I felt I must teach, a task I loved.

It was a real joy to me and to my staff when we were told the result of the examinations at the end of the first year. My school was second from the top in the whole of the Rhine Army. The only men who had gained more certificates were those at the colleges in Bonn and Cologne. We were all proud of the result and encouraged to go forward. Each afternoon I arranged cricket and football matches, also other games, and from time to time marched the men to a cinema in the nearby town for concerts and films. Later on I had a permanent cinema, and concert hall, built of brick in the grounds, the Germans carrying out, and paying for the work. No doubt they recognised it would be a good thing to do this in view of the future when the occupation ceased. In the evenings I organised dances, whist-drives, concerts and debates. The debates, on all kinds of subject, were very popular. We discussed pacifism, communism, conscription, 'ghosts, are they real?' and many other subjects. In addition to my own concert party 'The Merry Blue Boys', who gave many performances, we had visiting concert parties from home and from the various units and clubs. It was the best of all treatment for the men who were there, to keep all these various activities going on constantly.

I remember on one occasion I gave a lecture on the Empire, as we knew it in those days. I had a large map on the wall to illustrate my subject. The men were keenly interested. I little knew that behind the screen were Colonel Cumming, the commanding officer of the hospital, and General Sir William Robertson (afterwards Field Marshal Lord Robertson, commander-in-chief on the Rhine), who listened to all I said. Just before I dismissed the men Sir William came to me and with a smile and a handshake said, "That's the stuff to give the troops, Padre." I did not know at that time that he was very enthusiastic about lectures on the Empire.

Bishop Taylor Smith, the chaplain general, visited the Rhine Army, and he decided to hold a Confirmation service in the Lutheran church. The Church of England chaplain, who lived a good distance away from the hospital, sought my aid. I asked those men who wished to be confirmed to meet me and I told them the Bishop was coming and that I was anxious to help the Church of England chaplain. The men at once promised me their support. On the day of the Bishop's visit I had a big board placed in a prominent place in the camp and on it I wrote in chalk: 'Boys, I have arranged your sports and amusements. I have marched you to the cinema, will you meet me here, and march to the Confirmation Service held by Bishop Taylor Smith, the Chaplain General?' All the men turned up and I marched with them to the church and it was packed. We had a memorable service. Afterwards I had tea with the Bishop, and The Rev D.W.S. Parry-Evans, the assistant chaplain general, on the Rhine, and they thanked me for my help. Years afterwards I attended the Bishop's farewell dinner on his retirement. This was graced by the presence of Dr Davidson, Archbishop of Canterbury, the chief of the Imperial General Staff, members of the Army Council and many distinguished guests.

Later on, when I was the minister of the Caledonian Road Church, Islington, the Bishop came to address my anniversary meeting, and told the people of my work during the war and on the Rhine. In the vestry afterwards, I, feeling somewhat hesitant, asked the Bishop, "May I pay your expenses, my Lord?" He replied with a smile, "No, my boy, and here is a pound for your collection." That was characteristic of this great-hearted chaplain general, who had done so much for the army and the chaplains through the long years in which he had occupied his important office.

To create still further interest, I began a magazine for the hospital. I asked the men to send me articles and I had a remarkable response. One sent a weird story called 'The Avenger' by Vampire – another was very topical – 'The Doctor's Verdict'. There were many jokes and a few warnings about 'fair ladies', reminiscent of Solomon's advice in the seventh chapter of the Book of Proverbs; beginning with the words: 'For at the window of my house I looked through my casement, and I discerned among the youths a young man void of understanding' – then follows the description of what happened to him, with the stark message of the final verse: 'Her house is the way to Hell, going down to the chambers of death'.

On All Souls' Day, 2nd November, a memorial service was held in the Sudfriedshof (Military Cemetery), in memory of the British prisoners of war who were buried there. It was a snowy afternoon, the Germans had placed flowers and lighted candles on many of the graves of their own men. A great crowd of our men gathered for what I felt was the most moving experience of our Rhineland occupation – remembering those men who had died in captivity without knowing that the ultimate victory would be ours. We recited the 23rd Psalm, and those lovely words in the Book of Wisdom: 'But the souls of the righteous are in the hand of God, and there shall no torment touch them'. We sang with fresh feeling 'For all the saints who from their labours rest' and 'On that Resurrection morning'.

The lovely prayers from the Burial Order were repeated, the 'Last Post' sounded and we bowed our heads as we finally repeated:

> Father, into Thy gracious keeping,
> Leave we now Thy servants sleeping.

I wondered at the time what the German civilians thought, for they also came in great numbers.

How strange are the unexpected meetings in life! I was standing outside the Dom – Cologne's great cathedral – and the first man I met was Father McGuinness. I had not seen him since the day I left Salonica; what a lot we had to tell each other! What a joy to meet! We spent a happy afternoon together.

We made great preparations for the Christmas of 1919. I went with Colonel Cumming to buy a piano for our new cinema, which was ready to open, and with a gift of seventy pounds from General Robertson's headquarters we bought turkeys, ducks, suckling pigs and all kinds of food and drinks to give the men a real happy time. In the evening we opened the new cinema with a concert by my 'Merry Blue Boys' and I put on a special film. I provided the Christmas dinner for the family in my billet. So far as billets were concerned I could not have had a better one. I was well looked after and given every comfort. We became very friendly and I wanted to show my appreciation for all the kindness I had received. The other officers had the same experience and spoke very highly of the owners of their billets. To celebrate the New Year – 1920 – I took the Bahnhof Hotel for the whole evening and arranged a dinner for officers, non-commissioned officers and ward orderlies. We had turkey and the usual fare. We were waited on by the German hotel staff and I had engaged an orchestra to play during the dinner and for the dancing afterwards. I do not think that those present, if they are still alive, will forget that night.

I had a great desire to visit the unoccupied territory. I could not get permission for this but I adopted the methods of others who had made the trip, and I went unofficially in civilian clothing. I was passed through the controls and made my way to Dusseldorf, and toured the city and surrounding countryside. Returning, I decided to leave Dusseldorf by the midnight train. The green-uniformed security guards had been formed by the Germans and they were in force on the platform that night. I entered a carriage of the waiting train and one of the guards came in and examined my passport, which had been given to me by a German. He left, but stood by the door, apparently not satisfied, when there was a commotion. Another train had just come in from the frontier and then a porter and a woman arrived. There was a lot of luggage and the woman had only given the porter five marks for his trouble – a very small sum, owing to devaluation. He complained in vigorous language, and so did the woman. The security guard tried to intervene and lost all interest in me. My carriage door was open and the guard of the train blew his whistle, and the woman with her luggage was bundled in and almost fell over me, and off we went. The woman began to tell me of her troubles. She said she had come from America to bring her husband's body to be buried in the Fatherland, and she resented her rough treatment at Dusseldorf. I said to her, "Where is your husband's body?" She replied, "I had him cremated and his ashes are in the casket over your head." I forget what time we arrived in Cologne, but I had to get a taxi. The man I approached refused, until one of our red-cap military police compelled him to do so, and that was the end of an adventurous and perfect day. Afterwards I was able to give first-hand information on the condition of things in the unoccupied territory.

I have not written about the treatment given to the men. Most of them were up and about all the day. There were very few who were bed-ridden. That was the main reason why we had our school, recreation and amusements. The disease had a depressing effect and it was necessary to keep the men interested and active. Colonel Cumming, and his staff of doctors, were not only efficient, but understanding. After my experiences I made a study of the disease and I was determined to warn young people of the dangers of promiscuous intercourse and an immoral life. The opportunity came when I was asked by the British Social Hygiene Council, and then later the Central Council for Health Education, to join their panel of lecturers on the subject. I refer to this work which I carried out, elsewhere in my story.

Changes were becoming the order of the day, and demobilisation was being rapidly carried out. One day I received orders to report to the War Office in London. Colonel Cumming and his officers gave me a really wonderful farewell dinner. I was sorry to leave them and sorry, too, to leave the good friends in my billet, and so I departed from the Rhineland.

22

The Graves of the Fallen 1920–21

I reported to the War Office and received my orders to return to Flanders as senior chaplain for a district which covered the whole of the country from the coast to the German Frontier. Later on my work extended to France. Prior to my departure I was given a few days' leave, for which I was thankful. I crossed to Calais and went on to the General Headquarters at St Pol where I stayed the night with my old friend The Rev George Standing, who had succeeded Dr Simms as the principal chaplain. The next day I proceeded to Poperinghe. My headquarters were at the Kip-Cot Camp a mile or so outside the town. This was an old wartime camp of hutments and surrounded with trees. Colonel Sutton, the commanding officer of the district, met me on arrival. He was one of the best commanding officers I ever served with and was very popular with all ranks. His adjutant was Major Philip P. Kenyon-Slaney, who became a great friend of mine and who, after demobilisation, became a Member of Parliament. He died, to my great sorrow, at an early age.

There was a staff of a dozen officers at the headquarters and a large number of non-commissioned officers and men. We had many other camps throughout the vast area as far apart as Nieuport and Liege, and at such places as Ypres, Passchendaele, Tournai, and St Jean. We also had a Stationary Hospital at Remy, with five sisters and thirty-seven nurses, and my staff included chaplains, one of them a Roman Catholic.

Our task was a grim one. We had to endure much hardship and the isolation was a real test of character. Our days were spent in searching for the dead, exhuming the bodies of men in dugouts, trenches, ruined buildings and the open country. We also had to create big new central cemeteries. Our camp was well situated, and the huts were comfortable. There were large ones for recreation, officers, and messes. I myself became the president of the officers' mess, and took charge of the staff and catering. We had, in addition, a chapel well fixed up in a Nissen hut.

One curious thing happened: when we established this camp, there suddenly came a strange assortment of dogs. There were Airedales, Alsatians, Terriers, in fact all breeds. They came with string and chains round their necks. They were the dogs that had been left behind by demobilised soldiers, and they had been taken by the civilians. Some instinct told them that their old friends, who had always fed them so well, had returned, so they broke their chains and came back to their khaki friends. Eventually we had a pack of forty or so. I took charge of them and fed them. Soon I had farmers coming in search of their dogs and some strange scenes took place. "Which dog is yours?" I used to ask, and if a farmer pointed to one I would say, "Take it." But woe betide the man if he attempted to take the dog, for the whole pack could go for him and so, as a rule, he would depart. We hardly needed sentries as the dogs were always there to protect us and if any civilian ventured into the camp he did so at the peril of his life unless I, or some other man, was with him.

I remember one weekend, when the other officers had gone on leave to Brussels, being alone in my hut. Jack, an Airedale was my special companion and always slept in the hut with me. In the night a civilian, or sole deserter, came into my hut, no doubt to rob me, but he had not counted on Jack. I woke up when I heard a man yell, and there was a scuffle. The man ran out and I followed. Jack had a grip on his trousers. The man managed to roll through. I called Jack off and he still had a good part of the trousers in his mouth. That was the last time anyone tried to burgle one of our huts.

The dogs multiplied and Colonel Sutton said he could no longer keep so many, they must be humanely put to sleep. The men did not like this and I am sure they must have warned the dogs, for next morning when the execution should have taken place, not a dog was to be seen. They came back all right at night, and the colonel laughingly said, "What can you do with dogs like these?" So they were reprieved and the pups were sold by the men in the towns and villages around. It soon became a means of extra wealth for the charge was five francs and very often the dogs returned and were sold again.

I have mentioned the curious and rather mysterious matter of dogs but there was another which proved to be very serious and the cause of much tragedy. That was the human dogs – the bandits who terrorised the whole area, committing all kinds of crime, murder, lust, looting and sabotage. These were the deserters, who had escaped detention, and lived in ruined cellars and dugouts. Many were in the canal bank region of Ypres. We could only go out in armed groups at night and men were detailed to endeavour to round up these men. When caught they were tried by military courts-martial and if proved guilty received punishment for their crimes. I was myself shot at point-blank one Sunday evening at the Belgian Battery corner, outside Ypres. The man missed me and instinctively I went for him and he made off – only just in time, as a group of men hearing the shot rushed down the road to my rescue. The man escaped in a labyrinth of trenches which he must have known well – and escaped to be searched for and rounded up another day.

There was one group of South African deserters who had their hideout in the cellar of a ruined building. They committed a good many murders, one a most revolting one of a woman near Tyne Cot Cemetery which we were making; all they got were five francs which the poor woman had in her pocket. They fought at times amongst themselves and the gang was reduced to two survivors. These two were caught and put in the detention building, but somehow or other they set fire to the Provost-Marshal's hut which was near. They did not escape and eventually they were shot for the many murders they had committed. I went out one night in cars with some officers in a search for other suspects. The last night I was in Belgium a Belgian officer was brought into our hospital, terribly battered about by some of these bandits. They looted stores and when in gangs held up supply trains. We never expected to have to face these dangers after the war, when engaged in the task of exhumation.

The Chinese Corps contributed some grim humour to the life of their working camps, where they turned their hands to everything. There were a good many in our area, clearing the battlefield. The Mills bomb impressed them, at first, as a superior kind of firework. One afternoon, near the canal bank, one of them with a laugh, took the pin out of one and put it in the pocket of his pal – neither of them laughed anymore!

To return to our particular task. We were the pioneers of the Imperial War Graves Commission of which the Prince of Wales (now the Duke of Windsor) was the president. Our task was first of all to make the many war cemeteries and remove the known dead from small communal French and Belgian cemeteries and isolated graves and also, a much more difficult task, to make a systematic search for and identification of the unknown dead; but not even we who were engaged in this task could estimate, at first, what it meant. Not only had many thousand been buried where they fell in the confusion of no man's land; in wrecked trenches and dugouts; beneath the debris of villages and towns; in unsuspected fields, gardens and woods – but some earlier cemeteries had come into the battle line again, when our armies fell back, and had been shelled out or fought over for months or years.

I have the original list of hundreds of cemeteries and all kind of odd burial grounds and corners which I prepared. It is an amazing list with all kinds of strange names, 'Hyde Park', 'No Man's Cottage', 'Comedy Farm', 'Irish Farm', 'Bard Cottage', and so on. The more characteristic names come from topographical military or personal origins. We had a service of dedication for opening, extending or creating a new cemetery – also for burials, and one for the closing of a cemetery when completed. In my day only wooden crosses were placed on the graves, to be followed later by the beautiful headstones in the lovely stone of Remembrance and the Cross of Sacrifice, as can be seen in the cemeteries at Étaples, Tyne Cot, near Passchendaele, Delville Wood and many others, for there are in France two thousand four hundred and thirteen and in Belgium eight hundred and fourteen cemeteries and many others in all lands. These, with such lovely memorials as the Menin Gate, Ypres, and elsewhere, commemorate over one million of our dead, the majority of which are in France and Flanders.

These wooden crosses, thousands of which I saw erected, have become historical. They are a reminder for all time of what our men gave for us – life and love, hopes and heritage – these silent outposts of our Empire and Commonwealth. Here, officers and men lie side by side in equity. Richness of worldly wealth cannot assert itself here, neither rank or position; the poorest lad is a gallant and silent sentinel, as his officer that led him and fell with him.

It is interesting to note that the Germans adopted the same method. I was very much impressed when we entered Cambrai with the cemetery they had made. There are sections in this cemetery for the graves of soldiers of various nationalities. They had reverently buried our men and had erected wooden crosses over their graves. In the centre was a memorial stone which had inscribed on it, in four languages, the words:

'The sword divides, but the cross unites'.

We should never forget the help and generosity of the French and Belgian Governments in this almost superhuman task of the burial of our dead. As far back as 1915, I had buried men in their churchyards or cemeteries. We found that these were being rapidly filled by us, and it could not be continued. The two governments, France and Belgium, then decided that the new land required for our purpose should be acquired in perpetuity as a free gift. It was then decided that forty graves should constitute a permanent cemetery and it became possible to select sites near the front line, as well as further back, for 'authorised cemeteries'. Often we risked our lives to carry bodies, generally by night, back to burial grounds behind the trenches. I remember many such places, like Despair Farm on the Armentieres sector, where one night a German machine gunner found our range and I had to shelter in the grave of the man I had just buried.

The work of re-burial was one which needed careful planning. All the battlefields were examined at least six times, and places where fighting had been the heaviest, as many as twenty times. I found that the officers and men detailed for the discovery and concentration of scattered graves, gave to their task a skill, devotion and unselfishness beyond praise. This work needed special knowledge of many sorts, as well as past experience of the war, and sound detective instincts, no trifle could be overlooked, nor any claim missed. The dead, for example, of the 1914 and 1915 years had gone into action with more marks and badges than their successors, the khaki of some corps differed a little from that of others; and then there were minor details of battalion equipment, or changes on the eve of action, which had to be verified, recorded, and given weight in evidence. Identification discs often disintegrated too soon; but sometimes, for no apparent reason, over breadths of ground that had been gassed and shelled continuously, we would come across the dead of years ago with their last home letters still legible in their pockets – for each body had to be carefully searched – and we would also find pencils knives and watches, blackened it is true, but not destroyed.

I remember going with Colonel Sutton one day to Nieuport, and we witnessed the exhumation of five men of the York and Lancs Regiment. It was in the underground cellar of a ruined building. They were just skeletons lying around in the positions in which they were sleeping when the shell destroyed the building. One man had been reading 'Paradise Lost'. In his fingers were clasped about fifty pages of the book – wet and yellow – I took the book from his hand and saw what he had been reading in the hour of his death. I have the book as I write, and I quote the lines he was reading: 'Such high advantages their innocence gave them above their foes; not to have sinned, not to have disobeyed; in fight they stood unwearied, unobnoxious to be pained by wound, though from their place by violence moved' – then followed: 'Now night her course began'. Night had come for that Yorkshire boy – the night of death. I have often wondered what his thoughts were as he read those lines I have quoted. Although all the uniforms had almost perished I found in one corner the local weekly newspaper of the West Riding I came from and to which I had often contributed, and this helped in our identification of those five boys. But it took some little time to sort things out – and then I re-buried them.

Many curious coincidences were experienced by me. For example, early in 1915, whilst I was with the 38th Welsh Division, I buried a corporal and two privates at the back of the trenches at Ypres. It was the first burial in the corner of the field I had selected, and I called the place 'Bard Cottage'. In 1920 I held a service, closing what was then a cemetery containing the bodies of some thousands of men; my thoughts went back to that morning five years before, when I began the cemetery and buried those men at the peril of my life. In November of that year, Mr William Hopkins, and his daughter, arrived at my headquarters. They had come from Saskatoon, Canada, a city of which he was the Mayor. "Could I," he asked, "arrange for the exhumation and re-burial" of his son, and his son's friend who had been killed in the First Battle of Ypres. "Both," he said, "were fellow students at the Saskatoon University." I found, with the help of others, the bodies – and exhumed them. Mr Hopkins provided two coffins which we had made in Poperinghe and along with my men we buried the two men next to each other in the cemetery at Passchendaele. Mr Hopkins and his daughter, and a Canadian officer, attended the re-burial and I conducted the full service. His gratitude knew no bounds and he wished, in some way, to reward me for all my work, but I told him that no reward could be accepted. He then asked me it, later on, would I visit Saskatoon at his expense, but I regret that I never found it possible to do so and I expect by now he has passed away. Incidentally I know that he richly rewarded my men, but I turned a blind eye to this. What could one do under such circumstances? The men, of course, are grateful. It was the only instance of this kind that I know of.

The mother of Lieutenant H.C. May, who had been killed in action, came over from Kensington. Her son's body had not been found but, with the mother's faith, she was sure it could be. She stayed for one week and went home with a sad heart. We continued the search and eventually found the body in the area where she was sure that it would be. She had letters from his commanding officer when he was killed and later on she had met him and he had given to her the location. Within a week we found the body and I wrote at once and told the mother, but she could not return. I re-buried her son and sent her a copy of the burial service which I had conducted and she sent me a grateful and touching letter of thanks.

The mother of Lieutenant MacQueen came all the way from Glasgow, with her two daughters, to her son's re-burial at Vis-en-Artois. This was a very moving experience for me. I had known Mrs MacQueen for many years, little realising that one day I should lay her son to rest in that valley so far away – a place forever Scotland to her, and her daughters.

There is a saying that 'truth is stranger than fiction' and here is a story to prove it. The Rev J.T. Barkby, was a lifelong friend of mine. We both came from the same area in the West Riding. I little thought when I was a lad that I should meet him with his wife – a daughter of Sir William P. Hartley – and stand by the grave of his eldest son, named after his grandfather, Hartley Barkby. He was in the Royal Artillery and was killed at Maricourt and there he lies in the Casement Trench Cemetery. As we stood there the years rolled by and I could see a friend as I had so often seen him, one of the kindest and most generous of men and now, with his wife, stunned by grief.

My heart went out to him and I thought of Doddridge's lines:

O spread Thy covering wings around,
Till all our wanderings cease,
And at our Father's loved above
Our souls arrive in peace.

I looked after the boy's grave during the rest of my time in France. His father and mother have also arrived in 'our Father's loved abode' and their souls are in peace.

I could continue with such stories of life's surprises, coincidences that do happen and often under strange circumstances. We had a vast number of cemeteries to officiate in at re-burials, often we travelled one hundred kilometres a day. I had a car and driver and I took along with me two other chaplains, one being a Roman Catholic. All denominational differences vanished over the graves of the fallen, we were the forerunners of the United Church and we all shared in the same burial service. When the men had collected a number of bodies these were reverently placed in a row and we said our prayers and laid them to rest in the prepared graves; we thought, too, of those at home who were mourning the loss of their loved ones. It was all so moving. I can see those sacred spots, as I write, and feel again the emotions we experienced.

We had a special service for the closing of a cemetery, after its completion. I travelled to Liège to officiate at the closing of one there. After the service I paid a complimentary call on the Governor at the Citadel, and he kindly entertained me to lunch. He was greatly concerned about a smuggling racket in which two of our officers were involved. I took back with me a full report and the whole matter was thoroughly investigated, with the result that the officers concerned were cashiered. I saw them off after their trial and sentence. The complications which followed were very serious, and I have often wondered how they were solved.

From time to time we had visits from, so-called, 'very important persons'. Officers were detailed to show them round the various battlefields and cemeteries. I remember the Duke of Portland was one such VIP.

There were also the relations of the men who had fallen, visiting the graves. They were well looked after by the YMCA who had hostels in Ypres, Arras and all the principal centres. The Salvation Army also had a splendid and well-equipped chateau at Vlamertinghe. I visited these hostels a good deal to give any help that I could in finding the graves which the relatives had come to visit. I also conducted services for them on Sundays.

We did our best to keep our men happy and contented. I arranged concerts for them and collected a big library of books. I also arranged all kinds of games inside and out, whist-drives, football, cricket and boxing. On Sundays I held Holy Communion and voluntary services which were well attended. Then there was Poperinghe, which we often visited and where there were many attractions for all of us.

23

'The Unknown Warrior' and My Part in his Embarkation

Foreword

The burial of 'The Unknown Warrior' at a State funeral in Westminster Abbey took place on 11 November 1920 – two years precisely after the signing of the Armistice that ended the First World War. The permanent Cenotaph – designed by Sir Edwin Lutyens in Whitehall – was unveiled by King George V in the presence of 'The Unknown Warrior' that morning.

This was the first such burial in any nation. The burial of an unknown warrior under the Arc de Triomphe in Paris took place the following year. An army Padre, David Railton, was concerned for the relations of so many men who had died on the battlefields, but who could not be identified. Where could they grieve? He proposed to the Dean of Westminster – The Right Rev Herbert Ryle – only in August 1920 that an unknown warrior should be buried in the abbey: 'the Parish Church of the Empire'. Within three days, Ryle had replied – saying he 'warmly inclined to favour the idea', but that it 'must germinate'. Only in October 1920 did he confirm to Railton that the idea had germinated.

The account that follows is of the choice of the body – and recently, it has been proposed that DNA testing could reveal the identity of the warrior. Back in 1930, *Time* Magazine suggested that the identity was known; it never has been, nor ever will be, known. The body must be allowed to rest in peace. It remains of great importance in the abbey as a focus for prayer for peace, and for those who have suffered in conflict – visited by heads of State and of Government, as well as by more than a million visitors from all over the world, who pass by the grave of 'The Unknown Warrior' every year.

The Very Rev John Hall
Dean of Westminster Abbey

I must now proceed to tell the story of 'The Unknown Warrior'. It has been stated that this is the greatest mystery of the First World War. I have been interviewed from time to time by the correspondents of nearly all our great national newspapers, asking me if I knew who he was, could I say where he was actually found, who was responsible for the idea? All I can say was that he was chosen from the countless unnamed dead in France, and Flanders, that the nation might honour him, and this without distinction of rank, birth or service. There were in these two countries many thousands of graves of men whose bodies had been found, but, with all our endeavours, could not be identified – so over their crosses we inscribed 'Unknown British Soldier'. Here then is my story, told because of the younger generation, who go to see the tomb in Westminster Abbey and do not know how he was chosen and brought home.

Early in November 1920, we received orders from headquarters, for the exhumation of a certain number of bodies of unknown men. No one – and this is very important – was to know from which district a body had been taken. The graves which were opened in all the theatres of war were marked only by a cross which stated that an unknown warrior lay there. If the regiment or division in which the man had served were specified – and there were cases in which a man may not have been identified, but his regiment or battalion was known – the grave was untouched. In all some six bodies were finally taken to the headquarters at St Pol, near Arras. Those who awaited the bodies at St Pol did not even know from where they had come. The six coffins were placed in a hut, and each covered with a Union Jack. All night they rested on trestles, with nothing to distinguish one from the other. The door of the hut was locked and sentries posted outside. In the morning a general entered the hut. He placed his hand on one of the flag-shrouded coffins, and the body therein became 'The Unknown Warrior'. The five other coffins were taken from the hut and reverently reburied. The one selected to receive the tribute of the Empire was conveyed to Boulogne and embarked there on the British destroyer Verdun, to be brought to England. On the lid of the coffin, as it was taken on board, was placed a rare and valuable sword taken from the private collection of King George V. Out in the mists, six British destroyers were waiting to escort the Verdun to Dover. They formed up three ahead, three astern, and course was shaped for England. As the vessels slipped silently into Dover Harbour, a Field Marshal's salute of nineteen guns was fired.

Of course, one might ask from what cemetery the bodies were collected! That I cannot answer, and the knowledge I have will die with me. I suppose if the location was made known, there would be a flood of cameramen taking photographs of the cemeteries and saying, "From here 'The Unknown Warrior' was chosen," but apart from that, so great are the changes in the cemeteries in forty years that nature comes to the rescue, and destroys all identification marks. No! The location can never be revealed, but again I stress this great fact – the soldier lying in Westminster Abbey is British and unknown. He may have come from some little village or some city in this land, and he may be the son of a working man or of a rich man: 'Unknown to man, but known to God'.

On the morning of the embarkation ceremony, we motored from Kip-Cot Camp, Poperinghe, to Boulogne. We began the journey at 5am. It was a cold and frosty morning. Arriving at the starting point, we were marshalled into our places. I shall never forget the overwhelming solemnity of the procession. In it was Marshal Foch, French and Belgian officers of all ranks and ourselves of the British Army – generals, colonels, captains and myself – the only Padre to represent the many thousands of chaplains who had served in France and Flanders. The coffin, covered with the Union Jack, and carried by stalwart non-commissioned officers, was preceded by the bands of British, French and Belgian regiments. The streets through which the cortege passed, were packed with thousands of people, and so we passed on to the embarkation wharf. Home, they were taking this warrior dead, and all the trumpets sounded for him on the other side. I could, as I stood on the wharf watching the coffin being carried onto the cruiser, visualise the journey over the Straits of Dover and on to London's Whitehall where the massed crowds gathered round the veiled Cenotaph. I could also see the King with the Prince of Wales, standing beside the coffin on the gun carriage. What must have been the emotion as the King touched a button and the two flags fell, revealing the Cenotaph, followed by the two-minute silence which is observed, to this day, on Remembrance Sunday.

I could, again in my imagination, see the gun carriage make its way from Whitehall, with Earl Haig, Lord Byng, Lord French, Earl Beatty, Air Marshal Sir Hugh Trenchard as the pall-bearers, and then on to Westminster Abbey, filled with the great ones of this and other lands, and the mothers and fathers and wives of so many loved ones who had fought the fight and entered into rest.

Each Remembrance Day I visit the little crosses in the abbey grounds and stand by the tomb on which I read:

Beneath this stone rests the body of a British Warrior
Unknown by Name or Rank
Brought from France to Lie Among
The Most Illustrious of the Land
And Buried Here on Armistice Day
11 Nov: 1920. In the Presence of
His Majesty King George V
His Ministers of State
The Chiefs of His Forces
And a Vast Concourse of the Nation
Thus are Commemorated the Many
Multitudes Who During the Great War
Of 1914-1918 Gave The Most That
Man Can Give – Life Itself
For God
For King and Country
For Loved Ones, Home and Empire
For the Sacred Cause of Justice And
The Freedom of the World
They Buried Him Among the Kings because He

Had Done Good Towards God and Toward
His House

There he lies among the Kings and great ones of all times, speaking of life as nobly as all others, and it is true, as long as England stands in history this marble stone will tell the story of 'The Unknown Warrior'.

After the embarkation ceremony I returned to the Kip-Cot Camp and remained there on duty until 22nd March 1921, when I was transferred to the Stuart Camp, Arras. There I worked in the midst of the old familiar battlefields – a strange experience it was to visit once again the old trenches and dugouts and the places where I had lived among the horror and bloodshed, the snipers' bullets and high-explosive shells and where I had laid so many to rest.

One more strange coincidence before I finish my story of the graves of the fallen. I have previously referred to the grave by the roadside at Heninel of Captain R.A. Field MC. One afternoon I took a service at the YMCA hostel at Arras, and after tea I saw two ladies walking on the veranda. I said, "Have you been visiting the grave of a loved one?" They said, "Yes," and told me where they had been. Somehow or other I began to tell stories of brave and good men and I mentioned the cross on the roadside with the words on it: 'He feared death so little, because he feared God so much'. I said, "I am proud of my fellow Yorkshireman, whose name is on that cross."

"His name?" the elder lady asked. "Captain Field," I said. And then to my astonishment she replied, "I am his mother," and pointing to the younger lady she added, "and here is his sister." They had been visiting Captain Field's grave that morning. Afterwards they sent me his photograph. Strange it is how these coincidences happen, even in a far-off land, but there is a providence in it and I, who had often told the story of Captain Field, was privileged to meet those he so dearly loved.

I could write a book on the experiences I had whilst engaged in the sad task of laying to rest those whose memory is honoured in the land they loved. I left Arras on 9th May 1921, and was taken to the hospital at Calais to be treated for an acute ear infection, and a return of malaria which I had contracted in the first place in Macedonia. I was there for four weeks and was transferred to the Royal Herbert Military Hospital, Woolwich, where I received treatment for a further six weeks. I cannot speak too highly of the kindness and care that I received from the doctors and nurses at both these hospitals. My work had been very strenuous and I had virtually lived with the dead in the desolate areas of the old battlefields, so there is no wonder that one had to pay the cost in physical deterioration. Nature, however, is always on the side of recovery and I had a strong constitution which, for six and a half years of active service in all parts of the field had stood me in good stead.

I was one of the last to leave, and the Imperial War Graves personnel, comprised mostly of ex-officers and servicemen, took over as civilians. Every one of the cemeteries have been made as simply and soberly beautiful as British gardeners can make them. They will be lovingly cared for long after we have passed away. We can take hope and courage, remembering the supreme sacrifice of our honoured dead. We cannot, however, live in the past. We must remember that out of disappointment comes hope, and out of death comes life. Our loved ones are not dead, but having given their life they find it again in the land of the Eternal.

I only wish I could have been present when, in May 1922, the late King George V and Queen Mary made their pilgrimage to the graves of the fallen. At Terlincthun, near Boulogne, he gave a message which I think is the most moving every uttered by any monarch.

This message sums up all that I myself deeply felt, and so I must record it:

> For the past few days, I have been on a solemn pilgrimage in honour of a people who died for all free men.
>
> At the close of that pilgrimage, on which I followed ways already marked by many footsteps of love and pride and grief, I should like to send a message to all who have lost those dear to them in the Great War, and in this the Queen joins me today, amidst these surroundings so wonderfully typical of that single-hearted assembly of nations and or races which form our Empire. For here, in their last quarters, lie sons of every portion of that Empire, across, as it were, the threshold of the Mother Island which they guarded that Freedom might be saved in the uttermost parts of the earth.
>
> For this, a generation of our manhood offered itself without question, and almost without the need of a summons. Those proofs of virtue, which we honour here today, are to be found throughout the world and its waters – since we can truly say that the whole circuit of the earth is girdles with the graves of our dead. Beyond the stately cemeteries of France, across Italy, through Eastern Europe, in a well-nigh unbroken chain they stretch, passing over the holy Mount of Olives itself to the farthest shores of the Indian and Pacific Oceans – from Zeebrugge to Coronel, from Dunkirk to the hidden wildernesses of East Africa.
>
> But in this fair land of France, which sustained the utmost fury of the long strife, our brothers are numbered alas, by hundreds of thousands. They lie in the keeping of a tried and generous friend, a resolute and chivalrous comrade-in-arms, who with ready and quick sympathy has set aside for ever the soil in which they sleep, so that we ourselves and our descendants may for all time reverently tend and preserve their resting-places. And here, at Terlincthun, the shadow of his monument falling almost across their graves, the greatest of French soldiers – of all soldiers – stands guard over them. And this is just, for side by side with the descendants of his incomparable armies, they defended his land in defending their own.
>
> Never before in history have a people thus dedicated and maintained individual memorials to their fallen and, in the course of my pilgrimage, I have many times asked myself whether there can be more potent advocates of peace upon earth, through the years to come, than this massed multitude of silent witnesses to the desolation of war. And I feel that so long as we have faith in God's purposes, we cannot but believe that the existence of these visible memorials will, eventually, serve to draw all peoples together in sanity and self-control, even as it has already set the relations between our Empire and our allies on the deep-rooted bases of a common heroism and a common agony.
>
> Standing beneath this Cross of Sacrifice, facing the great Stone of Remembrance, and compassed by these sternly simple headstones, we remember, and must charge our

children to remember, that as our dear were equal in sacrifice, so are they equal in honour, for the greatest and least of them have proved that sacrifice and honour are no vain things, but truths by which the world lives.

Many of the cemeteries I have visited in the remoter and still desolate districts of this sorely stricken land, where it has not yet been possible to replace the wooden crosses by headstones, have been made in beautiful gardens which are lovingly cared for by comrades of the War. I rejoice that I was fortunate enough to see these in the spring, when the returning pulse of the year tells of unbroken life that goes forward in the face of apparent loss and wreckage; and I fervently pray that, both as nations and individuals, we may so order our lives after the ideals for which our brethren died that we may be able to meet their gallant souls once more, humbly but unashamed.

24

With the Territorials and RAF Balloon Command

Foreword

George Kendall is an inspiring character who made the most of the opportunities God placed in his way. He was equally at home amongst the personnel of the various battalions and regiments he served as an Army chaplain, amongst Royalty, senior church leaders and others among whom he ministered and the people of London whose life he shared during those important defining months during the summer of 1940 that have come to be known as the Battle of Britain. Whilst for me and other members of the Royal Air Force these months are characterised by the Few and the Many, those that sought to keep the aircraft of Fighter Command in the air, George Kendall reminds us of the important work of protecting London and of the cost to the citizens of those months.

George Kendall reminds us of the importance of pastoral care within the military community. As a 'living witness' he reminds us of the unchanging nature of chaplaincy, of 'preaching, friendship, atmosphere and games'. In our generation the Chaplain-in-Chief's Mission captures this as RAF Chaplains seek to serve the whole military community through prayer, presence and proclamation. In this way we build upon the strong foundation of men like George Kendall and seek to *ministrare non ministrari* – 'to serve and not be served'

The Rev (Group Captain) Timothy Wright QHC
Deputy Chaplain-in-Chief, Royal Air Force

After leaving the Royal Merchant Military Hospital I went on a short holiday to stay with my wife in Horncastle, Lincolnshire, and then proceeded to South Wales where I had been commissioned as a Territorial chaplain. There are all sorts and conditions of men in the Territorial Army. It is a sample of our national life brought under discipline. The men are in general respectable sons of respectable homes and the officers come from the professional classes – doctors, solicitors, schoolmasters and employers of labour.

During the next five years I served with the South Wales Infantry Brigade of the 53rd (Welsh) Division, and was attached to the 5th Battalion, the Welsh Regiment. This battalion saw service in Gallipoli, Egypt and Palestine, and on 9th December 1917, they furnished the first British Guard to be mounted at the Jaffa Gate of Jerusalem and were the first troops to enter the Holy City after four hundred years of Turkish rule. I had the honour of assisting Lord Allenby at the unveiling of the Obelisk on Pontypridd Common, to the memory of the gallant dead of this battalion. It was all so moving, and standing by the side of the victor of Palestine I noticed how he wept as he said to one poor weeping mother, "I too lost my only son."

The South Wales Infantry Brigade was recruited from the mining valleys. During the year I moved amongst the men, interesting myself in their spiritual and material welfare, my year's work culminating with the camp. I officiated at five camps held at Aberystwyth, Porthcawl and Tenby. The spirit of these camps was that of a holiday and the men from the coal mines appreciated the orderly open-air life under canvas.

At Aberystwyth I was appointed officer in charge of a large recreation tent and each evening found me visiting the various canteens and YMCA tent, arranging sing-songs and healthy competitions. The chaplain's work in all camps can be summed up under the four headings of preaching, friendship, atmosphere and games. The chaplain is a living witness in the camp and produces the atmosphere which helps men and through friendship much can be accomplished. The muscular Christian is always honoured and the inculcation of team spirit I find is a powerful asset. Some years ago I attended a conference of chaplains in the Eastern Command and London, at the Horse Guards. The general officer commanding-in-chief at that time, Lieutenant General Sir R.D. Whigham KCB, told us that in the army there was a growing freedom from drunkenness and impurity, and that this was largely due to the cumulative effect of the chaplain's work. A chaplain might not see the result of his individual labour, but the cumulative effect is great and the aggregate effect is also that his influence gives a soldier power to go forward.

At Porthcawl I spent two memorable camps. Here my units were divided and so I was provided with a horse. It was here I first made the acquaintance of Sir Thomas S. Marden KBE CB CMG, who commanded the division. He was keenly interested in the work of the chaplains. It was at his invitation that I had the honour of officiating at the unveiling of the Cenotaph in Cardiff – a proud and unforgettable memory. This service was broadcast throughout Wales and brought me several letters from people who had recognised my voice. At Porthcawl, we were a happy band of chaplains united in a common comradeship for the good of the men. I was the only Nonconformist and so my Sunday Parade services with band were very impressive. Here too, at our camp, I assisted the Bishop of Hereford at a great open-air service when the massed bands of the brigade accompanied the old hymns, and crowds of seaside visitors gathered on the outskirts. At one camp a Divisional Parade was ordered, at the close of which medals were to be distributed. The Bishop of Swansea was to be the preacher. I was not asked to take part at this service and so I held one for my own men. I think the general commanding had overlooked the fact that most of the men were members of the various branches of the Free Church. I had the same large crowd of men at my service, but alas, the attendance at the Divisional Parade was very poor. When the general asked the reason, he was given this reply, "The men do not know the Bishop of Swansea, but they do know Padre Kendall. He lives with them, shares their daily lives and knows their wives and children, and so they are loyal to him." That makes all the difference – to move about in places where men toil, and in their homes, sharing their joys and sorrows, you can leave the rest with the men. They will stick to you.

One camp that we had at the lovely seaside resort of Tenby, was a dreamland to all of us. How we enjoyed the route marches here and the bathing on the perfect sandy bay. The people of the town entertained us generously and a visit to the monks of Candy Island and a trip with Sir D. Hugh Morgan on his yacht were amongst my joys. The Rev George Standing CBE DSO MC, the assistant chaplain general to the Western Command, came on a tour of duty. What a joy to meet him once more and to see the affection in which he is held by all ranks. Here we maintained our Christian Witness and in the various services were able to influence men for Christ. I was sorry to leave Wales and the men and officers of the Welsh Division, for I had made many friends. These friends, too, helped me with the building of St George's War Memorial Church, and some of the officers attended the opening ceremony.

Again through army circles I made the acquaintance of the Earl of Plymouth, the Lord Lieutenant of the county, and I had the honour of attending the ceremony, with HRH the Prince of Wales, for the laying up of the Welsh Guards' Colours in Llandaff Cathedral. Afterwards, I marched with the Guards from the cathedral to Cardiff. At this memorable service I was reminded of the motto of the Welsh Regiment I served: 'Better death than shame'.

In between the camps I visited the drill halls in the mining valleys and I attended the various messes, especially that of the 5th Welsh, at Pontypridd. I always had a very high regard for Lieutenant Colonel William Dowdeswell and the officers I served with. Many have now passed away. It was a rich fellowship. I am glad that I had those five fruitful years with this division. It seemed so strange to me that having, for a time, service with the 38th Welsh Division in the war, and laying to rest many of those who were killed, I should be posted to Wales and live in the midst of the famous mining valleys.

I left South Wales in 1926, and was appointed a chaplain to the 131st (Surrey) Infantry Brigade of the 44th (Home Counties) Division, with attachment to the 5th Battalion, the East Surrey Regiment. The battalions of the brigade were scattered, and it was not possible to give the same close attention to the work as I was able to do in South Wales. I was able, however, to attend the annual camps which were held at Dover, Worthing, New Forest and Arundel. I think that I enjoyed the Dover camp most of all because I was able to have a horse and there was the added interest of the castle and the troops stationed there. At Arundel the Duke of Norfolk gave us every facility and entertained the officers. These camps were rich in fellowship with the other chaplains of the division.

After five years with the Home Counties Division I was transferred to the 47th (Second London) Division, and I served with the various battalions of this division until my transfer to the Army Reserve of officers in 1935.

My last camp, on the active list, was at Myrtle Grove, Worthing, where I served the 140th Brigade, and was attached to the Artists Rifles. Here I had the valued companionship of the present Right Rev and Right Hon Dr H.C. Montgomery-Campbell, the present Bishop of London. Dr Campbell was the senior chaplain of the division. It is a pleasure to me that I am still associated with him on the executive of the Public Morality Council, of which he is the chairman. These camps proved of the greatest importance to the chaplains, for we were able to get to know the officers and men intimately, sharing in route marches, field days, sports, as well as our usual religious services and welfare work for the men.

One feature of the life of a Territorial chaplain, which proved of great interest and help, was the conference we held each year at the Horse Guards Parade, when we were addressed by army generals and commanding the districts and divisions. Each year, too, the War Office took the High Leigh Mansion at Hoddesden, when all the chaplains met in fellowship for three days. The chaplain general joined us on these occasions and we had visiting bishops and other leaders of the church, also army commanders from time to time, to talk to us. Each morning and evening we joined in Holy Communion and evening prayers in the lovely chapel. We then had discussion groups and sing-songs in the lounge after dinner. Many too were the rambles we had in the charming countryside – unforgettable experiences to all of us.

The crowning joy and honour which I experienced was my invitation to the Levee at St James' Palace where the Minister for War duly represented me to King George V. I had met the King during my Windsor days so I was delighted to have the opportunity of taking part in one of the most colourful ceremonies in the land. The date was 1st June 1931, and I had full instructions sent to me of the part I had to play, and how I should be dressed. I went in uniform and I took particular care that I was properly dressed. The pageantry of it all impressed me. When I arrived at the ante-chamber I found it full of ambassadors, generals, officers of all ranks, and I looked round to see if there were any other chaplains but, apart from the chaplain general, I seemed to be the only one that day. When I entered I felt the coldness of the atmosphere – there were no greetings, no conversation. It seemed as if everyone was so keyed up and nervous that all the warmth of human companionship had vanished. Suddenly I broke the silence – it takes a Yorkshireman to do this – and I called out, "Cheer up, gentlemen, we are not going to an execution." That did the trick. A Guards officer laughed so much the he dropped his invitation card. He could not bend down to pick it up owing to the tightness of his trousers, so he whipped out his sword and used it, as a park-keeper does, to pick up the piece of paper. Anyhow, the silence was broken and the coolness disappeared, and we all began to laugh and talk. The transformation in that ante-room was indescribable.

The time came for the ceremony of the presentation. We were ushered by column into another room and there we were all inspected by a court official to see if we were properly dressed, and then one by one we entered the 'Presence'. King George, dressed in uniform, was on a dais, surrounded by his sons – the Prince of Wales, the Dukes of Gloucester and Kent, the chief of the Imperial General Staff, army commanders and officials. My turn came, my name was called, and in a moment I was in the spotlight opposite the King. All eyes were on me, and seemed to be watching my every movement. I made my bow, noticed a smile of welcome from the King, and gracefully backed out. Was I nervous? No! I thoroughly enjoyed it all. This ancient ceremony and pageantry appealed to me. I descended the red-carpeted stairs, where the Gentlemen-at-Arms were standing on each side. My companion was a Peer of the Realm, whose name I have forgotten. On reaching the entrance he asked the footman to call for his Rolls-Royce car; it glided to the door, he entered it and departed. I had no Rolls-Royce for the footman to call. I had travelled to Trafalgar Square by the No.29 bus from Holloway, which in those days was a sixpenny journey. I walked to the palace to and from the square and returned home by the same bus. My total out-of-pocket expenses amounted to one shilling – so ended my perfect day. I made the most of it, and the thrill of the experience remains. How little we know the issue to which our steps are leading, or the strange turnings that surprise us in life. I never thought that, when as a lad I saw Queen Victoria in Sheffield, I should ever go to the King's Levee.

On 10th October 1941, I reached the age of sixty, and retired from the army. I received a letter from the headquarters of the London District, expressing the chaplain general's deepest and warmest thanks for my work as a chaplain to HM Forces, and stating, what of course I knew and regretted, for who does not regret the passing of years – that on 10th October I should reach the age limit, and that the notice of this would shortly appear in the *London Gazette*. I was, however, to retain my rank as a chaplain to HM Forces and wear the uniform on permitted occasions – all this and a final note of gratitude.

I renewed my fellowship with the Chaplains' Department in 1957, when I was present at the annual dinner held at the United Service Club. This was attended by the chaplain general, the Minister for War, the chief of the Imperial General Staff and members of the Army Council. Our chief guest was HRH Prince Philip, the Duke of Edinburgh. I sat almost opposite him at the dinner table, and he remembered meeting me at the Windyridge Farm for delinquent boys, run by the Whitechapel Mission, and which he opened. He was also interested in my work, and my war service, especially when I was the senior chaplain of the Naval Division – the old names of Hawke, Drake and Hood appealed to him.

There is one thing that has given me great pleasure and kept me in touch with the services: for over twenty-five years I have been a member of the Royal Navy, Army and Royal Air Force Board, and at the time of writing I have been re-elected for another three years. By then I shall have reached the age of eighty. This Board deals with the appointment of chaplains, the care of soldiers' homes and welfare work, in the three services.

When the Second Great War took place I was too old for active service abroad, so I was appointed officiating chaplain to the 910 Squadron of the RAF Balloon

Command. My area was from London Bridge to Dagenham, including Dockland, and the barges with balloons flying from them, and situated on the Thames, at Woolwich – some eighty-one units in the most vulnerable and dangerous part of London. My headquarters were in East Ham and the group commander gave me the use of a motorcycle and side-car, and a driver. This made it easy for me to visit the balloon units in isolated positions. I visited them at all hours of the day and night and often shared meals with the men. I was always warmly welcomed, especially during the night. The group commander said that these night visits helped to keep up the men's morale. I am afraid, at times, when the bombers were over in strength, that mine suffered. I loved to visit the balloon barges on the Thames. In these there were splendid recreation rooms and the men were happy, even if they suffered at times from isolation. I had also the opportunity of visiting the gunboats with the ack-ack guns.

I had many strange adventures, and also escapes, from death. One night, for example, I was thirty yards nearer to a bomb which dropped than another man, yet I escaped and he was killed. The blast missed me, but he got the full force of it. The weekend of 7th September and 8th 1940, when the Germans wrought such havoc in the docks, was the most terrifying. They came over in waves – the warehouses, ships, balloons, all went up in flames and the destruction was indescribable. How one escaped the holocaust is a mystery. I saw many places come down in flames. Sunday the 8th was just as bad as the previous day, and I was thrilled to see our fighter planes in action. I was reminded of the old song: 'White wings, they never grow weary'. Those white wings were in the sky all the day; you could see them chasing the German planes and bringing them down.

That night, I was determined to go to Slough to visit my wife and children. I had bought a house for them in that town – safer than London, and yet not too safe, as subsequent events proved. I got on a bus at East Ham and reached Stepney when the siren sounded and almost immediately the bombers were over. I tried to find shelter in the vaults underneath a church, but it was packed to suffocation with people. I went outside and heard the scream of a bomb and dived behind a tombstone, falling into a grave which had sunk a few feet. In the background the docks were blazing. I little thought at the time that a short distance away a bomb had fallen on the Manse of a ministerial friend of mine in Stepney, The Rev W.R. Gilbert, killing him and the two deaconesses of the mission who were with him – I only heard of this the next day. There was a short lull and I went out into Commercial Road and there was the bus I had come in. The driver came up and said, "Who will drive with me through this hell?" I replied, "I will." I got in, the only passenger, and strange to say, a terrified dog. How he managed to drive his bus through the chaos of that road I know not. The bombers were over again, but still he went on – through Aldgate and the city, on to the Strand. There he stopped and said, "I am not going any further." I got out and wished him goodnight, and proceeded to walk from the Strand to Paddington Station – a walk I shall never forget. Arriving at Paddington I took shelter for a time in the fire station. There was a train going to Slough, I was told, when the bombing permitted. I waited and at last got into the train, and we pulled out. There was a woman in my carriage and she was in a highly nervous state. I was not much better after dodging bombs during my walk – and a long walk too. Again the bombs were falling and some had straddled the line a little distance from the station. The train stopped suddenly and the woman fell onto the floor, and I fell with her. What was happening on the line we did not know, but there were men at work – at work in the midst of so much danger. It seemed hours before the train proceeded. We were in darkness all the time and the woman – whom I never saw in the light and never knew who she was – seemed absolutely dazed. We reached Slough at 1am. I got out and fell over a pile of mail bags and sprained my wrist and arrived at my home with a blackened face. My wife was in bed, but she soon got up and I am afraid she had a shock when she saw me and a still greater shock when I told her of all I had gone through during the night of that terrible Sunday.

I lived alone in Central Park Road, East Ham, and my windows were shattered during that weekend. I slept on the floor under a table, over which I had placed a mattress. I had piled my books around this makeshift dugout, and rested my often weary limbs on another mattress under the table. This saved my life on 15th November of the same year, when a landmine came down and wrecked the house. The time was 4am. The bombing had been very heavy throughout the night and one street off my road had been totally destroyed and many people killed. I had been out helping all I could. There were scores of terrified people but the rescuers were soon on the spot. I had gone home to lie down for a time when destruction came to me. The rescue team were soon in my house and pulled me from under the table. I suffered from shock and a few cuts.

I never undressed in those days, and when I wanted a rest and change I went over to Slough for the night, but always returned by 6am train to East Ham. I remember one night a bomb fell in the garden of the house opposite mine. I went over to see if the woman, who lived there, was safe. I found her in bed with the ceiling on her. Her mouth was full of plaster and she could not speak until I cleaned it out. She got up and came downstairs and after a cup of tea, which I prepared, she said, "I shall do my ironing. I'm not going to let Hitler stop my work." That was at 3am and she got to work. Nothing could daunt these women in the Dockland area. They were as steadfast as rocks and a striking example to all that is best in life.

It was my sorrowful task to bury whole families of those who had been killed, and in the same grave. I remember one such family. The daughter, a very attractive girl, had been to a meeting that I had addressed. I left her at the gate and she went into the house to join her father, a schoolmaster, her mother and her brother. The siren had just gone and I had reached the bottom of the street when a bomb fell on the house and totally destroyed it. I buried all four of them in the same grave in the City of London Cemetery.

All through those long weary years I moved about amongst the people, as well as visiting all my balloon sites in Woolwich, Becton Gas Works and along the riverside to Dagenham. I had passed my examinations for Civil Defence, and this was of great value. I spent a lot of time with the old people in their Anderson shelters.

One could write a whole book on these experiences. They were days of stress but the heroism of the people of Dockland will live on through the ages.

25

With the Coal Miners

In my study I have four miner's lamps. One is the original Humphrey Davy Lamp and greatly prized. I suppose that many museums would be glad to have it. If this old lamp could only speak and tell the story of over one hundred and fifty years ago! The other three were given to me in South Wales. I prize them highly; they fill my mind with thoughts which lie too deep for tears. The gleams from these lamps have guided the feet and shed their light on the pathway and workings of many heroic men in the thick darkness of the mines. They are kindly gleams, safety gleams, without which no man could labour. I look at these lamps in my London study and my thoughts are far, far away, sometimes in the West Riding coalfield, sometimes in the South Wales coalfield, sometimes in Scotland, and in the Nottinghamshire and Derbyshire coalfield where all the eleven churches I served for some years were attended by the miners and their families. Just now I fancy I can hear an old hymn: 'Lead kindly light, amid the encircling gloom'. How those miners could sing that hymn. They sang it in the bowels of the earth, sang it in their churches, and always over the grave of a comrade. The little gleam of the lamp they carry often reminds them of the infinite Light, which lightest every man and in Whom is no darkness.

My old Davy Lamp speaks to me of its inventor. Born in 1778, the year 1815 proved to be the most memorable one in his history for before its close he had completed the invention of this lamp, and on 9th January 1816, history tells us that Parson Hodgson, a tough Tyneside vicar, went down a pit carrying with him a strange but simple new device – a lamp in which a flame burned behind a gauze protection. One miner swore when he saw the parson coming with his lamp, but like thousands of others lived to bless him. I presented a beautiful brass lamp to the Wesley College, Cambridge, so that the students could remember the many thousands of men who toil in the darkness of the bowels of the earth for us, and of the many who have died in doing so. There it stands in the lovely College Chapel. It speaks of the dignity of toil and of heroism.

I was brought up in the West Riding coalfield, and in my boyhood days I was strangely fascinated and deeply impressed with my surroundings. I was glad that I was called to serve for eleven years of my ministry in these various coal-mining districts. Whilst in Scotland I was always impressed with the experiences of Dr Alexander Irvine, who lived in the same area in which I also served. He has told me something of what he terms 'my schooldays in the underworld'. In his childhood he was hedged about with three of the worst limitations a child can have: hunger, dirt and ignorance. As an offset to this, he had a few things of priceless value: a good mother, a sense of humour, and a romantic bent of mind that could transform defeat or disaster into victory. When he was about fifteen years of age Scotland became to him the new Promised Land. There he was told he could escape from poverty and ignorance, so to Scotland he went. The British Army and the coal pits of Scotland were the ever-open doors, in those days, to three square meals a day. He got into the coal pits, but the meals were not so 'square' as he had anticipated. The pay was small, and the hours long – twelve. At first his wages were a shilling a day, "but then," he says, "I wasn't a miner, but merely a rehearsal for one, or a miner's mucker." Just when he was sick of soul and discouraged in mind he met with Henry Drummond, and all things became new. A new hope – a new determination. Something of Drummond's wonderful personality attached itself to him, and he began to fight for light. Drummond advised him to leave the pits at once. He did so, and in rags and dirt he went to Glasgow. Hungry, cold, wet and workless – "Yet aflame with the touch of Drummond," he says, "I walked on air. I owe more to contact with the great personalities than to schools and colleges. The only education worth having is an educated understanding." He suffered much in those coal-mining days – in mind, body and soul – but he knew those experiences were processes through which the soul finds itself. They never embittered him, and when he had shouldered his way out of the 'underworld', as he calls it, he never lost his sympathy with those he left behind. "I have worked," he said, "as hard as any man living, but no gulf divides me from them now when I find myself in another atmosphere."

The miners in Scotland are very dour, and there are many Poles amongst them. I got to know them well, especially their wives and children – the latter filled our Sunday School. I tried to bring all the brightness I could into their drab lives. It is over fifty years since I laboured amongst them. Harry Lauder knew them too, for he lived in Hamilton, and I knew him as a young man who used to sing at our concerts and who, I remember, once said in one of our soirees that there were three things he owed the most to in his life: the first was God; the second, his wife; the third, a kindly neighbour over the garden wall. I heard him at his final appearance on the stage in London. He was then getting, I think, one thousand pounds a week for his songs. As I gazed upon that little figure with his crooked stick and smile, and listened to that moving voice as he sang the old songs, I thought of the days of long ago and all that he meant to us in Scotland.

He sang that night 'Keep right on to the end of the road', and then a thousand voices in the theatre joined in that great human longing with him about the end:

> Where all you've loved and been waiting for
> Will be there, at the end of the road.

He had reached the end, as we all shall in God's good time.

From the coal miners in Scotland to those in South Wales, there seemed to me to be a big contrast, but I am glad that I had the experience. I can see a mountain village in the valley. It is surrounded by the eternal hills, nature's sentinels. If you follow one of the rugged pathways to the top of the ranges, a scene of wild beauty presents itself. Far away in the distance is the sea, almost at your feet, the valley. Ah! This valley. Let your eye follow its course, mining villages and towns, huge chimney stacks, engine houses and the surface machinery of the mines. There is a railway running through it and a long, white, winding road. It is very fascinating to stand there and give the imagination play. There is a graveyard in the centre of this valley. It is rapidly filling up and many are the processions to it. That winding road is often full of mourners, for the people die young in this valley and 'women are weeping and wringing their hands' – 'dead for bread'.

I have stood there at night and seen the myriad of twinkling lights, and round the lamp room are the men of the night shift with their lamps. You can mark their pathway to the cages where they wait to descend, and hear the throb of the drum as the steel ropes unwind, lowering the cages with the men down the shafts. In former years, when winter came, these men never saw the light of day until Sunday.

It was gleams from their friendly lamps, yes, from the very lamps over my study fireplace, which made them think of the best of all days in seven, and on the Sabbath morning they sang in Ebenezer with great fervour and yearning:

> This is the day of light;
> Let there be light today.
> O Day-spring, rise upon our night,
> And chase its gloom away.

I lived in a new miner's cottage in the Ely Valley, the total cost of rent, including all rates, being eleven shillings and two pence a week. I was the first to live in this house. It had a large garden and was virgin soil. Anyhow, I used a pick to dig it up and it seemed to produce nothing but rocks. I eventually gave it up in despair and had some splendid chicken runs instead. There was a gorgeous view of hillside and gorse from the back windows. Alas, when the rains came the house was flooded. One Sunday night when a ministerial friend from London was staying with me, all the ground floors were one-foot deep in water, and he helped me sweep it away and clean out the mud.

I was glad to live with the miners, and under the same conditions. We became very friendly and were real neighbours, especially on washing days when surveying the clothes lines stretched across every garden and full of the fruit of the washtub. Many were the conversations we had over the fence and we had plenty of callers asking for the loan of matches, stamps, writing paper, bread or any articles they were short of. There I found out the truth of the saying commonly used in the industrial and densely populated areas – 'it's the poor that helps the poor'. We did not lack any friends among the miners. They would help one to carry in a load of coals from the road and in fact help with anything.

To get nearer to the men I became chairman of the British Legion. There were a great number of ex-servicemen and we had a new headquarters built. I presided at all the meetings of the legion and helped those who were in need and there were many such cases, especially during the great strike which covered the whole of the coalfield.

During my service in the First Great War I decided that if I was spared to return home I would build a church in memory of those who have made the great sacrifice, and this I was able to do. I named it St George's. It was the only church erected as a war memorial in Glamorgan and is the 'Church of the Lamp' – the lamp of sacrifice and light.

We are all familiar with the Toc H founded by Tubby Clayton of Poperinghe fame. Padre Clayton was a fellow chaplain with me, and there is nothing more impressive than the yearly ceremony when the lamps of the new branches are lighted. The significance of the ceremony lies in the fact that it represents the spirit of light and love and brotherhood throughout the history of mankind, exemplified by rich and poor fraternising in the comradeship of mutual service. When the lamps are lighted there is a silence of twenty seconds, and a solemn vow is made to keep the light kindles by Him who is 'The Light of the World' and rekindled by those who died in the cause of Freedom, Love, Peace and Brotherhood, throughout the ages and in the Great War. As each lamp is lighted there is pronounced that moving and exquisite memorial prayer: 'They shall not grow old as we who are left grow old; age shall not weary them not the years condemn; at the going down of the sun and in the morning we will remember them'.

This 'Church of the Lamp' does not owe its origin to Toc H, but the idea is the same. How could the building of this church be accomplished? I knew not, but the God-given opportunity came, and the proposal to build such a church captured the imagination and moved the souls of our people in those mining valleys. One day we met on the hillside with the estate agent. "I want this site," I said, "to build upon it a war memorial church." He looked amazed, for I had chosen a magnificent corner site covering about one acre. "Do you want to have a cathedral surrounded by a graveyard?" he asked. "You have big ideas." Then I pointed to the east and west, north and south. "Here," I said, "I can build a church which will be a beacon to all, a continual reminder to successive generations of Him who said, 'Greater love hath no man than this, that a man lay down his life for his friends.'" As I spoke to him of the sacrifices of these men of the lamp he was deeply moved and from that moment I secured his whole-hearted sympathy. The land became ours for the nominal sum, and along with it the whole of the stone we needed, without cost. The agent has since passed away; he died suddenly one evening while sitting in his chair, but we live to bless his memory.

I laid the foundation stone with the words on it:

Their name liveth for ever more.

Mr G.E. Llewellyn, the agent, along with many others, laid a foundation stone. Many friends gave me donations to pay for the cost, but most of all I remember the unexampled generosity of some of those miners who loved the House of God. In the days of stress and anxiety which followed, they were to me 'the shadow of a great rock in a weary land'. Without them I should have despaired. They had hearts of gold, and I knew those hearts best in love for men. One came in with a gift of twenty-five pounds, others with five, and the miner's children with their pounds. Oh! The sacrifice, for times were hard and many had been unemployed for long periods. It was this wonderful spirit which made it possible for me to move the hearts of the wealthy to give, and the appeal was never made in vain.

I wished the opening of St George's to be worthy of the occasion. A month before the event I called at the Cardiff Civic Hall to see the Lord Mayor. A council meeting was being held, and by a strange coincidence there was a discussion on the debt of the city to the mining valleys. It was a profitable discussion in many more ways than one. At the close of the session I told the Mayor that I wished him to come and preside at the opening ceremony in connection with my new church. He was sympathetic, but replied, "I do not think it is possible, because it would establish a precedent for a Lord Mayor to leave the city boundaries during his year of office for any such event." I reminded him of his own speech in the council chamber that afternoon and said, "Here is an opportunity of practising what you have been preaching. You have admitted that your city depends for its prosperity entirely on the mining valleys. It is for you, as Mayor, to show your practical appreciation and establish a precedent? What does the strict letter of custom matter?" Anyhow, I persuaded him, and he came in his chain of office along with a distinguished company of gentlemen to honour us. Never was there such a day in the Ely Valley: the streets were decorated, the procession with bands and all kinds of public officials, organisations and churches was a mile in length and the church was crowded in every part. My friend, The Rev George Standing CBE DSO MC, the assistant chaplain general, gave a moving and appropriate sermon from the text: 'What mean ye by these stones?'

Another story, again of church building for the benefit of the mining community, is a striking proof of the fact that if you win the co-operation of the people, you can safely sing: 'Something accomplished, something done'. Opposite the principal colliery in the Ely Valley is 'The Little Church on the Hill'. It is known by this title far and near. The village where it stands had been erected for twelve years and yet no denomination had considered its spiritual needs. The people were 'as sheep having no shepherd'. I could never understand why this mining community should have been so long neglected. One day we 'viewed the landscape o'er'. From our observation post on the mountain path we could see the winding valley, the huge slag heaps, the three mineshafts, brickworks and by-product plant, and this cluster of houses forming, as it did, a very compact village, and we cried out, "Yonder village is ours!" And ours it became, so we began to consider ways and means. There was one freehold site for sale and so we consulted the solicitors and almost arranged to purchase it. I said 'almost', but the land was owned by the ecclesiastical commissioners of the disestablished church in Wales, and whether this august body objected to the Methodists owning the land to erect a church on it for the salvation of the village, I know not; the fact remains that when we sent in a sketch of the proposed structure we were politely but firmly refused the land. What a difference a friendly gleam would have made to us in those days. Anyhow, we secured a far better site on the hillside, and it has become a beacon of light ever since.

Several people were very pessimistic about this new venture. We had no members and no money. My faith, however, laughed at impossibilities, and to make a start, I had a sod-cutting ceremony and had the help of a brass band. This attracted a curious crowd, and the proposed new church became a constant source of discussion in the mines and elsewhere. On the day before the foundation stone laying ceremony I must confess that I was down in the dumps because no promises had come in, but on the actual morning the first letter I opened contained fifty guineas, the second ten, and at the close of the day I could announce a total of one hundred and twenty pounds. The letters I received were very encouraging and proved a real tonic. The opening ceremony was a red letter day in the history of the village and six months afterwards we had sixty members and a good Sunday School.

This 'Little Church on the Hill' completely transformed the life of the village, and it is the one and only centre for both religious and social activity. At the first Sunday School Anniversary the long procession of children through the streets was an eye-opener to those who had prophesied failure, and the first outing to the seaside saw a long string of motor buses taking nearly the whole of the inhabitants. The building was a blessing in other respects. It became a day school, run by the Glamorgan Education Authority, and it was also used for recreations, and soon the total cost was raised. I had two good football teams – one in Tonyrefail and the other in Coedely – and through my efforts land was secured for a recreation ground for all kinds of games, and it is now a park run by the local council.

I could tell many more stories of South Wales – of the day I carried the coffin of a miner's child some four miles up the mountainside to lay the little one at rest in the churchyard; of the bigamy case I helped to defend for a couple at the Swansea High Court; of the man who came to commit suicide on my doorstep at four o'clock one morning and of how I saved him – not only from death, but from imprisonment. All this and much more for any man worth his salt will do his best to help those amongst whom he lives and works.

My work amongst the Nottinghamshire coal miners came later on. As a kind of interlude after the London 'blitz', I took my wife and children into the country. The doctor had ordered me to do this to build up their health, and mine also, after the shock and privation we had suffered through the bombing. I served the mining community of Sutton and Kirkby-in-Ashfield, Newstead, Stanton Hill, eHuthwaite and Tibshelf. The work was similar to that I did in Scotland and South Wales, apart from church building. I lived among the people and, like the Prophet of old, 'sat where they sat'. Here too I served the British Legion, ministered to the local troops, married, buried and baptised. I was also the chaplain to the Newstead Sanatorium, and found plenty to do. Again I am glad that I had the privilege of working amongst the coal miners.

26

Soap-Box Orator (Hyde Park)

Foreword

T.E. Lawrence, after his legendary years among the tribes of Arabia, found it difficult to settle back into life in England. He'd endured so much, pushed himself to the very edge of his energy and considerable ability – and everything now seemed so tame. Partly to compensate for this duller life, he took to riding his motorbike around the roads of Dorset – unprotected and at full speed. It was as if he needed the wind on his face and the thrill of the chase to satisfy an inner craving for excitement, danger and self-sacrifice. He died tragically young whilst taking one bend too many at suicidal speed.

Michel Foucault, French philosopher of the late 20th century, turned this human craving for self-trial into what he called 'the limit experience'. Only when we push ourselves to the very edge of our possibilities, he argued, do we really discover who we are. Our 'default position', as human beings, is to settle for a comfortable and undemanding lifestyle, both petty and bourgeois. We should all, at some stage, be more adventurous. In his case, he sought to implement this idea by pushing at the limits of sexual experimentation. He died of AIDS.

So what exactly does a preacher do to push himself beyond the safe confines of his job? He's accustomed to plying his wares to a captive audience who sit quietly and politely in front of him in serried ranks. He stands six feet above contradiction – accustomed to hearing his own voice, unprepared for any contestation. What if that preacher has spent 10 years of his life on the battlefields of Europe? What if he's walked through the valley of the shadow of death; if death has been as close to him as his own shadow, what then? How can he now content himself with the strutting and fretting of a mundane existence? How can he settle for life, with its dull routines and repetitive duties, after such close contact with the sound and fury of war? George Kendall was faced by just such a barrage of questions. Throughout the inter-war years, he maintained a direct relationship with the army – serving mainly as chaplain in Wales, Surrey and London. Somehow, he also settled back into the day-to-day life of a Methodist minister.

During the Second World War, one of the ways he kept his raging spirit alive was to pitch his ideas into the open marketplace. Speakers' Corner at Hyde Park is to London what Mars Hill was to ancient Athens. Anyone with something to say could set out his stall and attempt to woo, win, convince or convert the ragbag of people who turned up – and he would certainly risk being booed, heckled, rejected and laughed out of court. All this while London suffered under constant attacks from V1 and V2 flying bombs – one of which actually landed at the corner. It must have felt just like riding a motorbike at 100mph, or blowing your mind with the drug of human interaction.

This chapter in the story of this remarkable man sees him in the arena of unqualified utterance; it shows him facing the public speaker's ultimate risk. His account captures perfectly the raw humour, the constant bustle, the risqué and the risky, the banter and the fun, the hostility and the bondings that are part and parcel of speaking in the open air. I stood at Speakers' Corner for some years and found it invigorating. My daughter cried when she heard the crowd shouting at her daddy, but I loved it. I rejoiced at the opportunity to commend something I was passionate about in an environment where the market would decide the value of what I was peddling. It was a mixture of Vanity Fair and fairground frolic. I can imagine George Kendall now, standing amidst the heaving crowd, claiming their attention with his equivalent of 'Roll up, roll up, roll up for all the fun of the fair'. He's thrown down the challenge and must now face his ordeal. Let him now tell us in his own words just how he got on.

The Rev Lord Leslie Griffiths
Superintendent, Wesley's Chapel, London

I acquired a love for open-air preaching in the early days of my ministry, in Lincolnshire, Scotland, and Windsor, and even more particularly in London. During my long years of service in the army I had an open-air pulpit in fields and woods as well as on the parade ground. North Northcliffe used to say to his staff, "Go out and find what the man in the street is thinking about." This is the best of all advice for journalists, and more especially for parsons, yet alas! So few take advantage of it.

I returned to London in the year 1926 and I was asked by the late Dr Winnington-Ingram, who was then the Bishop of London, to be chairman at Marble Arch, Hyde Park, of his Public Morality Platform, and for thirty years I served him, and his successors, Dr Fisher, now the Archbishop of Canterbury, and Dr Wand, now a canon of St Paul's Cathedral. What a strange fascination London has for us! I have heard it described as 'The City of Dreadful Delight', so mysterious, so overwhelming, so immense. It is the heart of the world, where all tides of human movement meet and mingle. Wherever you go the sound which fascinates and haunts you is the rumble of the tremendous human mill. David Grayson's description of the city with which he came to grapple, after his adventurous way along the sweet, dear, friendly road of the country, is true of London – 'All about on the streets, in the buildings, under ground and above ground, men are walking, running, creeping, crawling, climbing, lifting, digging, driving, buying, selling, sweating, swearing, praying, loving, hating, struggling, failing, sinning, repenting – all working and living according to a vast harmony, which sometimes we can catch clearly and sometimes miss entirely'.

There are various centres where great crowds gather and the most important is at Marble Arch. All roads lead to it – where 'every prospect pleases, and only man is vile'. It has become notorious in more senses than one. To one corner of it crowds are drawn as if by a magnet. It is the strangest corner in London, and stands at the north-east, facing the famous Marble Arch, and within view of Park Lane, the home of millionaires. In the time of Henry VIII, we are told it was the 'rendezvous of fashion and beauty', and in the seventeenth and eighteenth centuries a favourite meeting place of duellists. At Marble Arch stood the gallows of Tyburn.

Duels are still fought at this corner – stern and bitter, but not with pistols and swords, but words. If you want to know what men and women are saying about the great topics of the day go to Hyde Park. Say what you will about the tomfoolery by which you are surrounded on all sides, the speaker, call him soap-box orator, tub-thumper, or anything you like, if he has something of interest to say he has the world for his audience. Men and women, influenced by what is said and, for good or ill, are going to carry the thoughts that have impressed them, to the ends of the earth, listen there. I have had in my audience from time to time, students from India, Pakistan, Turkey, Persia, Japan, Africa, the West Indies, Germany, France, Spain, the USA and other countries. Many of them have had their notebooks out. I have had Peers of the Realm and Members of Parliament, Cabinet Ministers, actors and journalists. On one occasion I noticed the late Lord Allenby, on another Field Marshal Robertson, Sir James Jeans, Bernard Shaw and Sir Oliver Lodge. One night, when dusk was falling, I saw the familiar face of the Prince of Wales, now the Duke of Windsor. One surprise I had was to see two Roman Catholic archbishops from Spain accompanied by the Spanish ambassador. They stayed all the time I was speaking, simply because questions had been asked about General Franco, and his influence on Spanish life. I was afterwards invited to go and dine with them at the Embassy, but had regretfully to decline.

The unexpected often happens! You never know what you are going to hear or see, or are going to meet, in Hyde Park. I have met men I served with in Salonica, France, Belgium and Germany, South Wales miners and men and women from the provinces. One night a well-dressed young fellow stepped up to me and said, "The last time I met you was in Pentonville Prison." He had just finished a term of two years and was present at a service I had conducted in the prison. I often used to say that if you want to find your long-lost husband or wife, your wandering son or daughter, or even your creditor, go to Marble Arch.

What is the fascination, the strange drawing power of this famous corner? Nowhere will you find such a weird collection of scholars, patriots, revolutionaries, saints, freaks, cranks, oddities, lunatics and comedians. Some have called it a non-stop simultaneous show but it certainly is a modern babel. So long as you obey the park regulations, anyone can speak there, either on a platform, soap-box, chair or standing on the ground. There is no place in the world where such freedom of speech is allowed. Think of some of the platforms – I have counted as many as forty. You will find the Catholic Evidence Guild, the West London Mission, Open-Air Mission, the Latter Day Saints (Mormon), the Church Army and Salvation Army, the House of Israel, the Protestant Truth Society, the London Mission, the Pillar of Fire Church, Seventh Day Adventists, tramp preachers, the Divorce Reform Society, Islam, the Secular Society, the Public Morality Council, several religious groups, anti-socialist and socialist, conservative, as well as individual platforms demanding a redress of some grievance and some simply for amusement.

I always liked Mr Bonar Thompson, whose line was cynicism, chaff and ridicule. He wore a lop-eared black hat and a neat suit. He used to give stump speeches of famous men. I was always amused when with his soft, but pleasant, voice and captivating smile, he used to expound his views on civilisation. "Is it heading for disaster?" he used to ask. "No," he would reply, "it is doing very well. Look at all those buses going by. They're far too good for the people. Humanity is pampered and petted, a parasite living on the brains of a few people – the thinking few – who are grossly overworked. I need only say that I myself am practically dropping from fatigue." I remember too one of his often quoted jokes about himself which caused a great deal of laughter. "I, myself," he used to say, "never borrow ideas from contemporaries or antiquities, but others take from me. Only the other day I was reading Euripides and found there bits of myself; as for Shakespeare, he is simply full of me!" No one seemed to escape his eagle eye. He was always up to date, quoting from the newspapers and articles he had read.

Then there was 'Charlie' – I knew him well, and like the regulars in the crowds, I could always repeat his addresses. They were chanted like a chorus. When this annoyed him he would say, "Go back to your cheese and maggots. You are the cream of the underworld." This quip was always greeted with loud laughter. "I wrote to the Lord Chancellor," he would say, "and I said if you do not stop these evictions I shall come down with a few of my comrades" – all this would be repeated in unison by the crowd. Charlie was hot on the American debt. "Paying that blood money to America," he used to add – "is the greatest betrayal in history, the worst in our English annals." Then the crowd would finish his peroration – "absolutely immoral and against all Christian ethics." This always annoyed Charlie, and with indignation he used to retort, "You haven't got the brains of guinea pigs." Yes, Charlie was a great attraction to the crowds. I wonder where Charlie is now – his melodious voice is no longer heard?

Then there was the man who professed to know all the secrets of Freemasonry. How the crowd lapped it up! It was the same address every time. At the end he would say, "If you want to know the inner secrets please meet me at the gate" – and there he gave out his pamphlets to those who asked for them, expecting of course, some equivalent contribution. It is a park regulation that no one can sell anything, or advertise books or goods, or solicit money, but many risk this by the invitation to 'meet them at the gate'.

I remember during the period when May meetings were popular and attracted many people from all parts of the country. The so-called 'down and outs', who in reality were the worst lot of blasphemers I have ever met, used to get a platform and talk most movingly of their religious experiences. They looked so pathetic in their tattered suits and broken down boots and their addresses appealed to the visitors, especially the women, who one could hear saying, "Poor boys, they are the servants of the Lord, and we must help them." Once night, as I stood listening to them, I said to one of the women also listening, "Take no notice of such men. They are frauds and only want your money." Turning to me she replied, "You are a parson! You ought to be ashamed of yourself. Why do you not stand on that platform and help them in the Lord's work?" And that is all I got for my warning!

The communist platform was generally surrounded with many excitable hecklers. One speaker was a Church of England clergyman, who shall be nameless, for I was heartily ashamed of him. The speeches bristled with such words as 'capitalism', 'proletariat', 'class consciousness', 'economic determinism', 'syndicalism', and from time to time quotations from Karl Marx, and statistics – oh, marvellous statistics! It says much for the liberty of 'free speech' that this platform can carry on. In many countries this would be impossible.

I remember that one night I took up the cudgels with them, and I quoted the lines:

> Breathes there a man with soul so dead,
> Who never to himself hath said:
> 'This is mine own, my native land.'

One man, enraged at my remarks, took off his coat and wanted to fight me – I suppose 'he was a so-called lover of free speech!' I was not prepared to fight him in spite of his filthy abuse. He then came to my platform to pull me down, when he was touched on the shoulder by 'Pat', a well-known character, and a friend of mine. "Come over to the kiosk," Pat said. Off they went. I suppose he thought that Pat was going to sympathise with him, instead Pat knocked him down, and said, "Take that you red devil, for insulting our Padre." Of course, fighting is against the regulations, but sometimes passions run high. Through the years a good many men have been arrested through a breach of regulations, and I have seen them escorted by the police, usually followed by a curious crowd, to the park police station. Pat was not escorted that night but he was from time to time and on one occasion, he asked me to bail him out.

There were so many interesting characters occupying platforms and airing their views, that one could write a book about them. I was always fascinated by the Indian, lecturing on the transmigration of souls. He tried so hard to convert me to his belief. Then there was the 'Islam' platform. I never questioned the speaker about his nationality. He always held fur-line gloves and wore a raincoat and white turban. He would explain that the Holy Prophet Muhammad taught us to accept all the prophets – Christ, Buddha and others. We could believe in them all, and that should lead us to become a band of brothers. Sometimes he would come to my platform and, in a very courteous manner, ask me questions about the Christian faith.

There was 'Harry', who sometimes wore a clerical collar, and was also a familiar speaker on the Southend-on-Sea Promenade. I remember when he first made his appearance in the park. He used to give a religious address and lead the crowd in the choruses of Sankey's hymns. He was mimicked a good deal by the youths who surrounded him, but he persevered.

The Catholic Evidence Guild always maintained a good platform. Priests and trained young people vigorously advocated, often against much opposition, their faith, whilst Dr Soper, each Sunday afternoon, had the largest crowd in the park, showing himself a past-master in the art of replying to questions. I always felt impressed with the speakers who defended the faith from the Christian Evidence Guild platform. It was there where atheists and rationalists gathered in great numbers and discussion waxed fierce and long.

A favourite platform of mine was that of the Salvation Army – for the downright earnestness, and the wonderful way the major in charge managed the crowd, especially during the singing, captivated me. On several occasions I spoke from this platform.

I myself, before my retirement in 1956, addressed some two thousand five hundred meetings in the park. In this way I became a well-known figure. My first platform was a very high one, and on it I stood above all other speakers. Worked out with rough usage, another one was provided for me by Lady Barlow. One Sunday afternoon, however, a number of American soldiers came to me. They wanted to be photographed by their friends as 'Hyde Park orators'. The competition by these men, and their eagerness, resulted in several crowding onto the platform, which was smashed. The men responsible for the damage made good the platform.

It was always difficult for me to get men to fetch my platform and carry it back to the convent at Bayswater Road, where the kindly Mother Superior allowed me to store it at the bottom of the steps. I could give a man five shillings to make the double journey, and he would promise faithfully to see that this was done. Very often the promise was not kept. The man engaged would bring the platform, and then ask for the five shillings to go and get himself, as he would put it, a meal. He would not return, but one of his pals would come and demand another five shillings to take the platform back. I soon got wise to this trick.

I carried on this work all through the 'blitz' on London. The authorities said it was good for the morale of the people that we should try to carry on as usual. It was rather nerve-racking at times. When the siren went we left the platforms, and with the members of our audience, sheltered either in the Marble Arch underground station, or in the slit trenches, resuming our platforms when the all-clear was sounded. It is astonishing, looking back, to think of how speakers and crowds continued to throng the Marble Arch during those terrible days and nights.

The Public Morality Council, which I served at Speakers' Corner throughout the long years, was formed in the closing year of the nineteenth century, at a time known as the 'Naughty Nineties', when parts of the park were notorious for the immorality practised there, especially the area known as 'the pit'. Bishop Creighton – then the Bishop of London – saw the great need to cleanse the park and the London area, of all the pervading vice which was rampant. Probably he had been impressed by General Booth's book, 'In Darkest England' and the 'Way Out.' In this book were given many stories of the evils of prostitution; of girls who began in the West End, earning big sums of money and finishing in the notorious 'dust-hole' at Woolwich, selling their bodies for a crust of bread.

The council is formed of many representatives of national, religious and social organisations, and has for its objects, the raising of the standards of public morals by advocating obedience to conventional laws and needed reforms based on the common conscience of adherents to religion. The platform of the council is living witness for truth and righteousness, for civic virtue and social purity. It supplies guidance and inspiration as well as warning and exhortation to the youth of the city in this freedom-vaunting age – freedom that is all too apt to become licence. It has a distinctly religious tone and makes a great appeal to all that is noblest in the tradition and deepest in the faith of our nation.

I always maintain that to a speaker who loves his job there are few more thrilling experiences than to stand in front of five hundred or a thousand people in the open air. At the beginning, when you mount the platform and see in front of you a great open space and hear someone shouting from a platform on the right, and another on the left, it is not so delightful, but if you have a good voice, a little humour, you will see the curious passers-by stop, and gradually the crowd collects, especially if the heckler begins his usual tirade against parsons. You cannot resist the pull of the crowd once you get it. There you have the waiting, plastic raw material of humanity.

Carlyle once said:

Let a man but speak forth with genuine earnestness the thought, the emotion, the actual condition of his own heart; and other men – so strangely are we all knit together by the ties of sympathy – must and will give heed to him. In culture, in extent of views, we may stand above the speaker, or below him; but in any case his words, if they are earnest and sincere, will find varieties in outward rank, or inward, as face answers to face, so does the heart of man to man.

This I have found at Hyde Park, and I have found, too, the truth of the saying:

'Ridicule is like a blow with the fist; wit, like the prick of a needle; irony, like the sting of a thorn; and humour, the plastic which heals all the wounds'.

Speakers have to take everything that comes, and as magistrate Paul Bennett VC said once at the Marlborough Street Police Court, when hearing the case of a park offence: "A speaker needs nerves of steel and a hide like a rhinoceros." Again, in speaking of hecklers, he stated that in his opinion, women can beat the men and that often they exhaust themselves in vituperation. One particular woman troubled me for years. It was always difficult for me to stop her once she had started to heckle. I think I managed, at last, to quieten her. I suppose that in all public places, where there are crowds gathered to listen to speakers, you will find the unhealthy, obscene-minded and blasphemous element. Small groups of disreputable, depraved men, and lewd, leering women, go from platform to platform, and mingle with the more respectable people, poisoning the atmosphere, spoiling discussion and the healthy treatment of vital subjects.

I found this element a sore trial. I always wore my clerical collar and to some this seemed like a red rag to a bull. When the serious-minded old timers got to know me well they soon put this down and stood by me, for there are a good many who like to see fair play – reliable and decent citizens. Questions are asked on nearly every subject under the sun. On the Bible, religion, divorce, marriage, prostitution, homosexuality, war, free love, peace, politics, and personal problems. One night a man asked, "Do you believe in the Devil?" Now this man was an atheist who had been a trouble to me; in fact, I was fed up with him. I gave him a quick reply, "Yes, I do, and also in his agents, for you are one of his chief." The crowd cheered, and after that he remained silent. Another night I had a fierce struggle with a gang of unbelievers, until eleven o'clock. I was wedged in and bombarded with terrible questions, interspersed with vile abuse and oaths. Two came to my aid, one a splendid woman and the other a stalwart Irish Roman Catholic. I shall always be grateful to these unknown defenders of the faith.

Often I had questions about the parsons, and especially the bishops and archbishops' stipends. "Do you think," asked one man, "that the Archbishop of Canterbury should be paid ten thousand pounds a year?" I was not sure of the actual payment, but I replied, "Would you like ten thousand pounds a year?"

"Yes, I should," he replied. My reply was swift. "So should I, you fool, shut up." And he promptly shut up.

I persuaded Dr Fisher, the Archbishop, when he was the Bishop of London, to come and speak from my platform one Sunday afternoon, 29th June 1941, and he readily consented. Father Vincent McNabb also spoke for me on this occasion. Dr Fisher's address was on 'The moral health of the community'. I think the crowd was the largest I have ever seen at Speakers' Corner; all the other platforms were deserted. I had informed Scotland Yard of this meeting, and the police came in force to regulate the crowd and to make sure that there were no objectionable incidents.

Amongst the many speakers I have had on my platform are the Bishops of Willesden and Kingston, the Archdeacon of Middlesex, The Rev Joseph Christie SJ, Rabbi Dr A. Melinek, The Rev A.E.D. Clipson, Lieutenant Colonel O'Gorman, Dr R. Cove-Smith, Dr Nathaniel Beattie, Dr H. Davis, and The Rev R.Y. Baldry. I have shared the chairmanship with the late Rev P.W. Shepherd Smith, The Rev A. Jeans Courtney and The Rev William South.

From time to time, other organisations helped me, including the Alliance of Honour, when Mr A.B. Kent provided a splendid team of speakers, whilst Mr George Tomlinson, the secretary of the council, has often stood by my side. The late Father Vincent McNabb was a favourite speaker and he often came and helped me on my platform. He always walked to the park from St Dominic's Priory, Southampton Road, Haverstock Hill. He soared above the commonplace. His religious habit – of course black and white material – thick knitted white stockings, heavy-soled, black, old-fashioned boots, and a battered shapeless soft black felt hat, made him a picturesque figure. He had a keen, lined, ascetic face, with old-style steel rimmed spectacles, and a charming smile which won all hearts. The first time he came he impressed me in a strange way. I felt, as E.A. Siderman says in his book, 'A Saint in Hyde Park', that he was like a true apostle obeying the injunction to 'Go out into the highways and byways', and Siderman, who was Jewish, who I knew so well and who often attended my meetings, gives a true and moving description of this saint, on the occasion of the final meeting we had together. That afternoon he mounted the platform and said that those who spoke from it were doing vital work for the benefit of the community, and that he himself was greatly concerned about moral delinquency and sex licence. He then read the Ten Commandments, slowly and deliberately, one by one, and commented pointedly on them in relation to such matters as marriage and divorce, home life, the care of children, honesty, purity and kindred other subjects. The audience was gripped by his sincerity and intensity. It was the most realistic and practical explanation of the Commandments that I have ever heard.

Later on I arranged a great united demonstration at which Father McNabb, Mr Crook Palmer and myself were the speakers. All the churches were represented that night and the crowd was one of the greatest I have ever seen. Before this meeting the three of us met in a room at the Kingsway Hall, to discuss and make arrangements for the demonstration. After a long conversation of our plans, we knelt in prayer. It was like a real 'upper room' with the same atmosphere as on the Day of Pentecost. Two Methodists and a Catholic priest, praying for the success of this meeting. Is there any wonder that it was such a success?

The last time Father Vincent spoke on earth was on a never to be forgotten Sunday afternoon. He had promised to speak for me and he was, in spite of his health, determined to keep his promise. I little thought that within a few days he would be dead. He walked, as usual, from Haverstock Hill, and as he mounted the platform I could see that he was very ill, so I suggested that he should not speak, but he insisted. His voice was only a whisper, for he was dying of cancer of the throat. The crowd gathered closer to hear every word, and the emotion of those listening was beyond all words. He finished, lifted his hand in blessing and quietly departed to his Priory, never to leave it again.

I was glad to give my closing tribute to him in Siderman's book, and here I quote it:

Thousands have listened to him throughout the years, and especially during the war years;

a common suffering had bound them to him by a thousand ties. He looked towards the Marble Arch – it was past; he looked towards Heaven – it was near. He turned to the people and some were in tears. And then, as his voice, not the stirring voice of old, just a whisper, and the crowd straining their ears to catch every word – gave his final benediction. The silence could almost be felt.

I thought of the lines of Philip Doddridge, a Puritan Divine, who died in 1751 –

> I'll speak the honours of Thy Name
> With my last labouring breath.
> And speechless, clasp Thee in mine arms,
> The antidote of death.

And that is what happened to Father Vincent. He found 'the antidote of death'. Our common humanity will find at Marble Arch a memorial more enduring than brass, whiter than marble, richer than gold. For here was a saint, who had sublime self-restraint with mighty passion, modest without losing self-respect, humble yet without fear to face the cosmopolitan crowd, sometimes hostile but always won by his friendliness. His stature will grow more sublime as glittering errors fade and Truth finds her home.

Another Roman Catholic, who became a great friend of mine, was Father Joseph Christie SJ. He was introduced to me in the first place by Bishop George L. Craven, Bishop Auxiliary of Westminster. I met him at the Travellers' Club, where Lord Colum Crichton-Stuart kindly entertained us for lunch. Father Christie could only give me a few evenings during the season because he was in great demand throughout the country as a lecturer and broadcaster. He was an orator of great power and always attracted a large audience, and was a past-master in the art of answering questions. To my astonishment he told me that his favourite lecture was on John Wesley, as he had a great admiration for the founder of the Methodist Church.

The Rev Arthur E.D. Clipson, the superintendent of the Whitechapel Mission, was another speaker who always attracted a great crowd. The fact that he was in charge of the Windyridge Farm Home, near Colchester, for delinquent boys, and a centre for homeless boys, at Tulse Hill, gave him a subject which was of keen interest and of vital importance.

The Rev R.Y. Baldry, a Church of England clergyman, kindly gave me one night each week, and always proved to be an effective speaker, especially on marriage and divorce, whilst Drs N. Beattie and Cove-Smith from the Alliance of Honour, then under the leadership of Mr A.B. Kent, spoke frequently on various sex subjects and stressed the slogan – 'Chastity before marriage, and fidelity afterwards'. Medical men always attracted a great crowd because they had the note of authority.

The method I adopted was first of all to get the crowd round the platform. This required a lot of tact, patience and good humour. There were a number of regulars who always helped by asking questions. This aroused the curiosity of the passers-by. I would, when a fairly good number had gathered round, give a short address on various problems, and then introduce my speaker, and the meeting would by then be in full swing.

I was often alone, and then I had the meeting entirely in my own hands. I welcomed questions and if I could not give the correct answer I would say so, and add that I would look it up, as a doctor looks up his medical books when he is doubtful about a patient's trouble, and I would promise to give my answer the next night. I found, in my many visits to the park, how lonely London can be for people. One said, "I come into the park because I can always find someone to speak to. In my room I get so sick of my loneliness that I have to talk to myself." I always made a point of trying to be friendly to all and I have talked to many of these lonely souls, especially the aged.

One night, unknown to me, the Transcontinental Film Productions took a photograph of me on my platform. I was so wrapped up in my crowd, that I did not notice the operating camera men. One day, after a service in my church, a member of the congregation said, "You are a film star!" I said I had no knowledge of it, and asked where. She then told me that a film was showing in a cinema in Leicester Square, called 'The Knave of Hearts', and I was in it. I went to see the film, along with my wife. It was the story – a very unsavoury one – of a prodigal youth who had wasted his substance in riotous living with prostitutes and, as is usual, had come to the last dregs of despair. The youth, in the film, wanders into Hyde Park and there he sees me on a platform calling out with appealing hands uplifted, "Seek and Ye shall Find!" and a few other sentences. The photograph and the action were really excellent, but I objected to being put into such a sordid film, without my permission. I wrote at once to the director. In his reply he stated that he would love to see me one day and asked to be permitted to call on me on his next visit to London – he was then going to the USA. That was in 1954, and I have never seen him, nor heard from him since. He had arranged for the distribution of the film in America and would cut out the sequence showing me. I might say that I never received one penny for my part in the film, and I do not know if he fulfilled his promise. He should have had the courtesy to ask if he might use my photograph and my voice, and also he should have offered some payment.

I have often been asked, "Do you do any practical or spiritual good in Hyde Park?" I could tell many stories to prove the value of the work. The chief thing to remember is that you are in direct contact with all kinds of people who, after you come down from the platform bring their troubles and problems, asking for help and guidance. I know some looked upon me as a kind of relieving officer, asking for all kinds of financial help – from a few shillings for a night's lodging, to as much as ten pounds. The latter amount was asked for one night by a man I knew well, and who threatened to commit suicide if he could not get it that night as he was in trouble with the police. There are cases, where separated husbands and wives have been brought together again; where prostitutes have been helped to a new way of life; where wandering boys and girls have been found and returned home. I remember one such boy. He came to me at the close of my meeting. It was ten o'clock and he said that he had nowhere to go. He had been educated at a well-known Public School, and his father was a man in a very good position. This young man had left home, left his job and wandered about the nightclubs of London. He had been in some sordid places – often drunk. He had gambled and lived with prostitutes, and when he had spent all, he had come to his senses. I relieved his present necessity and got in touch with his father and he went home – sadder and wiser. The father and mother were grateful to me for my help.

There was the case of the servant girl from Liverpool. One night this girl stood in front of my platform. I noticed how pale she was, and the look of agony on her face. After my meeting she asked to speak to me. "I am in dreadful trouble," she said, "and I was about to go across to the Serpentine to throw myself in and end it all. I have been seduced by the chauffeur and he has left me to bear my shame alone. I have a very kind mistress and she is anxious to help me. I have been sending my mother ten shillings a week and my mistress says if I can find a home where I can go for my confinement she herself will continue to send my mother the ten shillings and pay my wages, and take me back into her service. Can you help me, sir?" I said, "Yes, I will help you. Go back to your mistress, and you will hear from me tomorrow." I at once got into touch with Miss Mylne, who was the secretary of the London Diocesan Association for Moral Welfare. She had often spoken of her work from my platform. She gladly placed the girl in one of her homes, without any charge, and there the girl remained until her baby was born. The baby was adopted, and the girl returned to her mistress. The mother, in far-off Liverpool, had her ten shillings, as promised. A life was saved, and new hope given to one wandering girl – and there are many such in London. That is my answer to those who think that all the work we did was mere talk. Did we do any real good? The answer is 'Yes'.

Looking back on my work in Hyde Park for the Public Morality Council, I am always grateful for the splendid help given to me by the successive Bishops of London. Both Dr Fisher, the Archbishop, and Dr Wand, his successor, sent me long personal letters of appreciation and thanks when I retired from the work of the council, and Dr Wand, who retired at the same time, kindly sent me a cheque as a personal present. It was so unexpected, and so generous of him.

I cannot help but mention the late Sir Thomas Maloney, the former Lord Chief Justice of Ireland, who was both a vice-president and treasurer of the council. He attended my meetings in the park and gave me every encouragement, financially and otherwise. Then there was the Dowager Lady Nunburnholme, who tried to make my life easier during the bombing of London. I think too of the late Lady Bertha Dawkins, the Lady Cynthia Colville, The Rev J. Schott-Lidgett CH DD, of Lord Colum Crichton-Stuart, Mr and Mrs Thomas Ogden, who from year to year gave great financial help, and my good friend, the secretary, Mr George Tomlinson – all these and many more.

An entirely new phase of my work in Hyde Park took place when Sir Drummond Shiels asked me to become a lecturer for the British Social Hygiene Council. I was asked to lecture on venereal disease. This was because of my wartime experiences, and the work I had already done in trying to combat the disease. The government and the London County Council were both anxious that this subject should be ventilated where big crowds gathered, as at Marble Arch. It is not an easy subject about which to talk under the circumstances, but I gladly three thousand people during one period of six consecutive nights. And that week was one of many others.

My subjects here:

'Sex – Its meaning and dangers'.
'Venereal diseases and their effects'.
'Facts of sex for men and women'.
'Social hygiene in wartime' and so on.

There was a good proportion of doctors and medical students, men from all the services, also girls from the services, and the usual group of sex perverts. Questions were asked, and answered both by myself, and a doctor, sent by the council. Later on this council was absorbed into the Central Council for Health Education, and I was put on their panel of lecturers. I extended the sphere of my open-air lectures to Tower Hill and Lincoln's Inn Fields. Toc H kindly lent me a platform and I went each weekday, during the lunch hour, apart from Saturdays, to Tower Hill, interspersed with occasional lectures at Lincoln's Inn Fields. The advantages I had at these places was the giving out of literature on the subject, supplied free of cost by the council.

The article I wrote for the Central Council for Health Education in October 1944 will give a clear picture of the work I endeavoured to do. It was entitled 'Fresh Air on Venereal Disease':

The venereal diseases, with their immediate effect upon man-power and their terrible legacy for future generations, are no longer to be left shrouded in secrecy, ignorance and neglect. We have brought into the open the discussion of the nature of the diseases, the way they are spread, their war-time prevalence and the urgent need for treatment; but can we not also bring it into the open-air? I think we can and should, and I therefore began an open-air campaign on January 26, 1943, and by August, 1944, lectures had been given on Tower Hill, in Lincoln's Inn Field and Hyde Park. The numbers present have reached as high as 500 at one lecture. The accumulated effect of this propaganda must therefore have been very great, and in the course of the season thousands of people must have been reached.

I found that straight talks upon the venereal diseases and their effects, or upon the meaning and dangers of sex, have proved of most value and that my experiences as an Educational Officer and a Chaplain attached to the Venereal Disease Hospital of the Army on the Rhine, have proved a good background to my talks. Following these lectures, my advice has been sought by many young men and women who, through shame or fear, had hidden the disease; and I have reason to believe that as a result many of them eventually went for treatment.

In speaking in the open air one must use the voice well, be direct in one's utterances, avoid piling on the agony, try to explain as simply as possible the germ origin of the venereal diseases, emphasise the dangers of promiscuous sexual intercourse and so-called sex adventures and, without undue moralising, stress that self-control means self-protection. I most strongly advocate sex instruction of the young by their parents in their early childhood, and by their teachers, clergy and youth leaders later on. In this connection I have given away at these meetings thousands of the excellent booklets issued by the Central Council, and these have done an immense amount of good.

These open-air lectures, addressed as they are to audiences of varied ages and experience, and of several nationalities, always lead to a stimulating discussion. So many ask questions and desire guidance that this is perhaps the most valuable part of the meeting. During these discussions the view is often expressed that further powers of compulsion should be introduced, that congenital syphilis could be avoided if blood-tests were carried out early in every pregnancy, and that a blood test should be made and a clean bill of health obtained before marriage. Questions about brothels always come up, but are easily answered.

The speaker's approach should be based upon an appeal to idealism. It is no good saying, "Don't do this or that." The positive side should be stressed and the ideal of a temperate life advocated. The effects of alcohol should be discussed, and the part it plays in blunting the finer feelings and lessening self-control.

The audience should be urged to keep the mind pure and the body healthy, for a healthy body is the best residence for a healthy mind. Self-respect must be prized as a directing force which promotes the true progress of the individual and the nation. As a parson I find that if I emphasise the sacredness of sex and the value of a godly life, I make a profound impact and the words of Tennyson have been of the utmost value.

> Self-reverence, self-knowledge, self-control. These three alone lead life to sovereign's power.

It was my privilege at the same time to address, along with the late Archbishop Temple, a crowded gathering of doctors from all parts of the kingdom and the USA in the Friends' Meeting House, Euston Road, a conference arranged by the Health Council. Many doctors who specialised in venereal disease also gave addresses and there was a general discussion. This was the climax of my work in connection with the Health Council, and my open-air lectures on venereal disease.

27

My London Service (1926-1944)

I returned to London in 1926, to serve for the next eight years the Caledonian Road Church, now part of the London Central Mission. The first time I met the Duke of Edinburgh he asked me where I laboured. I said, "Sir, in the salubrious area of Caledonian Road." It may have been 'salubrious' in the Victorian period, but it is far from that today. The large houses, once the abode of the rich, are now let out in rooms. There are some huge flats of the former period, known as 'City Mansions', 'Bruce Buildings' and so on. The side streets are mean and the houses dilapidated. Many new blocks of flats are, however, being erected, with all modern conveniences. The main line from King's Cross to the north runs through the road, and to cross the bridge when the engines of the expresses are belching smoke, is not a pleasant experience. To make the area more dismal still there are the warehouses, engineering works, electric power station and all kinds of factories from jam, pickles, tripe, rags and bones, and goodness knows what else. Bellowing cattle and flocks of sheep and herds of pigs were seen being driven through the streets to the slaughterhouses, and to crown it all there is the grim Pentonville Prison, which is no health resort.

All this was a great change from the valleys and hills of Wales. I arrived with my wife, Winnie, who managed us, and who we could never have done without, John Angus (Jack) my first-born son, a baby of sixteen months, and Topsy, our Welsh Terrier. We were kindly received by Dr Eustace Jackson, and Mr Robert Stather, both leading officials of the church, and the ladies kindly provided tea for us.

The Manse was a detached, double-fronted Victorian house with a walled garden at the back, and to cheer us up there was a fine view of the tower of Holloway Prison, which we could see from our bedroom windows. We were overrun with mice, but our cat effectively looked after these, and I expect, was thankful for small mercies. The church itself was a plain square building, with galleries all-round the pleasant interior. It was at the corner of the road leading to the famous Caledonian Market. This market was visited on Tuesdays and Fridays by thousands of people, who got off the bus outside our church or came by the underground railway nearby. I loved this market with its cosmopolitan crowd and stall-holders, and with its astonishing variety of goods, ancient and modern, for sale. It was said that one could buy anything from a pin to an elephant, from precious stones to marbles. There was also a crowd of butchers, fish merchants, greengrocers, soft-goods dealers, and antiques of all descriptions. I loved the piles of books, often heaped on the cobble stones, for many used the old cattle pens as a pitch. You could buy, in those days, hundreds of books for one penny each, and I managed to get, on more than one occasion, first editions for a few coppers. I loved also the picture dealers – pictures of all kinds, and yes! Even old masters. I remember once seeing the whole of a former Lord Mayor of London's pictures for sale – I bought several. One in particular, a lovely little painting of Bow Bells, I got for four shillings, and afterwards when I had to sell some of my pictures, it realised the sum of five pounds.

All that one bought were not the bargains the dealers proudly asserted they were. I recall one Christmas – a man had piles of big chocolate boxes all beautifully bound with red satin ribbon, and this was his patter:

> My dear friends, it is Christmas time and in the spirit of goodwill I have come along to give you a lovely surprise. Here are chocolates made by the best manufacturers, which have cost me a lot. I do not mind, however, the expense. I can afford it, and my one and only object in coming today is to give you a happy Christmas. All I am asking for these superb chocolates is one shilling a box.

Well, they looked a great bargain and the man was brimming over with benevolence and I at once bought two boxes. The huge pile disappeared as if by magic, for his patter had collected a crowd. I went home with my bargain and I said to my wife, "Here are some lovely chocolates for you, my dear, for Christmas."

"Why wait for Christmas?" she asked, "Let us sample them now." I opened one box and oh! What a surprise. I found it full of sawdust with two chocolates on the top. "Are you having a joke with me?" asked my wife. "No," I said, "a man with a spirit of goodwill sold them to me, and about one hundred others. I'll open the other one and see if it is the same." I did. It too was full of sawdust with two chocolates. There is no wonder that the man was anxious to clear his stock quickly, and make his speedy departure. He was not there when I returned in search of him, and there were many angry people anxious to show him another kind of 'goodwill' if they could only lay their hands on him. I got bargains at times, and I got 'done' – to use a colloquial phrase. The regular market people, however, were good to me, and to my church. They often gave goods for my bazaars, and dropped a coin in the collection box by the railings.

The church, Sunday School and the Scouts, Girl Guides and kindred organisations, were all in a thriving condition during this period, a great contrast to what I found fourteen years afterwards, when I returned for a further period of eight years. I had one of the best choirs in London, and a flourishing orchestra which played each Sunday afternoon for the Brotherhood – a movement very popular in those days. I remember that one afternoon Ben Tillett came and addressed a crowded church. During this period, I also introduced to my pulpit many famous preachers, amongst whom were Dr F.B. Meyer, Dr Dinsdale T. Young, Dr Leslie F. Church, Bishop Taylor Smith, Dr Jarvis, who was then the chaplain general, and Mrs Bramwell Booth.

I was honoured on many occasions when the Mayor and Mayoress of Islington, accompanied by the aldermen and councillors, attended a civic service in my church. I think the most notable of these was when Lord Ammon PC DL was the preacher. I have always been grateful for the long years of friendship, and the help I have received from Mr Sydney Walton CBE. On several occasions he has presided over and addressed my gatherings.

The late Mr Edmond Lamplough came along on a few occasions to preside for me. We had a mutual interest in the collection of relics, not only of John Wesley, but Lord Nelson. Mr Lamplough told me one day that I had 'the harvest of a quiet eye'. I think this referred to my love for choice and rare things. I have always had a great interest in antiques in old houses and churches.

I also had a very well attended Woman's Own, which proved to be a great blessing and comfort to many lonely and aged women. The Dowager Lady Nunburnholme kindly came on one occasion, to talk to them, and also other well-known ladies.

Once a year I held a special service for the police, and the church was packed with the men in blue. The police band accompanied the singing and various superintendents and officers of high rank read the lessons. This service always thrilled me and brought back the memory of my own police-officer father, who had died so long ago. The police were very good to me and I sometimes walked with them on the beat. It is a good thing to be well known to the police – not of course, if you are a criminal – and here is a story to prove it. One Sunday a very rich farmer from Australia was staying at the Hyde Park Hotel. He called the manager and asked him if he could tell him where my church was. The manager had not the slightest idea, but he was a sensible man and said, "I will certainly find out for you, sir." He sent for a taxi and told the driver to find out where my church was and drive the farmer to the morning service at eleven o'clock. The London taxi drivers are the best in the world for finding out the places which travellers wish to visit, and this one was no exception. He had no time to look in the Post Office Directory, but he did make a few tentative enquiries for the old farmer, and he found the place he wanted was somewhere in the region of King's Cross. Off he went with his fare. By the time he reached King's Cross it was nearly eleven o'clock, but taxi drivers will tell you that if you want to know the time, or the place, ask a policeman, as the song says. He stopped his taxi near King's Cross and said to the first policeman he saw, "Can you tell me where the Methodist Church is, please?" The policeman at once said, smilingly, "Oh, yes. Take the first turn to the left up Caledonian Road and you will find it at the corner of Market Road, the parson there is Kendall and I go myself to his church." The old farmer arrived, and I noticed him sitting in the back pew. After the service he told me that as a lad he had attended our Sunday School. He had emigrated to Australia and had made his pile, and this was his first visit, since he left, to the Old Country, and he had wanted to worship on his first Sunday morning in the church of his youth. I might add that the collection was well augmented by a substantial note, that morning – a thanks-offering for past mercies.

Experiences of this kind flood my memory. There was the evening when George Dale came to see me. I was a bit suspicious at first, because only a few days before a man of aged appearance and rather pathetic, had called and told me a rather long story of his religious experiences. I thought he had come to me for advice and consolation, as he said that he had been a member of our church in the past – unfortunately for him he mentioned the wrong church – and then came the climax. "Could I help him with a few pounds as he had got into serious difficulties?" I suggested to him that he should go to the church he had named, as I was not the minister of it, and he departed with a crestfallen look. I have, all through my ministry, kept in mind St Paul's words: 'Be not forgetful to entertain strangers; for thereby some have entertained angels unaware'. I am glad that I heeded this advice when George Dale, the stranger called, and that I did not turn him away because of my previous visitor. His appearance impressed me, the word 'gracious' could well describe him, and this was the reason of his visit – His father, bearing the same Christian name, had, before emigrating to Canada, served as a class leader in our church. He had spent the whole afternoon trying to find out where the church was but at last he had been directed to come to me. Now a very strange thing had happened. That very day I had been looking through some old class books and I had noticed the name 'George Dale'. And I at once showed the book to my visitor and asked, "Is this your father's signature?" His eyes filled with tears as with deep emotion he replied, "It is." You say, "What a coincidence!" I reply, "It is the Hand of God." George Dale, the son, was the premier fur trader of Canada, and he had come for the Hudson Bay Company sales, and here he was gazing at his long dead father's signature. He invited me to lunch at his hotel and took me to the Hudson Bay Company's sale – a very interesting experience. He came to all my services whenever he visited London and became an absent member of the church, giving very generous financial help, until he died.

Truth, it is said, is stranger than fiction, and I have seen this proved again and again in my experience of life. I had a similar experience, as the following story will show. He knocked at the door of my Manse one Saturday evening – a stranger, quiet, and with a certain wistfulness that intrigued me. "Could he see me for a short time?" – I was very busy, and I was getting rather tired of callers who put that question and then wanted their railway fare to Liverpool or Manchester, or any journey a good distance off – an old trick to get money. I had had so many during the past week. Anyhow, I asked him in. "I am a kind of tramp preacher," he said, "and I have just returned from a preaching tour in the Near East. I have preached in Germany, Austria, Poland, the Balkans, Greece …" – I don't know where else he had been, but he began pouring out to me the most astonishing experiences. "I am an American preacher from New York," he added. "Here are some letters of introduction."

"What do you want me to do for you?" I asked. "Well," he said. "I want to preach in your church tomorrow night. I must have some London pulpit. I have tried the leading ones, and I have been to all kinds of ministers. I have, however, pleaded in vain. You see I am a stranger, and I have been looked upon with suspicion." So he went on. He was very frank, very insistent, but all the time my impressions of the man were favourable. He had a personality, and there was an elusive quality in his character I could not fathom. I made a decision. "Yes! You can preach for me tomorrow night, and I will sit in the congregation." I gave him particulars, and his eyes lighted up with thankfulness and pleasure as he shook hands and passed out into the night. After his departure, and for hours in the night and the next morning, I wondered if I had done the right thing, and what my congregation would think. Sunday evening came, and half an hour before the service the stranger arrived. We had prayer together, and then he entered the pulpit. He conducted the service with quiet dignity. The sermon was not unusual, but again there was some strange, appealing influence in his manner. At the close he said, "We will have a prayer meeting." To my astonishment, no one left the church. It was in that prayer meeting that things began to happen. A young lady I had never heard speak before, got up and spoke of how her heart was strongly moved. Others followed, and then the stranger made an appeal, and down the aisle came the people crowding the Communion rail and seeking Christ and His power. The stranger passed out of the church. I have never seen him since, or heard of him, and yet from that night a new power came into my own life, and life has never been the same again. Once, I saw the play, 'The Passing of the Third Floor Back'. The story of the quiet stranger who made such a difference to those he lived with, so that life was never the same again to them, but enriched and made better. This stranger was just the same. Who was he? Where did he go? I shall never know!

How different this experience was to the Billy Graham campaign at Harringay. I attended the inaugural luncheon and listened to his plans for the meetings – what a time! What a luncheon! What crowd of ministers and laymen! I also visited Harringay several times, as well as private gatherings, including further luncheons and teas. All the buses, all the hoardings, in fact all London was posted with that one name in big letters and with the smiling, handsome face of the evangelist. There is no doubt that Billy Graham had a lot of personal magnetism and was also an orator of great power, and he knew the value of good human relations – and good human relations are the basis of good co-operation, and this the evangelist had from thousands of ministers and Christian workers. He certainly took London by storm, and especially at his final meeting, which I attended, at the Wembley Stadium. In Harringay all was so very spectacular – the spotlight, the platform stars, the great choir, the flowers, the counsellors, the crowds and the central figure of Billy – how that affectionate Christian name caught on. It was all so moving, surely the greatest mission of all times, which left the country, including the Queen and Prince Philip, who asked him to preach at Windsor, lost in wonder, love and praise. Will its influence abide? Anyhow, we were all stirred up – in many cases an earthquake experience – but having said all this – I believe in 'The still, small voice'; the stranger who came to my church had it – and the voice was heard.

Here is another story of one who was far from being an angel and, to my sorrow, I entertained her. There is a famous radio play called 'The Man in Black'. This is the story of 'the woman in black', and black she was. She came early one morning, dressed in widow's weeds and wearing a black veil. I asked her to be seated and she wept copious tears. I said, "Why do you weep?" She replied, "My dear husband, who has been my support and comfort for so many years, has passed away. Now I am alone in the world." I tried to comfort her and knelt down and prayed that she might receive Divine consolation. She then asked me if I would kindly officiate at the funeral of her husband and gave me an address in Brewery Road, not far from my church. "Would I," she asked, "have the service in the church?" She even selected the hymns her husband loved. I accompanied her to the door and then as an afterthought, she said that she had to go to collect some insurance money and also pay the undertaker some money on account, but unfortunately she was short of funds at the moment. Could I kindly lend her a pound or so until she received the insurance money due? I did so. Later on I called at the address she had given me, but I found that the woman was not known there and nobody had died at that address. I found out, afterwards, that in addition to myself she had called on another Methodist minister who had given her two pounds, three Church of England vicars, who had also given her various sums, and on one Baptist minister. They all went, at different times in the afternoon to call on the widow at the address given. The cleverness of the woman was to be seen in her timing of the calls – early in the morning, and the fact that we all lived near one another. She, with true instinct, knew that it was unlikely that any of us would call before the afternoon. The police caught up with her later on and then it was found that she had operated throughout London, telling the same old tale. Yes! This woman in black was a clever rogue. Her method was to visit a given area and obtain the addresses of various clergymen and ministers from the Post Office Directory, and after securing a plausible address, call on each one early in the morning and reap a big financial harvest. I forget what sentence she received but she richly deserved whatever it was.

At one period I had a constant stream of callers seeking the cost of a night's lodging or clothing. I asked a man, one day, how he knew my address, and he said that he was told by a man sleeping in St Martin's shelter, Trafalgar Square, that if he wanted help Padre Kendall would give it. I had many ex-servicemen who called. In some cases, seeing I was the president of the local British Legion branch, I could readily help. There were others, too, from my Hyde Park crowd, and some from the neighbouring prisons of Holloway and Pentonville. I acted from time to time as holiday locum for the chaplains both of Holloway and Pentonville, and so when some of the women and men were discharged they found their way to my doorstep. One woman, who had completed a sentence for blackmail, arrived at 10pm one very stormy night. I was alone in the house at the time and I did not feel too happy about her visit. She was wet through, so I got her some hot tea and food and listened to her story. I knew the real truth because I had visited her in Holloway, but she did not know that I had the facts of her case. She told me that her son was a doctor, and this was true, and that her crime was only one of false pretences. She talked on and on and it was getting very late, so I was anxious to see her go. "What can I do for you?" I asked. "Well," she replied, "I have got a room in Camden Town – can you give me fifteen shillings to pay the cost of the first week, and some clothing?" I went upstairs and bundled some of my wife's clothing and a pair of shoes into a parcel, and came down. "Here you are, and here is the fifteen shillings," I said, and ushered her out through the door, very thankful to get rid of her. My wife, by the way, was rather vexed when she returned home to find her depleted wardrobe. I never saw the woman again, but some years afterwards I saw her photograph in a paper and another sad story about her.

Mrs Kate Meyrick, the 'Nightclub Queen' as she was called, was in Holloway at the time I did duty there. The only time I came into contact with her was in the prison hospital. She impressed me as being a very resourceful woman.

There was one girl who was in for arson. She came from Norfolk, and had a mania for setting stacks on fire. The time for her departure had come and I had a long talk with her. I asked her, "Why did you set fire to so many stacks?" She replied, "I love to see them blazing, and I am afraid that if I return to the country I shall be tempted to do it again." I said, "Would you like to stay in London, away from the temptation?" She replied, "Yes." So I took steps to get her into domestic service. I succeeded in this. What happened to her eventually I do not know for I lost touch with her after I myself moved. I hope she settled down and was contented to light domestic fires, and not farmers' stacks.

Pentonville Prison stands like a grim fortress. It is, of course, a landmark in the Caledonian Road, and only a few yards from the church I served. The chief warden was an active worker in my church until he died. His son, who is still a member, is now an assistant governor of a very large prison. Some of the other officers used to be members of my congregation and many of their children attended our Sunday School. Because of this, and other matters, I had a great interest in the prison. It was always in my vision, and that of the many who lived round about. During the executions which took place from time to time, the prison was always surrounded by a curious crowd, and generally there was a death-like stillness, and many, including myself, prayed for the one who was about to pass from time into eternity. My period of service was intermittent, but one can learn a great deal, even under these circumstances, and I often envied the full-time chaplain in his responsible task. I always have a picture of the large chapel, known to thousands of men who have worshipped in it through the long years. The organist, in my time, was a brilliant player. He had been the organist of a big cinema and appreciated the opportunity of renewing his place at the keyboard. I used to allow him, in addition to accompanying the hymns, to play selections, and how he thrilled us with his mastery of the instrument! The service generally lasted an hour, and I used to allow the men to select the hymns they loved.

One particular favourite was 'How sweet the name of Jesus sounds' with the appropriate lines:

> It makes the wounded spirit whole,
> And calms the troubled breast.

These men were wounded in spirit, through their own fault, it is true, but one felt a sympathy for them and a yearning to lead them to a better life. I also shortened my service to enable the men to ask me questions on the religious faith. Their personal problems I could discuss with them after the service, in the quietude of their cells – it was, I think, a rewarding work. I always found the governor, and the prison staff of the greatest help, and I am glad that today, there is so much done educationally and in other ways, to rehabilitate the prisoners.

The romping children of the streets always fascinated me, and as I was one of the managers of four London County Council day schools and chairman of the Care Committee, I got to know them well. Often when I took my stand under a lamppost in the side streets, they would gather round and help me in the singing – this to the delight of their parents. We arranged many outings for them too – Southend-on-Sea, Burnham Beeches and Theydon Bois. How they revelled in these treats. I was often amazed at the talent of these children, which were displayed in their school concerts, Christmas festivities and the School Harvest Festival.

During a period of great depression, with a good deal of unemployment, I was able, through the kindness of many friends, to provide dinners, and I have taken a trolley bus load of children to buy each one a pair of shoes and stockings, also providing groceries for their mothers, coal in the winter and big Christmas hampers. To see the confidence the children placed in one, will be shown by this amusing story. It happened one year, on 5th November. The children had collected orange boxes and other wood to make a bonfire. These fires were forbidden in the streets, but who can stop children on such a night? There were too many streets to be watched. I walked down one street near the prison and I saw a big fire surrounded by children. As soon as I appeared they rushed up to me and said, "Mr Kendall, will you do something for us?" I replied, "What is it you want me to do?" And then came the request, and how they shouted it! "Will you stand at the corner of the street and tell us when the bobby comes?" And I did it – one could not break faith with such children.

In those days we were able to provide football and cricket pitches and also we had a tennis ground. It was a joy to me, in the New Year, to join the generous postmen of Islington, who provided a tea and a glorious treat for six hundred children at the Royal Agricultural Hall, Upper Street. The children had the added excitement of the World's Fair, which was held in the famous hall for several weeks at Christmas time, but alas, is now no more as the hall was badly bombed during the Second World War and is now used for other purposes.

I was always reminded of a very interesting and fascinating character, every time that I visited the fair. His professional name was Professor Zama. He was born in a caravan one year, with the caged lions all around, whilst the fair was operating in Islington. His mother was connected with the Wombwell family, who for generations had been linked to the Bostocks – how often I had visited the Wombwell-Bostock shows in my teens, and I once stayed with one of the Wombwells. The father and sister of Zama had both met their deaths whilst engaged in lion taming. Zama never went to school. At seven years of age he began as an acrobat and in due course became an animal trainer. He always said that he trained his lions and bears with kindness. Later on he was commanded to give a performance at Windsor Castle. One night, when dancing with a bear at the Royal Aquarium, which stood on the site where the Methodist Central Hall, Westminster, is now built, the bear suddenly hugged him and broke his ribs and injured his back. He was taken to Westminster Hospital, which was then a short distance away and now is levelled to the ground, and he was there for six months. Whilst he was there the nurses taught him to read and write. After he left the hospital he went to Camberley and there became acquainted with a Primitive Methodist local preacher. Through the influence of this man he became converted – it proved to be a real change of heart and life. There is little wonder that this happened, for Zama's mother believed in prayer and had done her best to train her boy to follow

Christ – this influence had a powerful effect and lived on. When Zama returned to the fair, he began religious services, which were held each Sunday afternoon for the seven hundred circus folk, and he cared for the children. He became an excellent preacher and his lecture on 'From Lion's Den to the Pulpit' used to attract great crowds.

I was privileged, from time to time, to do duty at the Whitely Village near Walton-on-Thames. This lovely village, set in beautiful woodland scenery, is a self-contained village of charming houses, with churches, hospital, recreation rooms, shops, post office; in fact, everything that the heart can desire to make old people who live there happy in their retirement. It is a paradise of beauty. Dr Winnington-Ingram, who was then the Bishop of London, was the chairman of the trustees. I remember talking to him about it at a garden party I attended at Fulham Palace. We walked together in his rose garden and he told me the story of the millionaire, who met such a tragic death, and how he had left his vast fortune to bless so many people in the eventide of life. The village church, where I held my services, was a perfect gem of architecture; in fact, the cottages and all the other buildings, with lovely lawns and flower gardens, all combine to produce a sylvan beauty that is unequalled in England.

In addition to my other duties, I served as president for one year on the Islington Free Church Council – a vigorous organisation in those days, and also president of the London North Christian Endeavour Federation.

Another great and historic event in which I took part, was the uniting conference of the three sections of the Methodist Church (Wesleyan, Primitive and United Methodists) on 20th September 1932. This was held in the Royal Albert Hall and was attended by the Duke and Duchess of York. His Royal Highness addressed the great congregation, congratulating the church, and bringing the greeting of His Majesty King George V and the nation. Never has the 'Te Deum' been sung with greater fervour than on this occasion.

Among the many meetings I have addressed was one held by the League of National Life, in the Central Hall, Westminster. This was addressed by the Bishop of Ely, the Lady Cynthia Colville, as well as myself. The Bishops of Bradford and St Albans, the Chief Rabbi, Canon Lyttleton, Lords Fitzalan, Howard of Glossop, Howard of Penrith, Gainsborough and Rankeillour, and other distinguished clergy and laymen supported the platform. The subject of my address, which was later published, was: 'The Enemy within our Gates'.

There was one interesting evening that I thoroughly enjoyed – a dinner with Edgar Wallace. I had long wanted to meet him for my brother-in-law Harry Lessware, who held a responsible position as the sub-editor of a South African newspaper, was one of those who had encouraged Edgar when he began to write his amusing poems which were printed in Harry's paper. Both were later on members of a band of journalists who became war correspondents in the South African War. I also knew that Edgar had married Ivy Caldecott, as his first wife, and the fact that she was the daughter of a minister of my church gave me an added interest in meeting this brilliant and prolific writer of crime stories – stories which I have so often enjoyed. The whole evening was spent in the telling of his experiences in South Africa and of his method of writing and stories for which he became so famous. In passing, I should add that my brother-in-law Harry did not survive the Boer War. He was coming home with Sir George White in the Dunvegan Castle, when he died on board and was buried as the boat was sailing through the Red Sea. Edgar Wallace, his old friend, lived on to attain great fame as a writer, but now he too has passed away. It was a most moving experience to be entertained by him that night.

I had another little church under my charge. This was at Highbury Vale and under the shadow of the Arsenal football ground. In 1927, we opened a new hall here. It was a thriving church and owed much to the devotion of the Allison family, the Albon-Crouch family and that of the Thornes. The Arsenal football team came, once, to open a Christmas bazaar for me. Alas! The church is no more, as the London County Council wanted the site on which to build the present block of flats.

How true it is that in this mortal life of ours sorrow comes exactly when and where we have expected sunshine and song. So it was in my case. After a long and serious illness my wife, Emily May, passed away on the bright morning of 21st September 1933. She had for years suffered from the dread disease of cancer, but her life had been preserved by radium treatment. The specialist had, a month earlier, ordered her into the London Hospital. There an operation was performed, but it was in vain. Her one wish was to return home, and this wish was granted. So for seven days she lingered and then passed away. Winnie, who cared for her so long and devotedly, and myself were with her at the end. Some little time before she passed into unconsciousness, she said, "Life is beautiful, and it is beautiful to know that all things work together for good to them who love God." That expressed her life. The whole of Islington mourned her passing, for she had rendered much service to the community, especially for the poor and aged. The church was packed with many sorrowing friends at the funeral service. She lies in Finchley Cemetery, with a marble cross over her grave and later on, in the church she loved, a memorial tablet was unveiled to her memory.

I continued in Caledonian Road until the following year, with Miss Stokes as my housekeeper. The closing meeting came, a very moving time, and I left for a holiday before beginning my duties in another part of London. In 1934 I became the superintendent of the Kilburn and Wembley Circuit, with churches in Kilburn, Harrow Road, College Park, Wembley and North Wembley. I had three colleagues, The Rev George Maland, a vigorous and earnest young minister, The Rev A. Walliker and The Rev J.W. Everingham. We were a happy team backed by some splendid laymen. I owe a real debt of gratitude to Mr H.W. Hagger, the leader of those laymen. He was ever faithful, ever sure.

Elsewhere I have written of the strange coincidence that I should be called to serve this group of churches which owed so much to the enterprise of The Rev George Shapcott, and with whom I stayed when I was a ministerial candidate. Kilburn itself, where I had the principal charge, was a typical London suburb, but since the war things have greatly changed. I lived in the Manse opposite Queen's Park in Milman Road. The park was well laid out and I spent many happy hours in it. The Manse was large, with a garden surrounded by trees. I was a member of the London Mission Committee which is responsible for all the Methodist churches and missions in the metropolitan area. After Methodist union, there came the problem of overlapping churches and this affected our work in Kilburn as there were two churches – the Primitive and Wesleyan – near to each other. This was solved by the sale of our Kilburn Lane church, the former Primitive Methodist, and uniting with the Fernhead Road, former Wesleyan Methodist. It is easy to write about this problem, but with so many conflicting views, it was not easy to solve. I managed, after much trouble, to bring about the solution. The same thing happened about our Harrow Road and College Park churches after I had left. All these union problems are gradually being solved, resulting in the strengthening of the Methodist Church influence.

At Wembley we had a beautiful church under the capable and wise administration of my junior colleague, The Rev George Maland. At North Wembley he had two old army huts which had been adapted into a church. There was still a debt of five hundred pounds on the buildings. I suggested to the trustees that we should build a new church but they said, "How can we?" I replied, "The old debt will be wiped out when a new church is built." They could not understand how this could be done. We had a full congregation worshipping in the hut – a splendid lot of earnest people – so I was anxious to erect a permanent church for them and above all, to the glory of God. One Sunday evening I was taking the service and I told the congregation that I was contemplating the erection of a new church, and explained my plans. The singing of the old hymns that night was particularly moving. I noticed a stranger in the congregation.

After the service I went, as was my custom, to the door to shake hands with the people, and there was the stranger, and this is what he told me:

> I was passing your church tonight and heard the congregation singing and it made me think of my father, who was a good Methodist, and my boyhood days. Something came over me which I am at a loss to understand, but it made me feel that I must come in and join you in the singing, and the service. I have been deeply moved. I heard your appeal for help towards the building of a new church and I will give you two hundred and fifty pounds.

There are two lines of a hymn which we often sing, and which flashed into my mind:

> Sometimes a light surprises
> The Christian while he sings.

That light had 'surprised' the stranger and it surprised me. I thanked him warmly and he passed out into the night. I have never seen him again, but he honoured his promise. I told Joseph Rank, who had given his millions to build Methodist churches and central halls, that story and he gave me two thousand pounds. The lovely little church was built by my colleague The Rev George Maland, after I had left, but I returned for the foundation stone laying and the opening. The old debt was cleared, and the new church paid for.

I felt so very lonely after my wife's death, and whilst I had a splendid elderly housekeeper, I needed someone who would share in my work. Winnie had been my wife's faithful companion for many years and a real mother to my son Jack, so I asked her if she would consider marrying me. She consented, and so I went to Dover, where she had been living with her brother, and on 3rd October 1934, Winifred Ada Norris and I were married in the Snargate Street Methodist Church and, after the wedding breakfast, we motored to London and to our home in Kilburn. The marriage was a really happy one. Winnie knew all my ways and also the ways of the ministry and, having all our interests in common there has always been that peace and harmony without which no good work in the ministry can be done. Our happiness was completed when a year later David was born. I remember so vividly that Saturday morning and the next day. It was the Sunday School Anniversary at my church and I was the preacher for the occasion.

I gave out the children's hymn:

> The world is very beautiful,
> My journey's just begun.

I sat there with tears in my eyes and a deep feeling of emotion for in my Manse there was a 'little pilgrim' whose journey had begun only twenty-four hours before. David stands over six feet and is a 'big pilgrim'. After several years at the Kingswood Public School, Bath, he is now reading Law at Christ Church, Oxford. He has been a real blessing to us and follows me in his love and devotion to our church.

The time had now come to decide the best for my eldest son's education. Methodist ministers have always to solve this problem for their children because of so many changes. Jack, therefore, sat for the entrance examination of the Ashville College, Harrogate, for being a Yorkshireman I thought a Yorkshire college would be ideal for him. He passed, and made the long journey. The little boy of those days, who had brought such brightness to my home, is now six feet two inches – a big man in every sense. I assisted in his marriage in Derby to Eileen Sonnex, and now a little baby named Jane – my first grandchild, brings joy to all of us. He is on the staff of the Rolls-Royce firm in Derby and no one is more welcome in his home than 'Dad' and 'Mum', as he calls my wife.

One Sunday evening, after we came home from the service, we found the lights on in the Manse. The house had been broken into by men, who probably thought I had the funds of the church in my keeping. All the rooms were in a sad state, beds stripped, drawers pulled out and their contents scattered, cases ripped open and my sermons scattered all over the floor. I hope they read some of them! The men took every present I had ever received and the mementoes of my father, rings and chains, who had died so long ago. The police came and searched for fingerprints, but the men were never found. A strange thing happened the next day. I was speaking at a women's meeting and one of the women chose the lesson – remember that none of those present at the time knew of my loss the night before – and what did she read? 'Lay not for yourselves treasures upon earth, where moth and rust doth corrupt, and where thieves break through and steal'. I had no treasure left to lay up!

I had burglars three other times in my London ministry, and the last time I had a visit from them I wrote out a notice and fastened it to my doors with this message:

> To all burglars of the night –
> I wish to save you further trouble
> Do not enter this abode,
> There is nothing left.
> Your pals have taken the lot.

This amused all the postmen and tradesmen, who called, but I have had no burglars since.

On 6th May 1935, I arose early and went to see the State Procession on the occasion of King George V's Semi-Jubilee. It was an historic occasion. I recalled the morning of the day he was crowned – the 22nd of June 1911. I had decorated my house in Colnbrook, where I was then living, and at 4am I left for London. I arrived outside Westminster Abbey at 6am and sat on the pavement until the procession arrived, and then I stood and cheered like an excited schoolboy. I did not mind the long weary waiting; there was the good humoured crowd and later the dazzling pageantry. I was better off outside than inside the abbey – I saw more and certainly heard more, for in the comments of the crowd you find the spirit of the nation. Now I was to see another great event in the King's reign. I remembered, as I stood there, how he had passed through a tragic illness with so much courage, dignity and unselfishness. There is little wonder that the multitude shouted, "Long live the King!" Alas! It was not long – a few short months and his reign would be over – for he passed away on 20th January 1936, at near midnight, and the whole nation was plunged into grief. I went again, not to the abbey this time, but to see his body lying in state in the ancient hall of Westminster. As I passed the coffin I noticed something which deeply moved me. It was draped with the Royal Standard, but over this was placed the white pall of 'The Unknown Warrior'. Nothing would have given the humble-minded monarch more solemn satisfaction than to rest under that symbol of lowly anonymous devotion. Crowned King and Unknown Warrior; in duty and death they were not divided. As I filed past the coffin to pay my homage, I remembered how the King had shown virtue of the highest order and had always maintained a tender consideration for his people and had also piloted his nation through a war unequalled in the world's history.

We sing sometimes:

> Crowns and Thrones may perish,
> Kingdoms rise and wane.

The throne of England stands secure when so many others have perished. During the King's reign, the Kaiser and other Emperors disappeared from Europe, but George V, with his wise counsel, his sincere love for his people, his unselfish service, maintained the honour of his name and his throne. My Windsor days came back to me, and I remembered the King's kindly smile and encouragement. It was a sad farewell.

It is not my intention to comment on the short tragic reign of King Edward VIII. When he ascended the throne I sent him a letter of congratulation, reminding him of the incident following the Battle of Loos, which I have already described, and on other occasions when we met. He was always fond of those who had served with him in the First Great War. His reply to my letter was not the usual stereotyped letter of thanks, but a personal one. In my opinion he would have been a good King, for he had a great human personality and loved his fellow men. He did not stand on ceremony and cared little for the restraints that some tried to put on him. This was seen in his visit to the coal miners in South Wales, how he went out of his way to speak a friendly word. He had the well-being of his country at heart, and that is why he abdicated the throne. I am personally sorry that he has been in the wilderness since, and I think the time has come when he should be at liberty to return home. In all our criticisms, we should remember those wise words: 'To err is human, to forgive is divine'. The curtain was drawn over Edward VIII's brief reign on 11th December 1936, and on that day the Duke of York, who wanted nothing better than the more simple duties of a Royal Prince, and the cheerful company of his own family and friends, ascended the throne and with his wife, whom he adored, was crowned with all the splendour and pageantry of this ancient land of ours.

The 12th of May 1937 was, I remember, a bright day. I had invited old friends from South Wales to stay with me and once again I got up at dawn, and with my friends I took my stand with the crowd of ordinary people, to see the Coronation Procession. I had often seen the King as a boy in Windsor, and now I saw him in all his regal splendour. I wondered what he was thinking – this shy and diffident man, as with Queen Elizabeth he listened to the cheers of his people. I little thought that in February 1952 – a cold winter day – that I should see him, as I had seen his father, lying in state in the Westminster Hall. The strain of war, in which he had shown such a bright example to his people, sharing their dangers and difficulties, had shortened his life and reign. There is no doubt that George VI maintained the stability of a throne, nearly wrecked by the upheaval of the abdication, through his sterling qualities and deep religious experience and also by the purity of his home life. History has shown that the British people will remain enthusiastically loyal to a King they respect. One could always imagine King George VI saying, "I will not disappoint my people." And he never did. As I look sometimes on his splendid statue in the Mall I think of the virtue made manifest in his life – a life faithfully lived, and peacefully died.

I was deeply grieved when my colleague, The Rev A. Walliper passed away. He was a lovable man and always willing to help in every way. His preaching was of the highest order and as he moved about among the people he brought them comfort and encouragement. I had laid his wife to rest a year or two before, and I knew how sadly he had missed her. Now life's fitful fever was over for him, and peace and reunion at last.

My ministry having finished in Kilburn, I moved to another London ministry in West and East Ham. I was appointed to take charge of two churches there in 1937. Before the Second Great War, we had two peaceful years when we witnessed much prosperity. Both churches were well staffed and the congregations very good. My

Manse, although small, was pleasantly situated as it fronted the park – a fine open space and well cared for, in East Ham. I was able to carry out the renovation of the West Ham church but alas, four years later it was destroyed by German bombs, also the two cottages which adjoined the church. We managed to carry on in a small room at the back of the church, for a time, but as the area seemed to be a special target for the German planes, all the work had to be discontinued. The site was eventually sold to the Borough Council on which to build a school.

East Ham was, for its size, the most thriving church in the borough. We needed a new Sunday School to replace the three large army huts which were filled with children – a well-managed school with a splendid staff of teachers. With a view to making this known, I arranged a bit meeting at which The Rev Ensor Walters, the secretary of the London Mission, was the speaker, and Mr Joseph Rank, the chairman. Although a millionaire several times over, Mr Rank was careful with his money. He came, not in a Rolls-Royce car, but a small and rather worse for wear Ford. We had a conversation in the army hut at the back, before the meeting and it turned onto newspapers. He said, "You parsons seem to be able to afford several, I can only afford one." He also said that the suit he was wearing had done duty for him for a number of years. He was then, I think, eighty-four – a big, tall and vigorous man. Looking at Mr Walters and myself, he said, "I will show you how to keep fit." He then proceeded to bend and touch the floor which his hands at the same time, keeping his legs straight. The two of us, then in the prime of life, could not equal him in this feat. We had still about twenty minutes to wait before beginning our meeting, so he said to me, "Come to the point you Yorkshireman – he was from the same county – what do you want me to do?" I replied, "To build me a new school."

"Have you any money to build it?" was his next question. "No," I said, "only what you put in the collection tonight."

"How much," he asked, "do you think I shall put in?"

"One hundred pounds" I replied. "You gave me this the last time you presided for me at Caledonian Road, and that will be the beginning, but I want more."

"More!" and he paused, "how much more?" I said, "Well, I think two thousand pounds will, with your collection gift and the gifts of my people, pay for what I want." He looked at me and smiled, and then said, "Get some plans drawn up and let me have them and I will see what I can do."

We had a rousing meeting and a packed church with many people standing in the vestibule. Mr Rank placed his one hundred pounds on the plate. I knew he would do this. Alas! The war intervened and the plans could not be carried out. It has now, and there is a new hall, partly named after me, 'Kenwood', and a fine modern set of school buildings. 'The Joseph Rank Trust', which Mr Rank formed, honoured the pledge he made to me, and paid most of the cost.

Our generous benefactor passed away some years before and of him I can say:

> Blessed are the dead which die in the Lord;
> Even so saith the Spirit; for they rest

from their labours and their works follow
with them.

I have a good deal to thank my fellow Yorkshireman for, especially the help and kindness he showed me during my ministry.

My family increased at this period. Raymond was born on 10th September 1937, and I baptised him a month later, on my own birthday, 10th October. Like his brother he is now a tall well-proportioned young man. He went, with his brother, to Kingswood School, and did well in his examinations. He had passed at the advanced level in Chemistry, and at ordinary level in Physics and Mathematics, and wanted to enter some firm as a research chemist. He had his wish granted by the Imperial Chemical Industries, and is now training at the Welwyn Garden City laboratories of the firm. A lovable boy, always willing to be of help, I am sure he will serve his day and generation well. I remember how his curiosity was aroused by seeing the sidesman take up the collection, and hand the same to me for prayers at the Communion rail. One day, to our amusement, he said, "Mum, the people put their money in the boxes and walk up to Daddy, and he takes the lot."

Rosemary was born nearly two years later, on 5th July 1939. She is our only daughter and very affectionate. Of course, we have made a lot of her, and that is only natural. She was educated at the Trinity Hall Public School, Southport, where many ministers' daughters are trained. On leaving school she entered the Belgrave Hospital for Sick Children. This is associated with the King's College Hospital. Here she trained to be a nurse. Rosemary was always passionately fond of children. She taught them in Sunday School and joined them in their games and now she is realising her ambition. It is not easy going, but a dedicated life brings happiness.

My wife always took our three children to church on Sunday mornings – two in a pram and David walking by her side, and when Jack was home from school, the party was complete. I little thought how this influenced others. She went because of her love for the church and because she wanted her children to grow to love it, and so they have. One day I received a letter from another mother with a family, and this is what she said: 'I have seen your wife going to church each Sunday with her little ones. I feel ashamed that I have not done so, if she can do it, so can I, and I am going to begin'. So she did, and others also. All this is a lesson in the value of cumulative influence and there would be far fewer delinquent boys and girls if this method, and duty, was adopted.

I remember once a very original, and inspiring lecture, which changed the life of The Rev Joseph Johnson – a man who became a leading minister and a great friend of mine. The title was 'Men who were spoiled in the beginning'. Joseph walked ten miles when a youth, to listen to the lecturer, and life was never the same to him afterwards. All things were changed and all things became new.

Two verses have had a great influence on me in my training of children. I do not know the author of them:

I took a piece of living clay,
And gently formed it day by day.
And moulded it with power and art,
A young child's soft and tender heart.
I came again, when years were gone,
It was a man I looked upon.
He still that early impress wore,
And I could change him never more.

I took a cottage for a three-week holiday on the sea front at Ramsgate. We were expecting a lovely time. The quaint cottage appealed to us, and right in front were the sands. We were there the Sunday war was declared, and when the siren sounded we were in church. I have never seen a church empty so quickly, as a rush was made for the underground chambers and tunnels excavated from the chalk. I tried to get in with my children but decided it would be far better for us to take the risk and walk back to our cottage. The policeman I passed called out, "Seek shelter at once!" Heedless, however, I went on and the all-clear sounded as we reached the sands. That night we scarcely slept and the next day I sent my wife and family to her sisters at Grafty Green, an isolated and lovely village some miles from Maidstone. It was a difficult place for anyone to live with a baby and young children, for it meant a three-mile walk, with a pram, to the nearest children's clinic. I visited them once in the three months they lived there and, after I had bought and furnished the house I have elsewhere mentioned in Slough, I sent a car for them and took them to their new home, where they remained for three years. In the meantime, I returned to East Ham to continue my work with the RAF, and the one church remaining. It was not very long before this church also was completely wrecked, and all I had in which to worship, with the people who remained, was a hut, but we carried on and in spite of constant bombing and danger, we were able to be, as the Psalmist says: 'A very present help in time of trouble'.

We often sang:

The Lord is my Light and my Salvation
whom shall I fear?
Though an host should encamp against me
My heart shall not fear;
Though war should rise against me,
In this will I be confident.

I had, about this time, a letter from Lloyd George, inviting me to go to see him. I always had a great interest in his life. I remember attending some of the great meetings he addressed when he began his parliamentary career and later on, especially on one memorable occasion in Manchester where I first had the privilege of meeting him, and also during the First World War. When I arrived at his London residence I found that others had been invited – leaders in various departments of national life. He gave me a warm welcome and I was moved to see the change in him. He had still the silvery white locks of hair and a captivating smile, but his face was lined and he looked his age. He seemed crushed by the fall of France and he was convinced that we could not win the war against Germany and Russia combined, and all his talk was on these lines. As he talked I thought of the words of the Psalmist: 'Why are Thou cast down, O my soul?' How different was all this defeatism, compared with his optimism of the First Great War! Was he jealous of Winston Churchill? Was he a disappointed man? We all know how wrong he was in his view. I tried to cheer him up and I hope that our conversation helped him. It was the last time I saw him.

I had been in East Ham for five years and then I removed a little further west to Brentford. Thinking that this would be a comparatively safe place for my family, I sold the Slough house and we removed to a commodious house which, with a lovely enclosed garden, I thought would be ideal for the children – but we were out of the frying pan into the fire, for one terrible night the whole house was wrecked with a landmine which fell on the opposite side of the road. The roof was blown off, the gable end destroyed, the doors blown to atoms, all the windows completely gone, and the internal walls destroyed. I was thankful that we had a deep underground shelter in the floor portion of the four-storeyed building. This had been well timbered, but in spite of that there was disaster. I, and my son Jack, were blown some distance. The children were all in a heap on the floor, and when I came round I thought the blast had killed them. It was a narrow escape for all of us from death. We were rescued by the Civil Defence men, who were soon on the spot, and at dawn the children were sent off with their mother to Hambleden, where the late Lord Hambleden kindly gave them a home for a time at his splendid mansion 'Greenlands', on the Thames. The children suffered from shock and were ill for some days, but Lady Hambleden, who was the Lady-in-Waiting to Queen Elizabeth, now the Queen Mother, did everything to help them to get better and to forget the terrible experience they had suffered. Lord and Lady Hambleden at that time had provided a home for the crippled girls from the hostel at Love Walk, Camberwell, and my sister-in-law, Hilda Norris, was a teacher on the staff and was with the girls at 'Greenlands'. This shows the unexampled generosity and kindness of Lord and Lady Hambleden.

It was a happy coincidence that my wife had the company of her sister in this time of need. Hambleden was an ideal place for the children. It is near Henley-on-Thames and the village of picturesque stone hoses, with the church and manor house in the centre, is surrounded by lovely meadows and woods. No place could have been more suitable for the children to recuperate. It was felt, after a time, that they should resume their schooling. 'Greenlands' was about two miles from the village, and the school. The Dowager Lady Hambleden, who lived with her son, arranged that my wife should take the children within easy distance of the school and Viscountess Daventry, the widow of Captain Fitzroy, Speaker of the House of Commons, who lived in a lovely house called 'Kenricks', kindly offered them a home. It used to be a real joy to visit them and stay for a day or two amid these peaceful surroundings, after the nights of bombing I had suffered from. I shall never forget the walks we had in the woods that surrounded 'Kenricks', but I was always haunted by the thought of my return to London and the sadness of the parting, for I never knew if I should ever see them again. It was a new life for my family, and all the people of the village showed their kindness and were very helpful, and this relieved my mind of a lot of anxiety. I had to suffer much hardship during the rest of the war. After my Manse was wrecked I stayed for a few weeks with Mrs Buck, and her two daughters, but they had, after many sleepless nights, to leave for Wales. The bombing raids on Brentford had become unbearable and many houses had been wrecked. A good many people had, therefore, evacuated and it became a dismal place. Eventually I slept each night under a big building which had been transformed into a deep shelter. About forty women, many of them old, slept there. There were two other men beside myself. We had bunks in tiers. I slept on the third bunk of one tier and the other two were occupied by women – one aged eighty and the other seventy-six. They said they were happy to have me on top, because they felt so safe! It didn't seem too safe to me, when the 'doodle-bugs', as we used to call them, were flying over. I generally arranged a sing-song for them and they seemed comforted by my evening prayers.

I had to get my food wherever I could find a place open. There was a little cabin for busmen and night workers, kept open all night, and I generally went there at 5am for a cup of tea and a couple of slices of bread and butter. For my lunch I had to search, and the only supper I had was a bun and a cup of tea at the Civil Defence canteen.

I had two churches to serve: one was small and just outside the grounds of the Brentford Football Club. The other, a stone Gothic cathedral with tower and spire. This had suffered from bombing, and the steeple was leaning on one side and had to be partly rebuilt. This church, which seated over one thousand people, could not be used, and the large main hall and classrooms of the school were the headquarters of the Home Guard. We had, however, the use of a minor hall, which in spite of evacuation was filled each Sunday morning and afternoon. My work, however, took me all over London, and I had many narrow escapes from enemy action as I travelled about. Once a bomb fell a short distance from me. I was saved by throwing myself flat on the ground in a gutter, with the result that I severely sprained my ankle. The bone was out of its socket and the whole ankle was swollen. This caused me a lot of pain, until it was put right by a bone-setter who still had a small operating room in Baker Street. On another occasion I was in a trolley bus when a bomb fell. The bus rocked and the windows were smashed, and I thought that the end had come – all in the bus had a shock, but no one was seriously injured. I ran into lampposts in the blackout, and once I plunged into a deep area, cutting my face, blacking my eyes and smashing my glasses. And so I could continue the story – but all who lived in London at that time had the same experiences and people got a little tired of listening to 'bomb stories'.

What a thrill it was when we heard the news of the Normandy landings. We felt then that victory would soon be ours. A still greater thrill – overwhelming in its intensity – came when Peace was declared and we knew that all our agonies were over. We had our Thanksgiving services and rejoiced, as only those can who have passed through the horrors of the war years. We were alive, and we had endured to the end.

The reconstruction period was not so easy for any of us, and I found this even more so when I returned to Caledonian Road to resume my ministry there. My first great task was to rebuild the Manse, in which I had previously lived for eight years. It had been damaged by bombing and half the front had to be rebuilt, and up to about eight feet of the side walls. The foundations had to be dug up and a deep layer of concrete put in to strengthen the walls. The upper part of the side walls had to be supported by steel girders. New chimneys had to be erected and the greenhouse, which was attached to the kitchen, was rebuilt. For nearly one year we had to put up with the inconvenience and we were nearly frozen in the wintertime as the wind came through the exposed walls. I was glad when it was all finished, but sorry that we had to spend a big sum of money over and above that allowed by the War Damage Commission.

The second task was to build a new room, new toilets and an electric light system in connection with the church. I laid plans for complete reconstruction and renovation. The cost was five thousand pounds. I received one thousand pounds towards this from the Joseph Rank Trust, also the proceeds of the sale of the Highbury Vale Church and the rest I got from special efforts, donations and large grants from the London Mission and our general chapel fund. So the whole of the cost was raised – which was no mean achievement so soon after the war.

Two of the bazaars we had were of special interest. The first of these I advertised to be opened by 'Nine' and 'Ninety' – The 'Nine' was my daughter Rosemary, who had reached that age, and the 'Ninety' was my old friend who had been a leader of the church for many years – William George Spicer JP. Childhood and age combines to bring about a successful effort. It was a real grief to me when my old friend passed away at the age of ninety-three, and I laid him to rest. He was a Justice of the Peace, and had served as a councillor on the Islington Borough Council. By profession he was an undertaker, and he had been selected to train the non-commissioned officers of the Guards, to carry the coffin of Queen Victoria when she was buried. William George Spicer was a link with the past and had a fund of interesting stories, personal and historical. The second bazaar was opened by the Lady Cynthia Colville DBE, the late Queen Mary's great friend and Lady-in-Waiting. I was particularly glad to have her with us because some years before another friend of hers, who had also been a

Lady-in-Waiting to Queen Mary, came to act for me in the same capacity. This was during Her Majesty's lifetime, and I was always deeply grateful to the Queen for her unfailing generosity in sending me each year so many splendid gifts. Lady Cynthia, the daughter of the famous Marquis of Crewe, has been a leader of many religious and social movements in places like the East End and the Caledonian Road. She is greatly beloved by all classes and I am grateful for her friendship and help for over thirty years.

In 1950 we celebrated the Centenary of our church and I produced a handbook, which had a wide circulation, giving the history of the church. It contained many interesting stories of the old days. This church has survived when no less than six others of various denominations have been closed during that period. Many distinguished preachers and laymen came along to share in our celebrations, which attracted crowded congregations. In the same year I celebrated my Jubilee as a preacher, and Dr Leslie Church and The Rev F. Bartlett Lang, the son-in-law of the late Mr Joseph Rank and the brother-in-law of Lord Rank, came along to share it with me. I was particularly glad on this occasion to receive congratulatory letters from Dr Fisher, the Archbishop of Canterbury and Dr Wand, the Bishop of London, and to my astonishment Father Joseph Christie not only kindly wrote to me, but sent me a present. My own church leaders, ministers and laymen were very generous in their tributes, and as I thanked God for all the way He had led me, I also felt profoundly moved at the kindness of all my friends. It certainly cheered me on my way and was a real help to me for the last six years of my active service. This Jubilee was for the period of my service as a lay preacher for six years, and forty-four years as an ordained minister. Six years later I celebrated my Jubilee as an ordained minister. My one desire, all through life, was to be spared to serve this length of time.

It was not easy work to build up the congregation again after the war years. So many were evacuated and many had died, but by persistent visitation and bright and happy services, we succeeded. The loyalty and devotion of the leaders of the church, and the members, have been to me an unfailing help and encouragement. I was very pleased to be once more appointed by the Islington Borough Council, as a manager of five London County Council day schools and vice-chairman of the group. These were different to the four schools I had served previously, and as they were in my area the opportunity I had of visiting the schools proved a great help. One got to know intimately many teachers and thousands of children. I saw that in the intervening years an exciting quality of the educational revolution had taken place. I found this of the greatest importance for the individual child. The schools were full of lively interested children, with a better chance of developing into mature men and women. They were learning to make their lives fuller and happier and were also being taught to make their proper contribution to the development of the community. The children felt that they were living in an age of opportunity. It was all so different from former years and I felt it was all to the good. What transformations have taken place in the long years I have served as a manager!

Again I was pleased to officiate at Pentonville Prison from time to time. Many men had passed through those grim portals since my previous term of service. The prison was more crowded than ever and many men were there through the laxity of morals, which always seems to follow war. I have often quoted the saying: 'If you cheapen human life, you cheapen everything else'.

One thing that has always astonished me is the great age that many live to in areas like Caledonian Road and King's Cross. I know that this is contrary to medical opinion. People also say that if you want to live long, then live in the suburbs or in the country. There is no place like London where there is so much smog, dust and dirt, and yet so many reach great ages. I have already mentioned one who died at ninety-three. I buried another old lady aged ninety-six, and then there was Mrs Robert Stather, whom I buried at the age of one hundred and four. I used to have a service in her house each birthday when her great-great-grandchildren, great-grandchildren, grandchildren and her surviving son and daughter came along to share in the happy day – such a crowd. We always sang the 23rd Psalm and the old lady's eyes – sightless for a few years – would fill with tears as we sang, "Surely goodness and mercy shall follow me all the days of my life." I buried her husband some fourteen years before this, at the age of ninety.

If you need anything further to prove what I have said, go into the cemetery where I buried these friends, and you will see a tombstone erected by the old Burial Board of St Pancras. It is over the grave of six people who lived in the King's Cross area and who lie in this grave together:

Ann Bowtell – Died 29th November 1890, aged one hundred and four

William James – Died 6th March 1895, aged one hundred and four

Sarah Wright – Died 26th September 1902, aged one hundred and one

Sarah Lamb – Died 19th November 1907, aged one hundred and six

Joseph White – Died 4th March 1909, aged one hundred

Mary Ann Fulbrook – Died 22nd February 1924, aged one hundred and one

The combined ages of these six people total six hundred and sixteen years, and yet they lived in the most congested area of London.

Another period of history came with the accession of Queen Elizabeth II to the throne. I went to St James' Palace to hear the acclamation read. It was a colourful ceremony. Afterwards I went to Buckingham Palace and was received by a court official and I signed the visitors' book. This was a privilege I prized. I little thought, when I saw her great-grandmother Queen Victoria, that I should, on the day of accession of a second Queen Elizabeth, go to the palace. I stood with the crowd to watch the Coronation Procession on 2nd June 1953 – and what a crowd! The years had passed since I saw the processions of previous monarchs. I was alone in those days, but this time I had three sons, a daughter and daughter-in-law with me. What changes the years bring! I wonder how many coronations my children will see? I ask the question, but at the same time say, with countless others, as we think of the devoted life and service of Her Majesty, "Long live the Queen."

Among other duties which I delighted in, was as deputation for our Home Mission Department. I travelled throughout the land for periods lasting some ten and fourteen days, visiting each year many cities and towns. I know there is much criticism today of the decline in church attendance, and yet I found that criticism unfounded. I think of a congregation of four hundred gathered on a bitterly cold afternoon, with a snow storm raging in Whitby, and a full church the same night. Of the packed churches in which I preached, especially in York, Liverpool, and Birkenhead; of the thriving mission in Scarborough, of the packed church at Weston-super-Mare; of the congregation, on a winter's night, in Salisbury numbering seven hundred, and of the many country churches which were throbbing with life and were the centre of all that is best in the community.

In the course of one's life there are many events, many journeys, that linger in the memory. Life itself is like the rising of the dawn and the setting of the sun, and so I found it in one journey I made. Let me describe it with all its associations. The coach was waiting for me on this occasion at Portman Square – centre of London's West End – it was raining heavily but the journey was anticipated with more than usual pleasure and the company remarkable in its composition and still more in the warmth of its fellowship. My particular companion was an inspector from Scotland Yard, no – I was not under arrest – we were one in the object of our journey, and one in the faith that never tires, for he was a good Methodist. We were bound for Glastonbury in Somersetshire, the ancient Isle of Avalon. It was here, tradition says, that the early Christian Fathers came with Joseph of Arimathea to found the first Christian settlement in this country and here too that Ina, King of the West Saxons, founded or enlarged a monastery which Dunstan, Abbot in the tenth century, did so much to advance. I was thrilled it is true with all the rich and sacred associations of Glastonbury, and the experience I had there, but it is of the journey and one incident on the way that has deeply moved me and will be unforgettable. There is no more delightful journey than this one along the Bath Road. In this island of ours how different each county is and how diverse its landscape, even the colour. Old World towns with winding streets, too narrow for modern traffic; and ancient churches and the Methodist chapels, quaint houses and lovely gardens, forest and downs, and later on the tors which many suppose are the burial mounds of our Celtic forefathers. The chief attraction for me and for my friend the inspector, himself a Somerset man, was Frome, the charming old grey town on the hills. It had been a stormy day with thunder clouds but as we came near to Frome there was one of the most glorious sunsets I have ever seen. Thick clouds with silver linings, the setting sun – a huge golden ball of fire and like the sun of old – 'I saw as it were a sea of glass mingled with fire' – and there in this setting was the fine late fourteenth century church in which is the tomb of Bishop Ken, of saintly memory

Surely it was on such a night in 1674, that he wrote:

> Glory to Thee, my God, this night,
> For all the blessings of the light.

All the memories of the good bishop are happy ones. He travelled a strangely eventful road. He was a stepbrother to Ann Ken who was gentle Isaak Walton's second wife. When Charles II visited Winchester he refused to give up his house to Mistress Nell Gwynne. He was fearless in antagonising William of Orange when he was chaplain to his Stuart Queen, insisting that a promise of marriage should be kept; and he would not take the oath of allegiance to King William, having given it to James. He was educated at Winchester where 'Manners make the Man' and at Oxford, as a fellow Winchester and chaplain to Bishop Morley, he wrote his manual of prayers for the use of the scholars of the college. Strange to say, on our return journey, we reached Frome as the sun was rising – such a daybreak with the dawn song of the birds and a broad cloudland flecked and shot with the glorious light of the rising sun – later on it was so dazzling that our driver had to wear his sunglasses.

Almost as one the inspector and myself were repeating:

> Awake my soul, and with the sun
> The daily stage of duty run;
> Shake off dull sloth, and joyful rise,
> To pay Thy morning sacrifice.

Frome will always mean to me the place of Bishop Ken. Is it not moving to remember as we sing the hymn of the rising sun, that good Bishop Ken was buried at sunrise one March morning in 1711, beneath the chancel window in the churchyard, having ceased to sign himself 'Bath and Wells' which Charles II had bestowed upon him because he was a brave little man who refused even his command to give up his house for Nelly to lodge in? So the coach rushed through the sleeping countryside. The bustle of life began as we neared Reading and we rushed into the traffic of London at eight o'clock. Night and morning we had been with Bishop Ken and glad we were to realise that the voice of prayer and praise is never silent but circles the globe. I have reflected on this experience so very often and it has always been a source of inspiration – would that each night we could recount the blessings of the light, then we should awake with joy and gladness to begin our daily duties. This is what we need in this day and generation.

My second period of eight years came to a close in September 1956. I had served for sixteen years in all in Islington, and the time of my departure was at hand. My total active service, since my ordination – in war and peace – had lasted. We had a moving farewell service and my wife and I were given presents. The generous people gave me a cheque to help to buy furniture, and to supplement the two hundred and fifty pounds given by the Retired Ministers' Fund. A rising young artist, Mr Roy Cumming, had painted my portrait in oils and this was also presented to me. As I gazed at the congregation, which filled the church, I thought of the many dear friends who had cheered me on my way. Some were with us that night; others I had laid to rest. This had always been a family church – the Collins, Sparkhalls, Dunns, Baileys, Grimseys, Davies, Drews, Cummings, Browns, Griffiths, Hastings, Lawrences – to name a few. My greatest grief was when I laid to rest Ernest Collins, one of the best and most generous of men I have ever met. He was for many years my circuit steward. There were also the surviving members of the Carnegie Street Church, the former King's Cross Mission, that had been completely destroyed by a landmine in 1941, and which I had in my charge. This church had been a great centre of Christian activity, with a Sunday School of some seven hundred. It had stood for nearly one hundred and twenty years. Alas, that this disaster should have come! The Exleys, Greens, Harpers and Pedders had, at great sacrifice and with a devotion beyond all praise, kept the congregation together in the Liberal Club, which they had rented, in Caledonian Road – All these memories – and now farewell!

How true are the immortal words of St Paul in his great epistle of Faith – the Hebrews:

> Seeing we also are compassed about with so
> Great a cloud of witnesses, let us run with
> Patience the race that is set before us.

The cloud of witnesses were with us that night.

I am now retired, living in a lovely little house with a charming garden, and I can gaze at a circle of trees on the front, and a row of trees at the back. I am happy in the companionship of a good wife, who has always kept my face to the light, and the love of three growing sons and my daughter. What more does a man want when the sunset of life comes? The things I have described have shown the strange, winding road of life that I have travelled. If I had my life to live over again I would choose that of the Methodist Church Ministry. Its fellowship is so wonderful – we are like a big family. Although I have retired, I am still busy, and I preach frequently. I was privileged only a short time ago to serve as a locum chaplain for eleven weeks at the London Hospital, and I was thrilled with this opportunity to visit the sick. I am still a member of the Royal Navy, Army and Air Force Board, and on the Executive Committee of the Whitechapel Mission, with its homes for homeless boys, and for delinquent boys. I hope to keep on until the end when 'life's long shadows are lost in cloudless love'.

There are two verses from one of my favourite hymns which Charles Wesley wrote, and which have always lived with me – I cannot better close the story of my life – of which half can never be told – than by quoting them:

> Captain of Israel's host and Guide
> Of all who seek the land above,
> Beneath Thy shadow we abide,
> The cloud of Thy protecting love;
> Our strength, Thy Grace; our rule, Thy Word;
> Our end, the Glory of the Lord.
> By Thine unerring Spirit led,

We shall not in the desert stray;
We shall not full direction need,
Nor miss our providential way.
As far from danger as from fear,
While Love, Almighty Love, is near.

G.K.
London, Feb 1961